IT COMPLIANCE AND CONTROLS
Best Practices for Implementation

James J. DeLuccia IV

WILEY

John Wiley & Sons, Inc.

Copyright © 2008 by John Wiley & Sons, Inc. All rights reserved.
Published by John Wiley & Sons, Inc., Hoboken, New Jersey.
Published simultaneously in Canada.

For general information on our other products and services, or technical support,
please contact our Customer Care Department within the United States at
800-762-2974, outside the United States at 317-572-3993 or fax 317-572-4002.

Wiley also publishes its books in a variety of electronic formats. Some content that
appears in print may not be available in electronic books.

For more information about Wiley products, visit our Web site at
http://www.wiley.com.

Library of Congress Cataloging-in-Publication Data

Deluccia, James J., 1977-
    IT compliance and controls : best practices for implementation/James
J. Deluccia IV.
       p.   cm.
    Includes index.
    ISBN 978-0-470-14501-2 (cloth)
    1. Information technology—Management.   2. Computer networks—Security
measures.   3. Computer networks—Standards.   I. Title.
    HD30.2.D456   2008
    004.068–dc22
                                                          2007045580

Printed in the United States of America

10 9 8 7 6 5 4 3 2 1

To my family

Contents

PART FOUR: Looking Forward

Preface

Intent: In this day and age, people, companies, and countries are measured by how well they succeed in their goals (profitable or self-sustaining) equally by the achievements of complying with hundreds of regulations and reams of mandates. The recognition of the enormity of this task and its significance to business viability is the first step towards developing a self-sustaining and integrated information technology control environment.

Information technology internal controls are of tremendous importance to business, governments, and civil services. These technology controls are employed throughout the world's hospitals, security services, and financial centers. A great chief information officer once described his purpose with regard to business continuity planning for a major healthcare provider in this way: "We do this not to save our operation, but to ensure we never lose a single life under our care." As IT has become the great enabler in terms of sharing information, the importance of information security, accuracy, and availability becomes paramount.

This reliance on information technology elevates the need for continuity of services, integrity of the operations requested, assurance of security, and privacy of processes. The controls placed on these technologies are accomplished through a concerted effort; however, by achieving a clear understanding of the control environment's purpose and value businesses may efficiently and progressively institute and manage the information technology controls. Understanding the business activities and their relative value, monetary or strategic impact, provides a way to ensure that appropriate levels of assurance may be obtained, expected, and supported by the IT environment.

Within the United States, several regulations, but most prominently the Sarbanes-Oxley Act of 2002, Section 404, requires organizations to improve and disclose the state of their IT internal controls. In addition, global awareness of the importance of internal controls and specifically IT internal controls continues to grow. In many regions, regulations are at least as strict as what currently exists in the United States.

These regulations on IT direction and management have the ability to disrupt business. These disruptions may be the result of a newly induced government mandate, a recent court ruling that impacts how a specific set of IT internal controls are interpreted, industry trade groups, or concerned stakeholders. No matter the source or the demands, organizations are being encouraged to have IT internal controls and to disclose these to the requesting parties.

The constant evolution of organizations toward efficiency, the embrace of technology, and global expansion to both new markets and resources makes having an enterprise-appropriate IT internal controls environment more important than ever. The old ways of tweaking point systems to meet new requirements or the rush of work prior to an audit are no longer feasible. The scale of organizations and the disbursements of systems and teams only exacerbate the deficiencies of point solutions and their compliance with regulations. Continuous and year-round information safeguards can accelerate or debilitate an organization's success in the world market.

The approach outlined in this book considers the intention of the organization and reflects the spirit of its core objectives. The organization's priorities are evaluated to determine the levels of controls necessary, an evaluation that considers the organization's current and future direction. After identifying all the most important areas of the business, a parallel process evaluates any mandated requirements and their aggregated requirements. Once these requirements are determined, the organization can achieve both compliance and due diligence.Therefore, it is able to protect not only customers, shareholders, and management, but also the families who rely on the product and on employment by the organization.

This book aims to provide insight into the complex world of government and industry mandates from around the world and to enable an organization to answer the question: How much control is necessary? An analysis of the leading influencers, regulations, available frameworks, and guidance documents makes up the first part of the book. Part II contains a practical way to evaluate the organization's IT internal controls needs and to merge these with the regulated mandates, as we develop a method to balance business with assurance. Part III contains a thorough breakdown of a core set of principles and the most prominent IT internal controls in place around the globe and an analysis of successfully implementing best practices. Part IV explores the future of IT internal controls, the challenges that lie ahead, and the technology being employed to enhance the quality and contribution of these environments. The appendix of the book provides valuable references to control publications and an alignment between over a 125 publications and the five Principles outlined in Chapters 9 through 13.

Consider the time frame in which you manage your environment and the time horizon placed on your organization based on incentive and established performance metrics. In today's digital age, time horizons have decreased. Shareholders and Wall Street constantly seek quarterly information results; monthly reports have to be closed; new product introductions, both internally and by vendors, occur almost monthly; threats and risks are uncovered on a weekly basis; daily events require immediate attention. This rapidly collapsed time horizon creates violent shifts in every direction that leave the organization expending significant energy, but making little progress in the organization's goals and future. The hidden agenda of this book is to emphasize the value of very long term technology control considerations and how these positively impact the organization.

Throughout the text, references to legislation, standards, frameworks, government discussion papers, and general data are highlighted and footnoted. Please continue to be a student of the trade and explore deeper into the areas that are most important to your organization. In addition to the references in this text, an open contribution forum is available at *www.ITComplianceandControls.com* that will act as a portal to the principles and important developments in the business of technology.

Acknowledgments

The shared experiences of life and the support and encouragement of family and friends enabled me to develop this book's ideas and merge them into a coherent whole. The support and love of my family provided me with the focus required for an undertaking of this size. I am most grateful for my wife, Jill, whose calming presence and time and effort ensured that my sanity and heath were maintained while I worked on this book.

While it is true that we are a product of our environment and every interaction must have some impact, here I will attempt to recognize particular individuals and organizations that materially affected my thoughts regarding this book.

The ideas, opinions, and field-tested ideas came from my direct experience with clients in organizations transforming their technology and systems into competitive business facilitators. These engagements ranged from the strategic governance of organizations to the tactical definition of metrics within billion-dollar e-commerce environments. Specifically I would like to thank Alaska Airlines, Chick-Fil-A, The Coca-Cola Company, CompuCredit, PepsiCo Inc., Synovus, TSYS, The Weather Channel, and their teams of extremely talented executives, managers, and technologists. Collaboration with colleagues, partners, and industry professionals provided additional support for and affirmation of the principles discussed in the text. I would like to specifically recognize the Association of Certified Fraud Examiners, Deloitte and Touche, the Information Systems Audit and Control Association, the Institute of Internal Auditors, KPMG, and Verisign.

In every organization with which I have worked, I have found that its strength starts with the passion and talent of its people. My greatest pleasure has come from working with these true professionals who seek only to grow and to improve the entire trade. I cherish the time, memories, and experience I have gained over the years. As it is impossible for me to cite every individual, I shall instead extend a huge thank-you and express my extreme gratitude for everything that each person has taught me.

A special thanks must be extended to those kind souls who listened to my rantings and helped condense this topic into a single bound text. Those individuals who provided guidance, suggestions, and encouraging words throughout this journey include David Bilko, Wayne Cook, John Dickerson, Fran Dramis, Clement Dupuis, Steven Jones, Salil Kurnani, Gavin Mead, Rajan Palaniswamy, Paul Parrish, Ward Pyles, Michael Raggo, Mark Ryan, Paul Sobel, and Dan Slodowick.

My greatest thanks goes to my family, who have supported and allowed me to bury myself into the office for months at a time while working on this manuscript. Special thanks go to the John Wiley & Sons team, especially Timothy Burgard, the most patient of editors; to Starbucks, for their copious amounts of caffeine per cup; and to Apple, for providing the rock-solid operating system that kept my manuscript safe and secure.

PART ONE

COMING OF AGE

In 2006, global nominal domestic product grew 60% over the past decade to $48.2 trillion, and over the same period global financial assets rose by 137% to $167 trillion, before adjusting for inflation.

Mckinsey Global Institute, Mapping Global Capital Markets: Fourth Annual Report, www.mckinsey.com/mgi/publications/Mapping_Global/index.asp

World Bank, World Development Indicators database, July 1, 2007, http://siteresources.worldbank.org/DATASTATISTICS/ Resources/GDP.pdf

Today's organizations reach beyond simple neighborhoods to around the world as a result of technology. Online sales and global distribution networks have exploded. This new age of complete integration carries both efficiencies and additional concerns. The concerns of respecting cultures and foreign business practices and adhering to unique governance and internal control requirements threaten the very efficiencies and the economies that nations rely on. This part analyzes the globalization of internal controls and how this interconnected world must be understood, acknowledged, and embraced in a universal fashion.

1

Operating in an Interconnected Universe

Key Topics Addressed in This Chapter

Globalization: opportunities and challenges

Interlinked business functions and networks

Regulation, mandate, and activism

THE INTEGRATED UNIVERSE

Entire industries, societies, and newly developing cultures are being created and older ones are being integrated into the most elaborate, global, intertwined, and automated technological system that has ever been seen. The significance of these computing environments in every enterprise, company, government, association, and affiliation of every size cannot be exaggerated. Yet the technological environment within which this evolution is occurring has few, if any, structured or defined boundaries. For any enterprise to ensure operational effectiveness and efficiency in the future, much less to avoid lethal syndromes and mortal traumas, it is critical that, at the very least, the board of directors and senior management understand the importance and significance of information technology (IT) controls. This is as vital today as it was for boards and management to grasp accounting control concepts 50 to 100 years ago.

The intention of this book is to enlighten those with fiduciary or senior responsibilities for the enterprise on the impact of the technological relationships being established around the world and to provide overview and direction for the IT controls their enterprise should establish. Throughout nature a balance exists where virtually all species live their daily lives in a complementary arrangement that is supported by complex interrelationships

3

among plant, animal, and nature. These relationships are more prevalent than ever today, when nation-states share ownership with public companies, globalized supply chains, third-party sourcing, and virtual networks and when the customers and suppliers and partners of every organization vary by regional culture and separate legal protections.

GLOBALIZATION

A world market exists in today's society and businesses. Businesses of all sizes are no longer selling or delivering services to clients in a specific region. The shrinking of the world and the newly available labor markets and consumers around the world extend the potential and challenge for every corporation.[1] In a world where a simple craftsperson may sell goods on eBay across the globe and extremely talented programmers are available from around the world on eLance.com, the reach and impact of online businesses is only just beginning to be felt. The availability of any and every mind from around the world to concentrate on a problem or to participate in a business transaction is both incredible and devastating to local economic supply–demand assumptions. The world will continue to evolve to adapt to these new global citizens, and technology will play a major part in this progression.

In principle, a local developer of a gadget or widget has a fixed market to service. This limitation may be the result of several factors: cost to transport, ability of the good to survive travel, and among other things the developer's ability to create sufficient items to support the market. Now consider the introduction of a medium that allowed a new market to become aware of the widget, its uses, and its benefits. Of course, the developer would see an influx of orders and after a point would have to expand the operations. If the product is time sensitive, the rational expansion would be to a place that is closer to the newest and largest set of consumers. With the right amount of technology, a small developer in New Delhi or Maybrook, New York, can become a multinational producer of goods in a blink of an eye.

Today digital media have allowed for massive commerce and the merging of minds from around the world for research and profit.[2] As the technology enables these activities to occur, the natural trend for organizations is to expand into the newly minted markets. Initially these expansions may occur by accident, as a result of the inquisitive consumer. Market forces that are actually *pulling* the company into new markets may be expanding beyond into a broader, more complex world. The implicit expansion of operations may occur regardless of a company's initial intentions, and the unintended consequences and profits must be considered.

In the new age of the Internet, where businesses can be developed in the quintessential garage and development and adoption of products can happen in weeks instead of months, it is important to recognize that these digital companies face challenges similar to those of the incumbent international firms. Companies that build such things as search engines, social networking sites, online office suites, or simply online gaming platforms must also cross the cultural divide. This divide is no different from that experienced by companies producing physical devices, such as dishwashers or silicon chips. Despite the cultural and legal challenges, physical and digital producers have access to markets and resources that outweigh the risk and expense.

EMERGING MARKETS: IMPACTS OF INDIA AND CHINA

The term *emerging markets* currently refers to powerhouses such as India and China and includes Eastern Europe, parts of Africa and Latin America, Brazil, Mexico, and Southeast Asia. The entrance of these nations into the global marketplace has a significant impact on resources, both natural and artificial. The world's natural resources are consumed just as artificial resources are, but with one exception: The artificial resources can be created anew to meet the demand. A discussion of the absorption of forest, oil, land, companies, equities, and human effort is best left to a different book with a different focus.[3]

By *artificial resources* I am referring to all technology deployed around the world and the complete representation of the complete online and offline network at once. Artificial resources are those created and implemented by countries, companies, and independent groups. These resources are leveraged by the community at large in some fashion, and as more users enter into the community, the existing resources must adapt to handle the increase in users. Inversely, the introduction of additional peers in this global community, using the artificial resources, naturally expands the reach, capacity, and knowledge of the community.

At the highest level, the nations of the world develop technologies and establish standards that allow for parties to communicate, collaborate, promote commerce, and maintain stability. The emphasis that nations place on their infrastructures directly benefits the citizens of that nation, but also become an asset to citizens elsewhere, including those in nations just emerging into the global technology community. The Internet, instituted with strict standards and an open model, allowed nonprofits, for-profits, governments, and individuals to add to the networked ecosystem.

The contributions of every company and individual have an additive effect on the whole community, which benefits from the introduction of additional peers in the environment. There is a tipping point throughout the community where improvements must occur to allow continued growth and elevate the experience. The entrance of billions of new peers into this community, such as from emerging markets, will challenge both the stability and the integrity of the Internet and in general the entire technology environment.

This is reinforced by projections from groups such as JupiterResearch, stating that an increase of 38 percent more people will actively use the Internet by 2011—that is roughly 22 percent of the world's population—or 1.4 billion people (using the current world population estimate).[4] The majority of these new users will be found in China, India, Brazil, and Russia.[5] The total effect of such a massive new user population will be muted if the network itself becomes exclusive and private, as is the case in some industries and communities that develop private or *dark networks*. A balance will be required where these networks either are developed on secondary networks not part of the public Internet, similar to leased lines and frame relay clouds, or are supported by priority processing through monetary perks paid to service providers.

The most immediate impacts will come from India and China, as the citizens, companies, and countries further rely on the Internet. The Internet will double and triple in size, complexity, information, and users over the next five years. The level of growth may be measured in several complex ways, but a simple way is to count the number of hostnames (systems/machines) online, which has grown nearly 400 percent over the past seven years .[6] The expected increase will impact the backbone infrastructure that businesses around the globe rely on for communication, commerce, and production. Beyond the dramatic increase in traffic, the reliance on the medium will become more essential. Even today international communications between parties and the near-real-time response times allow for individuals around the world to work and collaborate. So much of the global commerce and expansion is becoming reliant on this nascent global network that organizations, nations, and entrepreneurs must recognize the value and importance of this critical business platform.

INTEGRATION

The focus on core business processes, only recently possible as a result of the evolution of business process management and a focus on mapping out these environments, has led to the increased reliance on third-party service providers, or *business process outsourcing* (BPO), for outsourcing efforts. Another reason this has occurred is that through advances in technology, it is now more efficient and cheaper to outsource almost all but a firm's core business capabilities. Ronald Coase, Nobel Prize winner from the University of Chicago, has stated that the cost of a good or service is actually more than the cost of the actual good itself: You must include transaction costs into the cost structure, including search costs, information cost, communication, keeping trade secrets, and bargaining.[7] Through technology it is cheaper to contract out services, but only so long as these services address all of the enterprise's obligations. The ability to satisfy these obligations becomes expensive when rigorous compliance and controls are necessary. Today it is just as common to have outsourcing providers within the same country as it is to have them abroad. These service providers may provide consumer call centers, operate $2 billion manufacturing facilities for microprocessor companies, or conduct biomedical research.

Horizontal integration encompasses the basic building blocks of a business. This type of integration allows for organizations to have more than a dozen companies providing support functions from around the world. These functions may include finance (processing payroll through ADP or Ceridian), infrastructure (technology hosting environments), development and acquisition (software development), and logistical operations (warehouses and order management with UPS or FedEx). These integrations have several impacts on today's organizations and indicate the future makeup of corporate structures. The result of these available partners is a vast reduction of barriers to entry for any given market, reduction of specialty roles in a company, elimination of duplication within expansive organizations, and institution of standards and processes.

Through the leveraging of technology, any organization may outsource, domestically or abroad, nearly every component of the business—except those that damage the firm's future competitiveness, such as intellectual property (even this is being challenged by protectionist stalwarts like Boeing).[8] The availability of a worldwide hiring pool has allowed companies to accomplish what was once available only to the select few. The combination of massive knowledge with near-instant communications has opened the door for billions of human resources. These resources are able to enter the market, because the barriers to entry have been eliminated and elevate the availability of substitutes. Michael Porter's analysis in *Competitive Strategy* resonates with the current shift in the marketplace. The availability of fiber-optic cables placed around the world allows for the consolidation of services, such as call centers, but more likely marketing- and knowledge-centric tasks. The aggregation of these services allows for economies of scale to be achieved at the most affordable rate. As a result of standardization on the Internet, any switching costs between providers (whether internally or externally) are being eliminated.

As the integration becomes more refined, organizations will seek less specialized roles within companies, similar to the reduction of duplicate staffing that occurs during a merger or acquisition. The integration of services with the world market allows for the reduction in physical devices, systems, processes, and people. This trend establishes how critical the infrastructure, both internal and external to the organization, becomes for every enterprise and individual.

The integration and expansion of organizations into foreign markets requires vigilant awareness and monitoring of the laws that govern the organization abroad. While there are efforts in place between nations to reduce the complexity, an example would be the *safe-harbor provisions* between the United States and the European Union (EU); these are seldom complete nor broadly adoptable, given the conflicts between these laws, such as data privacy and IP concerns.[9] Beyond instituting appropriate controls to conform to the local laws where business occurs, other challenges arise with regard to copyright and intellectual property infringement. Regardless of the efforts of the internationally accepted World Intellectual Property Organization (WIPO), there are severe threats to organizations as a result of counterfeit goods, which amount to over $600 billion a year in lost revenue to the rightful product owner.[10] Organizations should establish data custodians and ensure that only necessary portions of data are shared and that the data are appropriately protected to the fullest extent wherever they travel.

Threats that appear due to the increasing utilization of resources from around the world by integration are the same as those that exist in standard supply chain agreements, and organizations must seek to manage these efforts.[11] An organization is susceptible to breaks in service if the Internet backbone experiences a service disruption, similar to that which occurred in 2005 when two major Internet providers had disagreements over contracts that impacted millions of Internet users. There are also direct and indirect risks that should be considered, such as if the service provider becomes a competitor or the third-party service provider becomes mired in a dispute and your business is injured as a result. This occurred when a data warehouse company that hosted the systems of thousands of companies had a problem with a single company. The company was a spamming company that made its money by sending unsolicited e-mails to users around the world, and it became the target of disgruntled hackers. These hackers crippled the spammer's site along with every other business running off the hosting company's servers.

Organizations must be aware of the benefits, trends, and threats that are introduced through embracing technology and the extreme reach of resources it provides. Elaboration on controls for these situations will be addressed in the *principle* chapters in Part three.

SEAMLESS SUPPLY CHAINS

Beyond the horizontal and vertical integration, another wave of change is the establishment of partnerships with clients. These partnerships allow for businesses to work more intimately through the linking of data networks. These linkages vary in sophistication and implementation, but the technology employed and the manner to secure this process are the same in nearly all cases. The linking of systems and teams allows for greater efficiencies, reduces the wasteful peaks and valleys in factories implementing *kaizen*, lowers cost of operations, and ensures that the relationship benefits from timely and correct data.[12]

Efficiencies are gained through the connection of technology environments in many industries and most demonstrably so with the retail and manufacturing industries. The world's largest retailer, Wal-Mart, with $348 billion in worldwide sales,[13] has a close relationship with the suppliers that stock its shelves. As an item is checked out of a store, a computer system communicates the store location and product information to the manufacturer to ensure that the next shipment of goods includes the replacement of that specific product item. This tight relationship saves Wal-Mart by not wasting resources storing extra inventory, removes the work normally involved with orders to suppliers, and keeps the shelves fully stocked.

Permitting suppliers and production partners to have access to sales forecasts and actual sales data allows for the streamlining of manufacturing cycles. Factories may be able to adjust production and capacity to reflect the expected sales and reduce their overhead costs through elimination of unnecessary overtime or downtime. The availability of the data requires a level of partnership where both parties benefit beyond operating efficiencies, as the partner represents an extension of the company that exposes competitive data and must therefore be safeguarded—even against its own customers who may be competitors of the company.

GOVERNMENTS GONE WILD

Regulation Bubbles

> During the boom, an individual would spend six months' salary on a single contract with the hopes that it would blossom into huge profits. This speculation continued and money was made hand-over-fist. That is, until the fundamentals around the contracts began to lose their mystique and investors began to understand the underpinnings of their investments. As a result of this transparency, the markets collapsed, investors were severely punished, companies languished, ripple effects spread to other portions of the region, and consequently economies were hurt by periods of recession.

This description is of the tulip mania that occurred in the Netherlands and the surrounding areas of Europe during the 1600s but is applicable to any period in history of bubbles or mania. Charles McKay does a great job of detailing these events in his book, *Extraordinary Popular Delusions and the Madness of Crowds*.[14] The South Sea, Mississippi, dot-com, and post–Enron-WorldCom-Tyco manias all experienced unsustainable levels of expectations of growth and returns. The eventual result of clarity with regard to earnings, control environments, and operations led to market resets. In each case a cycle of regulations, designed passionately and emotionally, was enacted to prevent a repetition of the egregious acts that made these events infamous.

Regulatory Evolution

The laws of society ebb and flow due to an enormous number of variables, but at a high level they are heavily influenced by the nature of the world, events that impact the citizens of a region, and the swing of the pendulum between open and close oversight. Given that the mandates imposed on companies change based on these dynamic forces, it may on the surface appear to be unmanageable for businesses to predict or reach a balance between these forces and the competitive marketplace within the organization.

In all societies, the political structures adjust to meet the current challenges. These challenges may involve a global threat or simply a need to instill financial structure in the markets to encourage a maturing of these industries. It is important to recognize that laws and mandates are placed in a reactionary and sometimes predictive fashion on businesses both local and foreign to a nation-state. Successful organizations lead and influence governments to shape the mandates in such a fashion that the regulations or mandates provide for the current needs (such as transparency to shareholders), which when developed by all participants will add value to corporations accretively. To that end, it is imperative that organizations proactively participate with domestic and international governance bodies to ensure that they are not caught with changing regulations that generate greater cost than benefit to society, the firm, governments, and stakeholders.

Regulatory Leakage

The threat of unintended consequences is the biggest danger to businesses and the effectiveness of any regulations. These penalties may stem from unclear legislative language, inappropriate or changing interpretation of the laws, aggressive sales efforts, abuse, market-shifting interpretations, or simply a lack of knowledge of certain requirements. These unintended consequences are severe and confuse the benefits and intent of most regulatory efforts. A prime example in the United States is the Sarbanes-Oxley Act of 2002 (SOX) legislation.

The costs associated with SOX are due to excessive implementation of first-year compliance technology as both audit firms and corporations scaled the learning curve together. While the costs after year 1 show a definite reduction in fees and effort, what is not considered is costs of companies that are being forced to comply due to business competitive needs. These organizations are being required to adhere to and demonstrate mandates that, according to the law, do not apply. This forced compliance is not the result of the legislators, the Securities and Exchange Commission (SEC), Public Company Accounting Oversight Board (PCAOB), or the audit firms. Instead, the forced compliance can be attributed to an effect where the legislative requirements trickle down to other companies in the supply chain. As we have already discovered, corporations and governments are intensely dependent and supportive of each other at many points of transaction and operation. This interwoven structure has required private, small, and foreign firms to adjust to the requirements outlined under SOX, which can be especially burdensome for small shops of under 100 persons and those that have cultural conflicts with the legislative requirements.

Regulatory leakage occurs as organizations partner and operate in markets that are foreign, whether they are abroad or simply in a different vertical market segmentation. The effect of regulatory leakage is greater control requirements for companies, which are potentially burdensome for start-up or smaller organizations. As a result of the leakage of laws, companies must fully evaluate every partnership, contract, and client relationship to ensure that all costs, risks, and opportunities to the business arrangement are made clear and provide a positive relationship to both parties.

The Rules are Changing

A recent challenge for governing bodies around the world is the evolution of data transmission and storage, and fundamental shifts in operations of business. These shifts have affected many of the assumed protections that consumers, citizens, and governments perceive to be in place. The truth is that the majority of the laws in society were not prepared for the explosion of an online business or civil society. Criminal activities have migrated from the streets and back alleys to the digital frontier and can range from coordinated for-hire teams to self-replicating code designed to damage the world's communications networks, or simply a group of teenagers attempting to purchase items at Best Buy online for a penny.

New threats are also appearing that never concerned anyone due to implied or natural safeguards, such as the data being inaccessible, or nonexistent, or simply a lack of a market for such data and information. In general, identity theft, corporate espionage, and the sale of credit data are becoming the latest threats and headline grabbers of society. These are the start of a very long list of risks that are becoming known to both companies and governments. In fact, the most recent damages and threats that have surfaced used to be considered low-occurrence threats that were mitigated through absorption. Today society is shifting from risk absorption to a risk prevention posture, but at present it is reacting only as new threat vectors are discovered.

The impact of these illegal acts are both accelerating as more data are aggregated and distributed through computer networks, and escalating in severity. The availability and aggregation of valuable data from all types of organizations increase the available targets for attackers. The severity of the digital threat is escalated due to the mature market that has developed around the exploitation of these systems. The initial annoyances of teenager script-kiddies have been replaced by sophisticated rings of criminal organizations out of Brazil, Russia, and terrorist organizations.

These ever-shifting teams have formed to create a community that has established an online marketplace for buying and selling pilfered information. Besides forming a marketplace, these organizations have teamed together to develop software attacks and exploits to use on their victims. An example is the development and distribution of comprehensive attack packages containing dozens of different attack modules that are able to exploit systems of varying types of security postures around the globe. The Gozi Trojan,[15] itself a single-instance configuration with a modular code base to allow for constant alterations, focuses on stealing user credentials and attacking online banking sites. It and custom attack packages are available for sale in the malware market. This represents a shift as attackers of systems have matured to focusing on high-value data targets with custom malware purchased online that possesses the ability to bypass antivirus, firewalls, and common consumer protection tools. A successful attack occurred in Sweden when such a package enabled attackers to gain access to hundreds of thousands of accounts before they were detected. It is only a matter of time before banks will be robbed online more frequently than with guns and fancy theatrics.

GLOBAL CITIZENRY

The trend toward international openness in corporate operations and government environments is being driven by government legislation under the umbrella of improving the financial stability of markets, as found recently in Japan by the Financial Services Agency, "Financial Instruments and Exchange Law,"[16] and the EU. In addition to regulatory mandates to management attestations, the power of large institutional investors is continuing to demand and influence controls and management activities of companies. The simple fact is that as more corporations and persons conduct commerce internationally, each nation will expect the same levels of service, safeguards, and courtesy as those provided domestically by the company. This means that organizations cannot simply ignore any nation that lacks a specific law found in another country; control safeguards will become only more ubiquitous to an organization's governance program. This absolute concept will only increase as organizations expand into further parts of the world.

Financial Stability of Market Mandates

The regulatory environment found in most developed nations is strongly correlated to the level of international investment and the velocity of the cash flowing through their markets. This market stability allows for the creation and enhancement of wealth and innovations. The progression and sophistication of organizational controls required in these markets are severe in contrast to unregulated markets and industries, but there exists a consistency in the principles employed by nations and the oversight bodies that guide these markets. This concept of financial stability is increasing in importance, as new markets emerge into the financial arena and global investors are attracted.

Japan, South Korea, and China have begun a process to provide greater reliance on and trust in their financial markets[17] through the mandating of adherence to International Accounting Standards in some countries and the adoption of SOX-like laws that require management disclosures and third-party attestations. The effects of the maturation of these markets are broad and impactful for every organization and person around the globe. The effects of these additional regulations shall provide greater access to markets and capital for businesses. While only a single example of the benefits of such legislation, the mandates shall also impose greater restriction and demands on companies from around the world—similar to foreign companies being affected by the SEC's requirements for adherence to SOX within the U.S.

Stakeholders Scrutinize Operations

A major focus of studies has been the increase in the retiring population popularly categorized as the *baby boomers* and the ever-increasing reliance on pension funds. The retirement funds of this giant population will be at their highest peak over the next dozen years, as these individuals shift from producing to consuming, and as a result gigantic funds have a need to invest in companies around the world. In addition, major foreign governments are investing in public entities worldwide. These two forces have accumulated large voting rights within mutual funds, public companies, and entire industries. As a result, these stakeholders have the ability to request, require, and enforce mandates on businesses. This stakeholder activism is akin to Carl Icahn and Ralph Whitworth's heavy influence on companies whose boards they reside on and own significant amount of company stock. The intention is to enhance shareholder value and allow for consistent generation of returns.

These stakeholders require a degree of transparency in the operations of the organization and flexibility. As a result, organizations must have complete awareness of internal operations and readily available data on request by these individuals. The advent of SOX and other international reporting disclosure laws has introduced a level of clarity into the operations, risks, and control environments for organizations around the world.

These influencers may be large pension funds, such as The California Public Employees' Retirement System (CALPERS) fund, entire nations such as China, or private equity firms with billions of dollars under management. Regardless of the organization of these influencers, each is able to influence the position, operations, and risk tolerance of companies.

SUPERSIZED CHALLENGES

Culture Clash and Resolution

The expansion of operations introduces the need to respect the regional cultures and operating requirements set forth by such industry and governmental authorities. Adherence to these laws and guidelines is expected regardless of a business's intention to expand into markets abroad. A great example is how Yahoo! was forced to adjust the type of goods for sale on its Web site to each market. Initially the company simply offered the same global content to all consumers, but after allegations were brought forward that it was violating local laws, the company introduced numerous safeguards to ensure only appropriate goods were made available to citizens of each region. Specific examples include Yahoo! adjusting its storefronts to exclude Nazi material from French citizens,[18] Google modifying its data collection and sanitization efforts to comply with the EU's Data Privacy laws,[19] and Microsoft MSN Search placing filters or deleting content on its China portal to comply with government requests.[20]

Whether intentional or accidental, globalization brings business operations into foreign markets with new oversight requirements. These requirements are unique to the region and may involve controls and safeguards not necessary in other regions. The resulting global compliance requirements will continue to exist, and as the implications of technology operations expand, the amount of governmental and institutional oversight will increase. The ideal approach is one that embraces the requirements together with the businesses' activities and long-term vision. Only proactively will organizations positively contribute to societies abroad and continue to be welcomed into a variety of markets. In fact, by embracing and consistently applying safeguards and best practices around the world to all citizens, corporations will actually demonstrate that additional laws and regulations regarding enhanced disclosure and oversight are not needed.

Ripple Effects and Death Spirals

In chaos theory, a popular statement is that a butterfly flapping its wings will kick off a series of events that causes a hurricane on the other side of the planet. While the application of chaos theory is appropriate in nearly all aspects of nature and artificial human creations, the simplest approach to understanding how it contributes to IT internal controls is through demonstration and example.[21]

The explosion of growth in India and China has enhanced the opportunity for fraud, speculation, and incredible positive growth. Together these create motivators for persons both to advance within the system and to take advantage of it at the same time. The development and maturing of these environments follows the paths taken by other developed markets, such as the United Kingdom and France.

The existence of these perceptions of control and safeguards introduces a false sense of safety and a raw market where the participants, both company and investor, define what laws will be created. This is clearly seen across the globe when fraud occurs in immature markets that have not legislated schemes that were proven successful in other parts of the world. In fact, the perpetrators of these acts typically are seasoned professionals who have moved from restrictive markets into more trusting nations.

The effects of fraudsters, here defined as those who commit an action to take unfair advantage of another party, create a ripple effect throughout the international legal landscape. These ripples trickle into every company that participates in each market. The negative effects of companies not adhering to best practice controls for all markets follow a sequence where each market creates duplicate laws to apply to its markets and fit its cultures. Unfortunately, the current trend of each emerging market exchange and oversight body is to create similar but not consistent laws of other nations that result in a regional patchwork of legislation that is incomplete when compared to other mature markets and alien to the culture.

Liability and Accountability

The integration trend with business processing centers introduces several complexities to the assurance of internal controls. These concerns result from the sharing of services, staff, and systems with other companies and potential competitors. At risk are the level of safeguards placed on the shared assets, which may not adhere to the company's internal practices. For example, internally the company may encrypt all data, but at the processor it may reside unencrypted, violating both company policy and exposing the organization to fines and consumers to damages. Such situations destroy/ decrease the firm's value.

The absence of legislative and judicial laws that protect business IP is a serious risk to organizations that outsource. These concerns may be addressed with the direct outsourcing companies, but too often services are sourced several times over and the legal agreements or moral restrictions established through a personal, close-knit relationship are lost or not relevant. In addition, in other regions, concerns over privacy, confidentiality, and trademarks may be perceived differently and therefore handled in a less appropriate fashion. The originator of the information is responsible for ensuring that data or IP processing is done in accordance with the laws and expectations of the originator and the originator's customers.

SUMMARY

The connectedness of systems with clients and partners must be done with careful regard to the threats that may be introduced to the organization. The organization must be completely aware of how the systems are being connected and the scope of the permissions being granted to both parties. Beyond the accidental release of confidential pricing or patent information, the organization may simply expose itself to technology-based threats, such as viruses and worms, through these connections. Other threats may appear based on the type of customers the client works for; malicious attackers or poorly monitored environments may expose the company to collateral damage. These threats can impact the organization materially, and depending on the source and contractual requirements, they may introduce punitive damages to the parties responsible.

ENDNOTES

1. Thomas Friedman, *The World Is Flat* (New York: Farrar, Straus and Giroux, 2005).
2. Estimated U.S. retail sales as of August 2007 for the second quarter as recorded by the U.S. Census Bureau are $33,645 billion. URL: www.census.gov/mrts/www/data/html/07Q2.html.
3. Robert A. Ristinen and Jack P. Kraushaar, *Energy and the Environment,* 2nd ed. (Hoboken, NJ: John Wiley & Sons, 2005).
4. U.S. World Census Population Clock. As of August 28, 2007, the site estimates there are 6,614,749,919 people. URL: www.census.gov/ipc/www/popclockworld.html.
5. Sehgal Vikram, "Worldwide Online Population Forecast, 2006–2011, "Emerging Economies Catalyze Future Growth," June 21, 2007. URL: http://www.jupiterresearch.com/bin/item.pl/research:concept/75/id=99411/
6. Netcraft: Web Server Survey Archives (August 2007). The Web Server Survey found 127,961,479 sites versus 25,600,000, which equates to 400 percent rounded up. URL: http://news.netcraft.com/archives/web_server_survey.html.
7. Ronald Coase, *The Nature of the Firm* (1937), Economica, New Series, Vol. 4, No. 16 (Nov. 1937), pp. 386-405. URL: http://links.jstor.org/sici?sici=0013-0427%281937711%292%3A4%3A16%3C386%3ATNOTF%3E2.0.CO%3B2-B&size=SMALL&origin=JSTOR-reducePage.

8. Boeing outsourced nearly 70 percent of the development of the 787 Dreamliner, the first time the firm has ever utilized so many offshore firms and exposed the manufacturing process. URL: www.businessweek.com/magazine/content/06_05/b3969417.htm.

9. Joel R. Reidenberg, "Resolving Conflicting International Data Privacy Rules in Cyberspace," *Stanford Law Review* 52, no. 5 (May 2000), pp. 1315–1371.

10. Fraud is estimated at a global scale for counterfeit goods to approximately be 5 to 7% of world trade, resulting in losses between $500 billion and $600 billion, according to the Association of Certified Fraud Examiners, WIPO, and government organizations. ACFE, "Report to the Nation 2006," URL: http://www.acfe.com/fraud/report.asp. WIPO—World Intellectual Property Organization, URL: www.wipo.int.

11. Michael Hugos, *Essentials of Supply Chain Management* (Hoboken, NJ: John Wiley & Sons, 2007), provides wonderful examples and detailed approaches to managing the global threats to organizations operating at a global scale.

12. Ibid.

13. Pulled from Wal-Mart 2007 annual revenues financial statements made available on EdgarScan. Wal-Mart Investors Resource Page: URL: http://investor.walmartstores.com/phoenix.zhtml?c=112761&p=irol-irhome.

14. Charles McKay, "Extraordinary Popular Delusions and the Madness of Crowds," 1842.

15. Gozi Trojan was a Russian attack program that spread through Microsoft's Internet Explorer. Greater details are provided on SANS Web site: URL: http://isc.sans.org/diary.html?storyid=2498&rss.

16. Financial Services Agency (FSA) of the Japan Government, URL: http://www.fsa.go.jp/en/policy/fiel/index.html.

17. Government efforts toward financial stability include Japan's Financial Instruments and Exchange Law, the Hong Kong Exchange's Code on Corporate Governance Practices, and the U.S. Public Company Accounting Reform and Investor Protection Act of 2002.

18. France ruled against Yahoo! to ban Internet Nazi auctions: URL: http://news.bbc.co.uk/2/hi/europe/760782.stm.

19. Google reduced the period that it retains user data from a maximum of 24 months to a maximum of 18 months to resolve concerns by an EU-appointed working party, the Article 29 Data Protection Working Party. URL: www.epic.org/privacy/ftc/google/gres_a29_061007.pdf.

20. The Microsoft Encarta Encyclopedia article highlights filtering and blog-post deletion per request of government agencies. URL: http://encarta.msn.com/encyclopedia_761582857/Search_Engine.html.

21. James Gleick, *Chaos: Making a New Science* (New York: Penguin, 1988).

2

How Technology Enables the World Market

Key Topics Addressed in This Chapter

Collaboration and technology

Evolution of networks and data access

Technology pioneers

PROCESS IMPROVEMENTS

The productivity of a single worker today is vastly superior when compared to a similar individual of equal capability 10 years ago, and 10 years prior to that. This productivity is attributable to information technology and to those who rely and depend on IT to satisfy ever-increasing complex business processes and relationships.[1] At the macro-U.S. level, economists broadly agree that economic productivity gains that surged around 1995 through 2003 at 3.90 percent were largely attributable to technology: the development of new industries, the acquisition of hardware/software, and the services that are attached to these products, which are higher than periods prior to 1995 according to publications by the Federal Reserve Banks.[2] The period following the post-2003 resurgence is at a macroeconomic scale trending downward, which implies that the U.S. general economy is receiving a decrease in gains from the technology industry.[3] A diverging set of hypotheses on the macroeffects are too tangential to the topic of this book to discuss, on the economy after the massive buildup within corporations, but a consensus is beginning to emerge on the gains within companies. Technology has contributed efficiency gains in productivity, as indicated by the growth through the mid-1990s. The projected harder times after 2000 resulted in companies purchasing less technology and focusing more on streamlining their business processes, which in some cases required cutbacks in staff. Technology itself, given partially, allowed companies to make these cost-cutting and streamlining efforts a success.

The concept of *general-purpose technologies* (GPTs) has developed as a contributor to the global corporate efficiencies achieved by technology. This term is usually applied to innovations, such as electricity and the combustible engine, that have a pervasive and wide-ranging effect on how firms do business or even how people live. Information technology, also called *information communication technology* (ICT), is compared to electricity in that the industry provides a measurable growth, but the true efficiencies and gains are delayed into the future. This delay in efficiency gains by companies is the result of their building on the IT environment itself. The situation is similar to how electricity itself provides the supportive structures for air conditioning and other marvels of today.[4] Examples of these ICT additions that provide contributory effects include the buildup of customer databases and massive repositories that allow for new product lines and product extensions and can even transform an existing business.

Examples of operational improvements can be identified everywhere in the world today. A good example, and one that has probably been experienced by every reader, is the length of time it generally takes to process a mortgage application. In the United States, mortgages managed by the government-sponsored entity (GSE) Fannie Mae, once took quite a while due to the manual work involved. A response to a simple mortgage insurance billing query from the GSE once took up to 45 days. Today, by embracing technology, the same process takes 30 minutes.[5] This gigantic improvement in the level of effort is true throughout the world where technology has been employed. The constant striving for lower costs, better products, safer work environments, and consistent operations all center around the ability of technology to enhance, measure, or correct business processes. The efforts of Six Sigma, Lean Management, and just-in-time (JIT) manufacturing are all possible through technology.

The simplest example of a function of technology may handle repetitive tasks that require consistent precision, a type of work that used to be handled by a single individual or team of skilled laborers. The business and its customers accepted a certain amount of errors, defects, and mistakes, given the difficulty of the tasks and the likelihood of human error. Once that same process is handled by technology, the organization experiences higher productivity, near-zero error or defects, and more satisfied customers as technology is more reliable in situations where tasks are definable or repetitive. This single improvement allows the customers to rely more on the company and therefore elevates the services of the company and allows for greater complexity to be applied to the service provided throughout the supply chain process. As a whole, the entire ecosystem of business functions and delivered services is both increased and more reliable. A single improvement in the processing of a single area within one business can have a huge effect on the market and the competition and on the new expectations of customers and regulators.

The capability of an organization to respond to market forces and create new markets, or blue oceans, is a cornerstone of sustainable and successful corporations. The ability to innovate requires the organization to pay attention to its people, its culture, its structure, and its technology. Technology, the tool of today, must be considered when innovating. A study conducted by Accenture demonstrated that innovative companies are twice as likely to use technology as a competitive advantage, and nearly 77% consider technology throughout the innovation process.[6] These results further emphasize that technology must be considered as part of the business value, not simply a commodity or enabler.[7] A 2004 study conducted on behalf of the Financial Executives International (FEI) emphasized this point. It was found that firms that spent above average realized a performance gain by a factor of six over the average firm. This performance gain was achieved by applying technology and managing it not as a cost but as a service contribution that can enhance margins.[8]

Yet these improvements come at a cost. Technology has enhanced the nontechnical workplace while introducing another cost category. Technology also is evolving at an incredible pace, forcing businesses to enhance the very technology that was put in place to enhance existing operations. While this is a very circular puzzle, it is an important one, because it is the driving force behind the increased use of technology around the world. The technology that drives these improvements gives rise to a new set of issues and risks that must be managed. To state this another way, technology begets more technology, and therefore controls beget more controls. The best safeguards are those that satisfy the simple requirement of achieving sufficient balance between safeguard necessity and the value of the information at hand.

COLLABORATION ENHANCEMENTS

The advent of the Internet forever changed how businesses operate. The introduction of a single infrastructure that allows for all parties from around the world to communicate, and the development of web-facing technologies, has created an entirely new marketplace for businesses, governments, and (unfortunately) criminals.[9] According to the 2006 Internet Crime Complaint Center annual report, the amount of frauds is growing and the financial damages are increasing on a relative basis.[10] Today technology allows for collaboration on such a grand scale and in such a friction-free manner that the concepts of borders, time zones, and languages become irrelevant.

Technology has given people throughout the world the ability to communicate instantaneously with each other over the Internet using ubiquitous instant messenger technologies, free international Internet phone services, and real-time online whiteboard applications virtually cost-free. This blending of knowledge, society, culture, and work ethos has yet to be fully understood, but we do know what happens when cultures are isolated from the rest of the world. A good example is in the book *Guns, Germs, and Steel* by Jared Diamond,[11] in which the author states that geography is a critical component in varying advances in civilization. Any physical separation—say a mountain or an ocean—that is insurmountable for the population, and as a result completely isolates the population, causes it to lose the benefits of knowledge sharing and thus fall behind in its ability to advance when compared to societies that had heavy interaction with neighboring settlements.

As this disruptive ability to collaborate across national and geographical boundaries changes our global landscape, there has been a corresponding climb in creativity and capability around the world to tackle once-impossible and unimaginable challenges. The near-real-time communication networks have expanded the available labor resources and reached consumers who were once unavailable. Today teams are formed with international players who all contribute throughout a project—whether that may be developing the latest Intel chip, creating a software application, filming a movie, or attacking the world's poverty challenges.

Throughout modern history, technology has played a crucial role in society's growth. Technology replaced paths with roads to allow for vehicles, boats, and trains, and then air travel extended the ability for interaction and expanded teams. Collaboration has been evolving through the ages from letters, to phone lines, e-mail, and now real-time free and reliable collaboration tools.

This increase, of course, did not occur overnight but is the aggregate effect from decades of development and some seemingly unintentional consequences. Consider the fact that without the dot-com-boom-bust in 2000, the fiber-optic cables that are essential to the infrastructure for business process outsourcing and real-time communications would never have existed. They exist now only as the direct result of the speculation in the Internet market that opened up the world to this new technology. This single event linked the world's populations, and through the expansion of Internet technologies, a global collaboration evolution occurred. The ability to bridge the gap of both culture and geography has expanded the global workforce. The continued application of technology will further this expansion to the overall benefit of the world.

PROGRESSION OF NETWORKS AND DATA

At the start of the technology evolution, businesses initially stored all digital data for the organization, as limited as it was, on systems that were physically accessible only by a small group of persons who were knowledgeable about the technology and motivated to protect the data. Eventually, with the introduction of networked dumb terminals and then fully independent desktop workstations, this single key to the basement safeguard became ineffective to protect the data. The distribution of access and information extended the ability for the organization to connect greater numbers of people from varying functions. The more persons who contribute to the system, the greater the value that system has to that same group, as efficiencies and improvements are made through transparency in the operations. As companies moved from an environment that supported only dumb terminals that did not store the data locally but pulled the data from a central server), to one that supported independent workstations, the explosion of productivity increased. This productivity growth, initially considered a productivity paradox given the lack of immediate returns on IT investments, occurred in relation to the immediate access of information and the ability for companies now to conduct business with greater speed and general efficiency—something not fully understood until recently.[12] In addition to this unprecedented amount of information, the increased range of access into systems continued to expand in concert with the digitization of company information.

Once organizations began offering access to their data through the public Internet, the absolute safety and integrity of the data was placed into question. Today technology allows for constant access and update of data. These updates may occur through BlackBerry devices, iPhones, through Web 2.0 interfaces running on an employee's TiVo device, or simply through a web browser at the home office that is connecting to a server in India to review the latest medical charts.

The correlation between technology and networking of systems that distribute information is directly related to the efficiency businesses gain by implementing these technologies. Therefore, these systems do provide an absolute bottom-line contribution that can be attributed to technology. While there is a positive correlation between technology networking and efficiency, there is also a negative correlation that the increased presence and reliance on technology increases an organization's exposure to the risks that exist due to the technology. An often-cited study in *Contingency Planning and Management* magazine found that 40 percent of companies that shut down, resulting from an unplanned business continuity outage, for three days failed within 36 months—a threat that can occur through supply chain relationships or technology failures.[13] Examples include the loss of power in a data center—a frequent challenge for companies in the western United States, and the loss of connectivity to a BPO providing critical services to the organization resulting from a fiber cable being damaged on the ocean floor.

Many situations can break the carefully laced-together network of software, hardware, and cabling around the world. Many of these events are natural and accidental, but malicious activities also cause intentional damage to organizations. Everyone, from experts to the media, was talking about these little bits of malicious code that were self-replicating, worms and viruses. It seemed daily in the late nineties and right after the millennium that these pieces of code were released with the aim to infect as many servers as fast as possible. The direct cost to corporations to recover from these events measured in the billions, as the infections virtually disabled infected hosts. A recent study confirmed this trend as direct damage caused by malware (viruses and worms are considered a part of malware) yielded "only" $13.3 billion globally from $14.2 billion in 2005 and $17.5 billion in 2004.[14] To put this into perspective, the "ILOVEYOU" Microsoft worm in 2000 caused $5.5 billion in damage.[15] Today attackers use these tools to infect a few choice systems within an organization to pilfer hundreds of millions of bits of information. This information may be valid user accounts, banking account numbers, credit card numbers, government secrets, and anything else that has monetary value. The use of Trojan software on targeted corporations is growing popular and more effective. For example, the attack on Monster.com (a single server with single piece of malware) garnered approximately "1.6 million entries of personal information belonging to several hundred thousands of candidates."[16] These pilfered accounts were then sent fake e-mails asking for the user to forward banking information, all under the guise and authority of Monster.com's logo and domain name in the communications. The costs of these types of attacks on the organization are minimal from an IT perspective: one system to clean or replace. A company's direct costs can be tremendous given the possibility for litigation, fines, and lost customers. In addition, firms that are victims to such attacks are participating in the reconstitution of the lost funds for consumers to transfer the liabilities back to the company, which can amount to a hidden tax, considering that the cost to U.S. consumers that can be attributed to malware was more than $7 billion over the last two years.[17]

Integrity of communications is imperative beyond the financial aspects of business and consumers, but also includes those that process medical information and allergies, and multinational conglomerates that use systems to determine pressure and valve calculations for operating nuclear power plants. The availability and confidentiality of their data are critically important to organizations that rely on this information to maintain profitability and support their clients. Therefore, the supported business functions of these now-interconnected systems rely on the trust provided by IT controls. This interconnected environment introduces a second layer of control requirements for businesses, as a recent study stated that a U.S. resident has about a one-in-four chance of becoming a cybervictim.[18]

This focus on the integrity, availability, and confidentiality of the data is emphasized as governments around the world continue to develop laws and mandates that adjust to the new threats that exist within a globally interconnected digital world. The rush to ensure appropriate and applicable laws to deal with the digital threats has continued as the threats left unmitigated have begun to impact society. Two key examples highlight how politically and socially explosive the threats within technology may be when left alone. The impact of identity theft immediately and maliciously affects the clients of your company. These customers must wrangle with credit agencies, debt collectors, and investigative services to undo the damage caused by criminal attacks on your organization. The average loss per person has been estimated at $3,537, and only about 61 percent are likely to recover their loss, according to a Gartner study.[19] Another impact of poor general IT controls within an organization is due to financial accounting system manipulation, which can harm the entire corporation's employee base and public stockholders as the news of such deficiencies is disclosed.

MIRACLE OF CONNECTIVITY

What are the underlying technologies that have launched your business into new markets and greater productivity? What are the critical components that have enabled technology and society to reach such an integrated state? The huge number of contributors to our existing interconnected society makes it impossible to acknowledge every one. Instead, in an attempt to highlight a few core concepts, a discussion of a few of the major components follows.

"It's the network" is a common saying of a phone company within the United States. While the company is focusing on its cellular infrastructure, the truth is, it *is* and *was* the network.[20] The network, casually referred to as the Internet, represents the technology that interconnects the world's devices together. These networks, or as phrased by Tim Berners-Lee, "abstract information spaces," were designed to allow traffic to share pathways, and through references (hyperlinks) extend the network. As a result, with every addition to the network, the available network itself grew.

The network—the Internet—would not be possible if the world did not finally agree on a common approach/standard. The eerie acceptance of standards and uniformity that makes up the Internet was the tipping point that has allowed the world, business, and persons of every culture and generation to connect and work together. This acceptance is loosely tied to the fact that the early-adoption companies selling and purchasing the backbone hardware mostly had a monopoly. The rapid expansion of the network—fueled by the insatiable demand for access by businesses and the world's populations—did not allow for competing approaches to be developed. This is evident in many examples, but the simplest is the protocol TCP/IP, which was developed by the U.S. military and not by a multinational team. The speed of implementation can also be attributed to the success of businesses that focus on this online environment and to the establishment and longevity of participants in the market. Overall, the openness of the technology implemented and the near-fanatical work of the World Wide Web Consortium (W3C) help to ensure that the ability for everyone to contribute and expand the possibilities of the Internet will exist far into the future.

To summarize, the importance of this ecosystem and the parts that make up this new world is unquestioned. More pointedly, as Berners-Lee stated quite eloquently: "We nurture and protect our information networks because they stand at the core of our economies, our democracies, and our cultural and personal lives. Of course, the imperative to assure the free flow of information has only grown given the global nature of the Internet and Web."[21]

ENDNOTES

1. According to "Information Technology and the U.S. Productivity Acceleration," a study published by the Chicago Fed, those who use technology gain productivity per worker. These trends extend beyond the initial introduction of such technology and have a cumulative effect. URL: www.chicagofed.org/publications/fedletter/2003/cflsept2003_193.pdf.

2. Dale W. Jorgenson, Mun S. Ho, and Kevin J. Stiroh, "Will the U.S. Productivity Resurgence Continue?"*Federal Reserve Bank of New York* 10, no. 13 (December 2004).

3. Dale Jorgenson, Mun Ho, and Kevin Stiroh, "Potential Growth of the U.S. Economy: Will the Productivity Resurgence Continue?"*Federal Reserve of New York* (2006).

4. John Fernald and Shanthi Ramnath, "Information Technology and the U.S. Productivity Acceleration," Chicago Fed Letter, 2003.

5. Other examples include a loan approval formerly taking 1 day reduced to 10 minutes, mortgage insurance underwriting shifting from 2 days to 15 minutes, and invoicing falling from 2 days to 2 minutes. "Loan Underwriting Portal 2005 Computerworld Honors Case Study." URL: http://cwhonors.org/laureates/finance/masshousing.pdf.

6. Accenture Study, "The Innovator's Advantage: Using Innovation and Technology to Improve Business Performance" (2003). URL: www.accenture.com/Global/Research_and_Insights/Policy_And_Corporate_Affairs/CompaniesTechnology.htm.

7. Joint study conducted annually by CSC and FEI/FERF continually indicates the financial benefits of technology that are embedded in the operations of the organization. URL: www.csc.com/solutions/management-consulting/knowledgelibrary/3275.shtml.

8. GMA study, "Information Technology Investment and Effectiveness Study—The State of the Industry 2004" (2004). Research conducted by Computer Sciences Corporation. URL: www.gmabrands.com/publications/docs/2004gmaitstudyreportfinal.pdf.

9. L. A. Gordon et al., CSI Computer Crime and Security Survey, Computer Security Institute (2007). URL: http://www.gocsi.com/.

10. The Internet Crime Complaint Center—2006 Internet Fraud Crime Report focuses on U.S. frauds that are filed through online forms. The data are analyzed and portions are discounted based on the information provided by the user. It is estimated that 1 in 7 online frauds are not reported. URL: http://www.ic3.gov/media/annualreport/2006_IC3Report.pdf.

11. Jared Diamond, "Guns, Germs and Steel: The Fates of Human Societies" (New York: W.W. Norton, 1999).

12. A report prepared in the early 1990s by Erik Brynjolfsson, "The Productivity Paradox of Information Technology: Review and Assessment," indicated that investments did not return immediate results and that questions were raised on the measurement approaches. URL: http://ccs.mit.edu/papers/CCSWP130/ccswp130.html.

13. Online Survey Results: 2001 Cost of Downtime, Eagle Rock Alliance Ltd., Aug. 2001. http://contingencyplanningresearch.com/2001%20Survey.pdf (accessed November 2007).

14. "2007 Malware Report: The Economic Impact of Viruses, Spyware, Adware, Botnets, and Other Malicious Code" (June 2007), http://www.computereconomics.com/article.cfm?id=1225. Computer Economics.

15. Wikipedia contributors, "ILOVEYOU," *Wikipedia, The Free Encyclopedia*, http://en.wikipedia.org/w/index.php?title=ILOVEYOU&oldid=155786518 (accessed September 7, 2007).

16. "Monster Attack Steals User Data." BBC News article, published: 08/21/2007, URL: http://news.bbc.co.uk/2/hi/technology/6956349.stm.

17. "Net Threats: Why Going Online Remains Risky" (September 2007), online article published by Consumers Union of U.S., Inc. URL: www.consumerreports.org/cro/electronics-computers/computers/internet-and-other-services/net-threats-9-07/overview/0709_net_ov.htm.

18. "Net Threats: Why Going Online Remains Risky" (September 2007). URL: http://www.consumerreports.org/cro/electronics-computers/computers/internet-and-other-services/net-threats-9-07/overview/0709_net_ov.htm.

19. A Gartner study of March 2007 determined that 15 million Americans had their identity stolen in a 12-month period and identified the average costs and recoverability of these funds by consumers. URL for press release: www.gartner.com/it/page.jsp?id=501912.

20. Bo Carlsson and Gunnar Eliasson, "Industrial Dynamics and Endogenous Growth," *Industry and Innovation* (December 2003). "In one set of simulations we examined the effects of various features of technological systems on economic growth, particularly the role of networking, absorptive capacity (receptivity), and connectivity. . . . The simulations showed that it is important to be connected to a network. The basic reason is the imbalance between the limited knowledge and experience in each firm, and the greater knowledge existing in the economy at large. Thus, in networks the yield on each investment, whether in physical capital or knowledge, rises as a result

of knowledge spillovers, and the economy grows faster. It does not seem to matter much who the other network members are; the important thing is that networks expand the range of options available to each participant and increase the experience base upon which decisions can be made. The performance of the economy clearly declines when both connectivity and receptivity are reduced."

21. Tim Berners-Lee, speech to Congress (2007). URL: http://dig.csail.mit.edu/2007/03/01-ushouse-future-of-the-web.html.

3

Importance of IT Controls

VALUE: BEYOND "BECAUSE IT IS BEST"

The idea that the recent attention provided to information technology controls is new and just a fad, or nightmare, is mistaken. Across the globe governments, industries, and stakeholders alike have asked, required, and expected diligence over the systems that make up their enterprises.[1] In the United States alone, the government has explicitly required oversight and safeguards numerous times. The two most recent, giving Sarbanes-Oxley a rest for a moment, are the Fair Credit Reporting Act (FCRA), and Office of Management and Budget Circular A-123, "Management Accountability and Control." Interestingly enough, the circular defines management controls in a way that is echoed around the world:

> Management controls are the organization, policies, and procedures used by agencies to reasonably ensure that

- programs achieve their intended results;
- resources are used consistent with agency mission;
- programs and resources are protected from waste, fraud, and misman-agement;
- laws and regulations are followed; and
- reliable and timely information is obtained, maintained, reported and used for decision making.[2]

At this point we realize the business and global implications that technology and its associated services provide to society. But there are other important attributes of IT controls, such as the assurance that the environment is secure from tampering and that both government and customer expectations are met regarding delivery of services, as well as additional nonsecurity- and nonregulatory-focused benefits.

INFORMATION SECURITY

A common statement within the security profession is that if you are secure you *may* be compliant, but if you are only compliant you are certainly not secure. This statement is both truth and false. Any organization that does just enough as detailed by a regulatory checklist or an internationally accepted IT controls standard, such as COBIT (Control OBjectives for Information and related Technology), will not be secure if it is done without perspective of the organization's own systems, business, and risks. In fact, it is likely that such an organization will not even mitigate or address the threats that the regulation had intended. However, an organization under the exact same requirements and resources can become secure if it embraces the intent and opportunity to truly elevate the organization to a more mature and secure operational posture.

There is absolutely no secure solution that can address and mitigate every known and unknown attack against an organization. An organization may be successful only if it institutes a layered approach to security and controls. These are the backup plans for businesses, the spare tire in our cars, and the old credit card sitting in our wallet "just in case" we are unable to use our major cards at a location. The logic in formulating these backup plans is simple: You do not want to be caught without a net, and that is the very essence of layering the security safeguards in an organization.

The expense for companies to maintain security programs is typically part of the total information technology budget allocation for an organization, and Forrester estimates firms plan to spend 7.5 to 9 percent on information security alone.[3] A report issued by Deloitte Touche Tohmatsu detailed that corporate audit and certification costs made up 34 percent of these information security allotments, down 12 percent from 2005.[4]

Attackers, like businesses, only do what makes sense; they attack something using a sequence of steps that is likely to produce a result that exceeds the cost of the effort. This cost may very well be jail time, if they are caught, or it could just be a few late evenings. The benefits could be an advantage over competitors by having insider sales or product information, a fresh set of access codes for online sites, or cold hard cash. The constant return on investment (ROI) calculation done by companies instituting controls must forever weigh the attacker's perspective. This effort must take into consideration two critical points: first, the value of the data to the company, their competitors, and the criminal markets; second, the cost of the safeguards and their ability to limit and safeguard the data.

INFORMATION ASSURANCE

Operating in a state of noncompliance, consciously or unconsciously, nowadays results in fines, public disclosure, stock price volatility, and loss of business. In the marketing world, these points are called *FUD*: Fear, Uncertainty, and Doubt. Concentrating and operating an organization in such a fashion is by far the worst approach to reaching an optimized level of operations and meeting the challenges of a competitive marketplace, which results in an organization incapable of sustaining operations. Business is about embracing risk in an intelligent manner and not hiding from risk under our desks. While the upside of affirmative safeguards is tremendous and limited only to the organization's ability to execute and adapt, the negative risks are real and must be considered in every calculation and new venture.

An organization that is found out of compliance in the government space will lose access to lucrative contracts and the ability to fulfill third-party service contracts. This causal impact is an often-overlooked risk to organizations and results where regulation requirements apply to nonspecified parties by the mandate, but are included from contractual business agreements that extend the duties of the entire supply chain. When an organization outsources work, the companies it outsources to are expected to be compliant. If the parent organization becomes out of compliance, it loses the contracts and all the support companies lose the business.

The term "poster child" is applied to a company that is notable for actions that are considered egregious by society. Such events may be of such proportion—such as the Veterans Administration losing personal information on nearly 26 million veterans[5]—or of such belligerence—consider Enron (fill in any corporate fraud here)—that they become the basis for lawsuits, legislation, and industry reform.

Fines, fines, and more fines are levied on companies in a brutal fashion if they are deemed noncompliant. Penalties of this nature can occur in two ways: The organization is audited, fails, and is given a financial penalty, or an event occurs that demonstrates (in a most public fashion) that the company was noncompliant. This latter scenario is by far the worst, as it results in the most severe penalties, the longest-drawn-out proceedings, a high likelihood for burdensome regulation, excessive oversight, and being featured in the *Wall Street Journal*. In either case, additional oversight will be an unplanned expense to the organization and other noncompliant systems and processes are likely to be identified. Beyond oversight fines and fees, the organization may also be assessed contractual fines relating to breaches of confidentiality and service to customers. At its best this damages the near-term financial performance of the company. Earnings can be materially impacted as a result (consider TJMaxx, MCI WorldCom), and the company may become less able to perform acquisitions or adapt rapidly enough to market changes, or it may be forced to shed lines of business if extensive government oversight and approvals are imposed (ChoicePoint). All of this culminates in a loss of market capitalization to the firm, reduces its ability to acquire funds in the public market, and can lead to the demise of the entire firm (CardSystems, Enron).

VALUE BEYOND REGULATORY MANDATES

Business agility and responsiveness are factors in understanding an organization's appetite for risk. This appetite may be manifested in an aggressive acquisition plan, as demonstrated by some major pharmaceuticals, Cisco, or the Internet darling at the time of this writing, Google, which has been acquiring companies at a dizzying pace. Balancing the business strategy and the risk absorbed by the organization can be routine for one that is growing organically, but for one that is acquiring or divesting assets, it is a very challenging problem. Risks associated with these activities can be mitigated through a mature control environment, specifically those mandated by certain countries. These control environments provide visibility into the organization, promote an environment of open communication, and allow for adequate due diligence to properly inform management of the costs of the new strategy. The adoption of a control environment ensures that due diligence of the technology assets is done completely and that all valuations reflect these findings.

Operational efficiencies can be achieved when organizations have established and maintained a proper control environment and avoid distracting key resources to address compliance and audit demands unexpectedly. It is reasonable to have occurrences where key team members must participate cooperatively, but these instances should truly leverage the innate value of these teams, and not involve repetitive or overlapping requests. Organizations can do a better job of understanding how their operations are divided among the budget and any compliance or security-associated expenses. The more clarity that exists, the better the organization may identify areas of efficiencies and improve the effectiveness of the operational audit process. At the launch of any project or initiative, organizations must require proper accounting of the technology environment and capture the components related to audit, security, compliance, safeguards, and data management. By reducing cyclical spikes, an organization will be able to focus on the business priorities while addressing stakeholder concerns. Beyond efficiencies gained from not reprioritizing teams, an organization will also be able to minimize surprises and losses. Those organizations that have visibility into the operations of their key functions are able to identify developing threats and plans of action before a material impact occurs.

A study conducted by Deloitte Research identified significant and measurable efficiency gains and cost savings within a supply chain study.[6] These figures provide valuable inspiration on how true performance contributions may be highlighted in other areas and industries. The percentages below illustrate a single industry, but provide a clear basis of connecting business objectives and quantifiable results that may be reported regularly to executive management:

- 49 percent reduction in cargo delays

- 48 percent reduction in cargo inspections/examinations

- 38 percent reduction in theft/loss/pilferage

- 37 percent reduction in tampering

- 30 percent reduction in process deviations

- 14 percent reduction in excess inventory

The study also found a

- 12 percent increase in reported on-time delivery

- 30 percent increase in timeliness of shipping information

- 43 percent increase in automated handling of goods

- 50 percent increase in access to supply chain data

Once an organization is comfortable with its information systems, and these systems are supportive and sufficiently adaptive, its ability to increase risk exposure through more acquisitions and organic growth is enhanced. This ability to embrace business opportunities is enabled by the output and consistent reports provided to management about the control environment. Transparency of the control environments of acquired units prior to and after merger is critical to developing a realistic integration plan that includes how the company handles the security, audit, and compliance concerns.

IN THE END

As businesses expand their operations and leverage relationships with partners, clients, and vendors, the sophistication of the technology and the associated control environment that oversees them are directly correlated. While it is possible to implement technology without IT internal controls, the result is usually an underperforming organization that is not the leader in its market and is subject to fines both from oversight organizations and through loss of business due to poor adherence to service-level agreements.

The organization also is more likely to be a negative influence on the community that relies on and is supported by its services. Therefore, the ideal balance is between business and controls, which may be achieved only through a keen understanding of the business objectives, the business-specific risks, the expectations of third parties, and prudent placement of internal controls.

The value contributed by IT and its partner controls has tended to be quantified with risk models, negative predictions, and what-if analysis scenarios. The tangible benefits of the technology environment have not been communicated. Companies must seek to identify these benefits and communicate them accordingly. A process of identifying benefits provided by IT and then quantifying those benefits using specific data points (in order to eliminate assumptions and guesses) and measurable sources by applying confidence values on sources, identifies subjective/objective types of data and attributes a correction factor to adjust for human nature. Benefits of efficiency gains provided throughout the organization by IT can be demonstrated only if technology itself is measured against defined performance metrics and hard milestones.[7] Organizations that realize, define, measure, and communicate the value of IT will be able to allocate budgets properly year over year to extend and enhance the business's competitive posture.

ENDNOTES

1. Jan Heier, Michael Dugan, and David Sayers, "A Century of Debate for Internal Controls and Their Assessment: A Study of Reactive Evolution," *Accounting History* (November 2005): 39–70.

2. Alice M., Rivlin, Director. White House Circular A-123, "Management Accountability and Control." URL: http://www.whitehouse.gov/omb/circulars/a123/a123.html.

3. Khalid Kark, "2007 Security Budgets Increase: The Transition to Information Risk Management Begins," Forrester Research (January 9, 2007).

4. Deloitte Touche Tohmatsu, 2006 Global Security Survey. URL: www.deloitte.com/dtt/research/0,1015,sid=2211&cid=121523,00.html.

5. Veterans Affairs Data Security announcement disclosed a breach occurred in August 2006 involving 26 million veteran identities. URL: http://www.usa.gov/veteransinfo.shtml.

6. Deloitte Research, "A Risk Management Study: Disarming the Value Killers" (February 2005).

7. Process modified from online article, "Efficiency Gains: Can You Prove It?" by Rebecca Wettemann (May 2005).

PART TWO

INFLUENCE AND EFFECTS

It is a riddle, wrapped in a mystery, inside
an enigma; but perhaps there is a key.

—*Winston Churchill, radio broadcast in October 1939*

4

Death of Siloed
IT Strategy

Key Topics Addressed in This Chapter

Stages of siloed technology development

Marrying business and technology

IT CONTROLS PERMEATE BUSINESS OPERATIONS

Technology exists throughout businesses, and the IT controls utilized to maintain these operations are vital to the success of the organization. Controls are used in these ways, among others:

- Sales systems track validity of orders.

- Accounting ledgers validate that all input is authorized and approved.

- Security systems repel corporate spies, criminal organizations, and hackers from damaging the business.

- Continuous availability is maintained for online customer sales.

- Business process outsourcing companies operate in virtualized networks and segments securely contributing to projects.

- Student records at universities are properly coded and stored for backup purposes.

The evolution of environments where technology is introduced to gain efficiency and consistency in operations begins as a grassroots project where users develop automated solutions for daily tasks. The expansion of such efforts into the enterprise occurs for even the most sophisticated and global enterprises. *Knowledge workers* of today embrace technology to enhance company operations and improve on their own ability to deliver better results.[1] The growing trend of online tools and services, such as online software systems, Web 2.0, social and viral technologies, collaboration, networking, mindshare sites like Google's popular online office suite, and the recruiting site Jobster, increases the likelihood for rapid introduction and adoption of tools within an organization. This entrepreneurial spirit supported by technology is credited as being the source of success for companies around the world, including innovative stars like 3M and GE.[2] The negative effect of such breakthroughs in productivity and capability from grassroots initiatives is the tendency for these to be localized within small groups or divisions of the enterprise. In addition to these innovations and introduction of leading-edge technology, an organization must continually manage the data and environment; often these are two trains moving in opposite directions.

Siloing—the segmentation of usage and management of technology and tools developed or introduced by a core group of users—creates duplication and waste with regard to a company's information security technology strategy and controls.[3] The problems experienced within a single department also arise in other areas throughout the business. Therefore, the business may have dozens of parallel efforts under way aimed at achieving similar results. The time spent exploring, researching, developing, implementing, and managing these duplicate multidirectional grassroots solutions causes a negative return when considered at the macro-level of the organization. These micro-initiatives throughout an organization are difficult to scale, and the lack of integration and documentation for these ad-hoc processes further restricts the organization from leveraging the work of others. Beyond the scalability, lack of process consistency across an organization, and the introduction of untested technology, an organization must address the eventual industry or governmental establishment of IT controls that will require all businesses to substantiate each initiative and produce the appropriate oversight and control documentation.

The entrepreneurial spirit that produced the grassroots solutions and helped an organization grow and enhance customer experience is not the root cause of the problem. The silo effect turns up in organizations around the world that have departments charged with addressing individual specialty areas for IT control assurance requirements. This situation arises in nearly every organization that suddenly must address a new regulation or mandate. The establishment of the Health Insurance Portability and Accountability Act of 1996 (HIPAA) caused human resources executives to institute technology controls over their systems and operations. Firms in the healthcare market have even begun supplanting the existing corporate IT strategy in order to take advantage of the U.S. Nationwide Health Information Network (NHIN).[4] Another example occurred with the advent of the Sarbanes-Oxley Act (SOX); organizations were forced to develop departments to manage all of the SOX requirements within a special group. The European Union's introduction and improvement of its internal control environment requirements have caused similar responses within European and international organizations.

The resulting impact is the existence of IT control responsibility— accountable to meeting a requirement, budget, and technology purchase— spread between every major business line in the company to involve human resources, facilities, accounting, and risk management. These are naturally occurring and certainly warranted technology initiatives within organizations that have minimal or no control environment established, but they prove counterproductive for organizations that have embraced a corporate IT strategy and compliance program. Single instances of business vertical compliance responsibilities (i.e., the chief financial officer creates a new group to address SOX or the vice president of international affairs establishes a safe-harbor team) allow for clean tactical management of an isolated set of requirements. An organization that has more than one of these initiatives will suffer from a lack of structure that would otherwise be available if the responsibilities of the organization were taken with a strategic mind-set. Compliance responsibilities may include partner service-level agreements (SLAs) internal codes of ethics, internal business process standards, domestic legal mandates, industry trade group guidelines, and international regulations. Impacts may include any of these costs to the organization:

- Separate and costly audits of each division for a single mandate.

- Companies are unable to respond to business requests in a timely fashion.

- Internal staff is distracted for a greater period during audits.

- Possibility of identifying an ineffective control environment.

- Teams must build proper documents or absorb grassroots initiatives to the detriment of outstanding projects.

To achieve the greatest benefits from the natural ability of grassroots efforts and to maximize responsiveness for controls and business, organizations must evolve away from silo strategies toward a concise and complete control environment. This evolution is necessary and is happening throughout the world. Those organizations that evolve will compete and operate more effectively in the global marketplace. Another benefit of this alignment is the elimination of the negative costs experienced during merger-and-acquisition activity or general expansion and contraction of business lines. Siloed organizations forced to consolidate their enterprise strategy based on the introduction of a burdensome level of requirements often end up with an unnatural consolidation that is not ideal for cost savings or long-term efficiencies. In these situations, unfortunately, a race to the bottom occurs as control environments lacking an enterprise strategy are adjusted and manipulated to address tactical requirements without regard for the appropriateness of the systems and controls.

Organizations that maintain a central IT control strategy are more agile and better able to handle market shifts in expectations. The Hackett Group has a wonderful running benchmark of organizations grouped as *typical* and *world class*. Its studies show that organizations that "rely on standardization and reduced complexity to more effectively manage compliance costs," and generally organizations with strong control environments (whether natural and self-sustained or the result of embracing worldwide regulations), had lower costs associated with SOX Section 404 criteria and other internal control regulations.[5] Organizations that were unprepared initially experienced exorbitant costs to comply with SOX.

AGILE TECHNOLOGY CONTROLS

The alignment of IT strategy with the business involves understanding both the near-term and the long-term needs of the organization. This includes addressing the dynamic ability to change as an organization, and rapid establishment of controls supported and required by industry, management, and governments.

The ability to respond rapidly to the necessities of the market and business is a strong measure of the *agility* of the organization. In order to be agile, an organization must have confidence in its operations and their flexibility. This measure indicates the organization's capability to embrace outsourcing or optimization of business operations and allow for the replication of environments consistently as mergers and acquisitions or international expansion occur.

The efficiency of operations and the IT control environment must support and enhance the business's mission and direction. The enterprise controls in place must complement the objectives while ensuring that the intent of the mandate and threats identified are adequately managed. In addition, the instituted control environment must not unnecessarily burden the enterprise. Globalization of IT controls and IT strategy with business objectives allows for efficiency in all operations, and the act of embracing the risks through clear and appropriate control definition provides assurance and consistency. Business agility therefore may be considered a function of the organization's flexibility, or the ability to adjust rapidly to the needs of partners and customers.[6]

Operating internationally or domestically introduces risks of all types to the organization. Management of these risks is essential to ensuring the continued successful existence of the company. The control environment provides a framework that permits the identification of risks that may affect the organization and allows for the continued management of these risks. The IT controls should address the most important risks to the business by optimizing and maximizing the control environment in the organization to provide visibility and assurance regarding the mitigation of threats. Risks must be measured through a defined process that considers all the stakeholders of the organization, both internal and external.

BALANCING BUSINESS OBJECTIVES

Information technology environments and their controls are constantly evolving to adapt to constant shifts in the application of current technology and the rapid and ever-changing business needs. The current operating and technical posture of the organization represents only a flash in time, and as influencers—both internal and external, place demands on the organization the control environment must also respond. The evolution of the systems and their controls to respond to these influencers represents the target or future state of the organization's control environment. Balance and coordination of the organization's current and future concerns allow for it to achieve both compliance with regulated concerns and operational needs.

An organization can understand its current and future posture by self-evaluation, comparison against peers, and measurement against standards and frameworks. Businesses must implement unique solutions that complement the business and client needs, which are unique by industry but not completely by company. It is not appropriate simply to take a framework and drop it in the organization, as each company is unique. A blending of the frameworks, published standards, and guidance documents must be done with care and awareness of the business. The identification of areas of similarity and contrast provides every team and set of controls with a necessary balance and sanity check. Teams within companies tend to work independently without outside influence and almost in competition with peers. While independence provides certain moments of *original thought*, as sought endlessly by John Nash, the challenge of trying to reinvent the world of enterprise controls without incurring an unnecessary amount of waste is difficult.[7] The firm that is able to leverage the work achieved and published by organizations previously from around the world will gain from its experience and can leap frog the development path attributed to the development of such safeguards.

Benchmarking allows for the comparison of an organization's functions to other organizations in similar situations but not necessarily similar industries. It provides a method of comparison that allows any organization to identify and achieve reasonable targets and to work toward an optimal set of performance metrics.

The employment of benchmarking allows organizations to institute a thorough measurement process against a relevant group of common organizations or functions. Benchmarking provides organizations with an understanding of what can be achieved. Through exposure to other companies, it identifies additional areas for improvement and increasing value. Benchmarking internally using self-evaluations and self-assessments is possible but limiting; external benchmarking provides exposure to a wide variety of ideas and approaches.

Benchmarking sources can be found in numerous freely available resources. Public papers produced by industry-watch groups, universities, and case studies provide excellent guidance on what other organizations are doing to achieve similar results.[8] Organizations can interpret the information and apply it based on the business and the unique nature of the control environment. Governments also provide specific mandated controls and guidance documents that organizations can adapt to their needs.[9] These provide very useful templates and thorough discussions on concerns that are applicable to many organizations. Besides benefiting from the freely available analysis and control environment guidance, the organization following these controls can further mature and better prepare to enter into foreign markets. A business that embraces published guidance is better prepared to address the mandates of the future.

Benchmarking is done to identify two specific metrics:

1. Where the industry or those who are challenged by similar business environments are with regard to IT controls and technology.

2. Determine which regulations and business objectives are of material concern to the organization.

The percentage values or relevant CMMi score will be generally lower for compliance to legislative requirements when compared against industry and professional society leading practice guidances. Thus, an organization cannot merely be compliant and consider itself to be meeting the business objectives or long-term mission. The competitiveness of an organization's control environment should be tracked against peers that face similar challenges and not simply legislative requirements.

ACTION STEPS

Business owners and active participants in the IT components of any business have many available sources and references to enable performance measurement and benchmarking. Broadly there are two main sources for this type of free data—government-sponsored and non-government-sponsored publications.

Nongovernmental sources consist of every trade group, study, interview, and report that is not a mandate or requirement. These are extremely valuable as they provide a wealth of knowledge that is both extremely affordable—usually free if used internally—and readily available. Industry studies, surveys, case studies, interviews, and research reports issued by the Institute of Internal Auditors, Information Systems Audit and Control Association, Association of Certified Fraud Examiners, SANS Institute under the Global Information Assurance Certification process, and National Security Agency (Security Configuration Guides) are excellent references for any benchmarking initiative. In addition, many of these organizations allow for online benchmarking and for individuals and corporations to issue surveys and questionnaires to the entire member base, permitting further specificity and value in the benchmarking effort.

Government works provide very detailed requirements that are extremely specific and well researched. However, they are developed mainly for government institutions, so a level of interpretation is necessary when applying them to private organizations that operate within different risk, technology, and legal bounds. Excellent resources include government oversight studies and guidance publications by these organizations and committees. Businesses may embrace these guidelines but should be aware of the scope and applicability of the guidance, as some are centered on a single concern. Government mandates should be considered as the floor or starting point of any control environment standards program. The publications are broadly well written, thorough, and provide a wide breadth of control implementation approaches as compared against private sector safeguards. While these government resources are not restricted by border (although their audit requirements and compliance mandates may be,) such globally accessible guidelines and standards of practice are extremely valuable. Any organization may access and incorporate these into their programs to prepare for future adherence to laws or simply to prevent reinventing the compliance program wheel. Organizations in Germany may access the framework established in Japan, and those in the United States are able to learn and advance their programs using those detailed in the Netherlands. This cross-border usage is conducive to our global society and allows for the further advancement of global convergence of IT internal control requirements and expectations.

The complexity of technology environments can grow rapidly in an organically expanding business but can expand exponentially through acquisitions. This complexity is not simply a function of the number of additional users or systems, but includes the appliances, software, authentication methods, operational procedures, monitoring systems, host platforms, standards of communication, maintenance structures, and redundancy required in highly available environments. Such complexity in technology and organization can become a source of high costs to the point of being wasteful when additional controls and operational procedures are laid on top of these acquired environments. The key to controlling the systems and the costs of operations is simplification and then consolidation. You must first simplify your systems (remove complexity) environments and then consolidate them (remove duplication). Finally, once these acquisitions are completed effectively, it is possible to overlay an IT security and control system and have cleaner audits and compliance records, and therefore lower costs.

ENDNOTES

1. Peter Drucker coined the phrase and expounded on it throughout his career as a recognized management leader.
2. GE and 3M consistently achieve innovative company awards due to their established programs that encourage, support, and reward innovation and attention to detail. Recent (April 24, 2006) *BusinessWeek* study. URL: www.businessweek.com/magazine/content/06_17/b3981401.htm.
3. "Information silos arose gradually as information management evolved over decades. Operational departments ranging from Accounting to Manufacturing to Warehousing developed specialized databases to satisfy their own complex departmental needs." The article provides a nice breakdown of silo effects on call center capabilities. Although dated, the article still resonates with the challenges of today. Lisa Chiranky, "Technology Advancements Bring Information Silos Out of Isolation,"*Telemarketing & Call Center Solutions* (March 1998).
4. Nationwide Health Information Network Homepage. URL: http:// www.hhs.gov/healthit/healthnetwork/background/.
5. The Hackett Group provides research and running comparisons of world-class organizations. The available research areas include "Complexity Cost Impact," "Sarbox & Finance Cost," "World-Class HR Metrics," "World-Class IT Metrics," and "World-Class Procurement Metrics." Expansive research is available to all Hackett Group clients. Direct URL: www.thehackettgroup. com/portal/site/apresearch/menuitem.b024ed6253e0100ad91dc21066f069a0.
6. "Business Agility = Speed × Flexibility" is espoused by Nicholas D. Evans, *Business Agility: Strategies for Gaining Competitive Advantage Through Mobile Business Solutions* (Upper Saddle River, NJ: Prentice-Hall PTR, 2002).
7. John Nash continually sought for an original thought, and unfortunately rediscovered theories and truths previously discovered by others in the field.
8. The Center for Internet Security has specific technical benchmarks available at URL: www.cisecurity.org. The Information Technology Process Institute has broader benchmarking information available at URL: www. itpi.org.
9. Freely available government documents within the United States are in the NIST library. Specifically valuable in this context is the NIST SP800-53 publication, "Recommended Security Controls for Federal Information Systems."

5

A Regulated Environment

DEFINITION OF INTERNAL CONTROL

Internal Control Advantage

Beyond the competitive advantages of technology and the importance of the safeguards to ensure that these systems operate consistently to deliver service and support revenue, there exist legal necessities that encourage the same type of IT internal controls. The next listing highlights advantages of having an IT enterprise control environment:

- Consistent language throughout the entire enterprise facilitates clearer communications, better success rate for projects, and complete metrics.

- Standardization of technology, infrastructure, and software enables businesses by:

  - Supporting rapid expansion of an organization, as scaling is accomplished simply by reproduction and not reinvention.

  - Lowering total cost of ownership (TCO) by reducing the number of specialists within the organization.

  - Increasing the effectiveness of the help desk support center by focusing on a single technology platform.

- Lowering licensing and maintenance costs, because of discounts from bulk purchases from vendors of the IT enterprise controls.

- Enabling simpler integration with clients, partners, and acquired entities due to stricter due diligence requirements; also establishes a process for integrating with those not adhering to a centralized approach.

- Greater visibility, success, and savings in projects.

- Increased productivity of end users resulting from less downtime, patching/maintenance of virus outbreaks, and timeliness of processing of jobs in applications, as reliability and consistency will be more assured.

- Increased productivity by information technology (IT) teams resulting from the lack of mission-critical interruptions during planned activities.

- Spin-off advantage is that internal business improvement projects are achieved on time or ahead due to the lack of such interruptions.

- Reduced interruptions resulting from fires (emergency projects, audit activity, security breach) that negatively impact IT strategy by introducing delays and complexities.

Commonality among International Expressions of Internal Control

Around the globe, the concept of internal controls and what is considered relevant with regard to technology internal controls is generally consistent across businesses and professionals. This is due to the overall global acceptance of the components that make up an internal control and that of an IT internal control. The European Union (EU) has issued directives and guidance through Directives 4 and 8, but no EU-centric definition exists at this time. Instead, over two dozen definitions are in place within the European bloc.

In the United States, internal control has been defined by several authorities. The most widely adopted within the United States and internationally recognized is from the Committee of Sponsoring Organizations (COSO). The initial publication addressing internal controls and an organization's control environment, the *Integrated Framework*, was published in 1992 and includes this definition:

Internal control is broadly defined as a process, effected by an entity's board of directors, managers and other personnel, designed to provide reasonable assurance regarding the achievement of objectives in the following categories:

- Effectiveness and efficiency of operations.

- Reliability of financial reporting.

- Compliance with applicable laws and regulations.[1]

Outside of the United States, nations, oversight bodies, and enforcement organizations have produced variations in the definition to fit their needs. In some cases the definitions directly reference other internationally recognized definitions and frameworks, while others do not. In Japan, for example, a new framework was initiated in 2005 that affirms portions of the COSO definition just quoted. It also includes specific additions and a focus on technology usage within an organization and the response of an organization to risks.[2]

Canada has established several mandates and through numerous published works has defined the bounds of internal controls for organizations. The mandates do not explicitly state a specific published framework to adopt to become compliant, but instead focus on a *principles structure* to allow the organization to construct its own appropriate framework. The language within the published works regarding internal controls echoes that found in Japan and the United States but highlights specifically the need to "provide reasonable assurance regarding prevention or timely detection of unauthorized acquisition, use or disposition of the issuer's assets that could have a material effect on the annual financial statements or interim financial statements." This expansion is consistent with many of the security and privacy requirements found in U.S. guidance documents.[3]

The Canadian Institute of Chartered Accountants also has published a series of guidance documents to facilitate adherence to these new internal control requirements and has summarized the Canadian internal control definition in this way:

> Internal control is widely taken to mean the processes established by management to provide reasonable assurance about achievement of the organization's objectives regarding operations, reporting and compliance. Internal control is designed to address identified risks that threaten any of those objectives. The Canadian Securities Administrators (CSA) definition of internal control over financial reporting specifies objectives relevant to financial reporting.[4]

Organizations for the accounting and internal audit profession source their definitions directly from COSO, the Office of the Comptroller of the Currency (OCC), and the Securities and Exchange Commission (SEC). While the OCC focuses primarily on the financial transactions and operations of an institution, the scope still includes the need for an effective risk management system, internal procedures and policies, and accurate record keeping. Expanding beyond the OCC specifications, organization's should include an effective system of controls as defined by COSO.

The Autorité des Marchés Financiers (AMF) Working Group in France—the Financial Markets' Authority—published a report in 2005 as a response to EU discussions on internal controls in reaction to the legislative activities within the United States and Canada. The report echoed many of the concerns and requirements of the other nations, but emphasized corrective efforts and measures requiring properly functioning assets at a process and security level. In addition, the report highlighted the fiscal utilization of assets within an organization as a requirement.[5]

Given the different regions, cultures, and situations that initiated the need to define internal controls, the definitions are remarkably similar and generally differ more in form than in substance. Each of these definitions has a strong consistent theme, which can be summarized in this way:

- Internal control is a process—continual and everlasting—and as a result, organizations must operationalize, document, and measure.

- Controls should afford reasonable but not complete assurance. The implication is that a measure of risk exists and is included in the assumptions of safeguards.

- Controls should ensure efficiency and effectiveness in operations to enable cost reductions, greater productivity, and dependability.

- Controls should ensure reliability of information.

- Controls should ensure compliance with relevant regulations and principles.

Recognition of such universal applicability and the embrace of an internationally acceptable definition would strongly promote an international perspective in any organization and allow for the global satisfaction of multiple laws and requirements. This is an important fact as over time the enforcement of and attention to internal controls ebbs and flows, like most politically sensitive topics.

REGULATORY ACTIVITY AND INTERNAL CONTROLS

Internal control requirements are nothing new. They have been implemented by various parts of government, business, and society for decades and even hundreds of years. The mandates in Exhibit 5.1 are a representation of such requirements for a sample of nations and demonstrate the legal substance and the trend of increasing importance, especially over the past decade. Many legal mandates focus on specific industries; for instance, the Sarbanes-Oxley Act of 2002 (SOX) focuses mainly on U.S. public institutions or those with public debt.

Exhibit 5.1   Annotated History of Internal Control Regulations
and Related Publications

1892	Lawrence Dicksee, *Auditing*
1934	United States, Securities Exchange Act of 1934
1948	AIA Committee on Auditing Procedures, Special Report on Internal Control
1957	Saul Levy, Special Report on Internal Control
1977	United States, Foreign Corrupt Practices Act
1979	AICPA, Report of the Special Advisory Committee on Internal Accounting Control (aka Minahan Report)
1993	Canadian Deposit Insurance Corporation, Standards of Sound Business and Financial Practices: Internal Control
1994	COSO publishes *Internal Control—Integrated Framework*
1995	Canadian Institute of Chartered Accountants, Guidance on Control
1997	European Monetary Institute, Internal Control Systems of Credit Institutions
1998	Basel Committee on Banking Supervision, Internal Control Systems in Banking Organisations
1999	Institute of Chartered Accountants in England and Wales, UK, Internal Control: Guidance for Directors on the Combined Code
2002	United States, Sarbanes-Oxley Act, Public Company Accounting Reform and Investor Protection Act of 2002
2002	The Netherlands, Corporate Governance in The Netherlands 2002: The State of Affairs
2003	LSF, Loi sur la Sécurité Financière (Law on Financial Security)
2003	FEE, Discussion paper
2003	Bill 198, Ontario, Canada, Keeping the Promise for a Strong Economy Act (Budget Measures), 2002
2004	COSO, Internal Control over Financial Reporting—Guidance for Smaller Public Companies
2004	IFAC in cooperation with CIMA, Enterprise Governance—Getting the Balance Right
2004	Hong Kong Stock Exchange, Code on Corporate Governance Practices
2005	Hong Kong Institute of Certified Public Accountants, at the request of the Exchange, Internal Control and Risk Management—A Basic Framework
2005	Institute of Chartered Accountants in England and Wales, UK, Internal Control: Guidance for Directors on the Combined Code, revised
2005	ISACA, COBIT version 4.0
2006	Japan, Financial Instruments and Exchange Law
2006	COSO, Enterprise Risk Management—Integrated Framework

Regulations and mandates are needed for many reasons, but most simply they exist to prevent a negative event from occurring (in some cases from occurring again). Regulations are designed to ensure that markets and participants have confidence in the system and the organizations they are relying on. The lack of confidence in any system handicaps the entire system at once. Unfortunately, as we discussed earlier, many of these laws were born in haste and passion due to a lack of morality by a firm or entire industry. Examples of these events include Japan's Seibu Railway, Kanebo, and Livedoor.

GLOBALIZATION OF REGULATIONS

Locally every business and organization must be aware of the laws for their region and industry. They also need to consider the laws that are being applied to the organization that are required as a result of contractual agreements, despite that the law is explicitly written for their business partner. This is discussed in Chapter 1 under "Regulatory Leakage," but some specifics are necessary before we examine some of the most prominent IT control mandates and laws.

Just as laws are *trickling down*, meaning that legislative requirements are being applied and adhered to by parties not explicitly defined under the law itself, businesses are furthering these validation activities through vendor audit programs. In addition, the global volume of laws and requirements is increasing across all industries and nations. This acceptance of foreign nation mandates and foreign industry oversight group requirements is resulting in a consistency in compliance control programs. It is also setting a precedent that business managers in every industry must recognize: The world marketplace seeks assurance, and whether a customer or a vendor, the need for attestation exists. As a result, a set of global best practices is emerging, and companies that follow these are preferred by governments and private industry alike.

Federal Mandates

The Sarbanes-Oxley Act of 2002 was adopted immediately after the headline-capturing accounting scandals of the likes of Enron and Tyco. The legislation served many purposes but specifically required the institution and management of an internal control environment. Section 404 of the act and the Public Company Accounting Oversight Board (PCAOB) through Auditing Standard 5 (AS5) established the guidance and methodology to evaluate the general information technology controls that make up the internal control environment.[6] Section 404 has been greatly criticized, due to the discretion afforded to audit firms and the lack of specific requirements offered by the oversight body. As a result, initial compliance costs greatly eclipsed every estimate, from the initial SEC estimate of $92,000 to an average cost of approximately $2.9 million to a company in 2006.[7] Lessons learned from organizations dealing with Section 404 can be adopted throughout the entire enterprise to enhance every aspect of the control environment.

The process of associating business processes and their values, and relating these both to IT general controls and to balance sheet items, is essential to identifying a company's most important processes. Numerous studies demonstrate that a company that has a strong existing internal control environment does not incur burdensome auditing and compliance expenses to ramp up for legislation such as SOX.[8] Another study demonstrated a direct correlation between companies disclosing material deficiencies and poorer-quality earnings.[9] Therefore, it is reasonable to conclude that, if an organization already has a strong control environment, it will be mature enough to address additional disclosure requirements, will have more accurate financial records, and will be able to return value to stakeholders with minimal impact on business operations.

The mature control environments required by SOX can be leveraged to and from other regulations that the organization must adhere to throughout the world. This has been largely successfully done by organizations within the United States that operate in the financial sector, as they must also maintain reports on their compliance for the Gramm-Leach-Bliley Act (GLBA), the Federal Financial Institutions Examination Council (FFIEC) book requirements, and stock exchange listing requirements.

Globally the adoption of IT internal controls occurs through varying levels of legislation, international trade agreements, stock exchange mandates, and business-initiated requirements. In all parts of the world, governments have instituted regulations that require companies to have an internal control environment. Although the expected level of control varies for each nation and region, the constant theme throughout these mandates is the need for management of risk. The majority of mandates from around the globe outline the most appropriate approach as the institution of a risk-based methodology. In other words, controls should be adapted to the business and its inherent market risks.

Throughout the European Union, very practical and market-responsible legislation is in existence and under review. The EU's structure allows for both high-level (akin to federal legislation in the United States) and regional state-level laws. The agreements made by EU member states are guidelines that mandate the enactment of regional implementation laws.[10] In Australia and Japan, there are laws that strongly reflect the guidance and framework put forth by the International Standards Organization 17799 (ISO-17799). This standard is considered a very strong framework to manage business and information systems, and has been augmented with the introduction and adoption of ISO 27001. In addition, Australia and Japan have introduced SOX-like laws to enhance disclosure and operation of risk management within companies.

Regional Mandates

Conducting business between regions requires as much knowledge of the regional legal environment as operating in separate hemispheres. Every region has the right to institute laws that protect the local citizens, and while these may be of varying degrees of complexity and sophistication, they are required. Companies must acknowledge the requirements of neighboring regions, their laws, and their cultural differences. Given the transparency of borders online and the ability of consumers to purchase and acquire services internationally, companies must match the behavior of their consumers with their compliance programs.

An example is when companies within one region provide safeguards and services, such as disclosure notification, but elect not to provide such services to neighboring regions. The cost to expand a compliance program beyond a specific region is negligible compared to the costs of establishing and maintaining the program. Therefore, organizations should elect to apply such services to all clients who face the same risks. This equal treatment ensures that countries from one region are not required to *duplicate* legislation from other regions—an action that only increases the cost to the companies, as these new regulations are not the same as the first ones. By affording customers equal treatment regardless of their global location, consumers and regulators understand the company is working in their best interests. Such a situation has occurred within the United States more than once, where firms selectively treated consumers differently (providing customer Group A with free security services and denying Group B the same services—despite the fact that both groups were exposed to the same risks). As a result over three dozen state laws have been enacted, and two countries have elected to establish legislation to protect their citizens.[11]

This trend is likely to continue for the other laws that require good controls and disclosure. Regrettably these laws are not reactions to the fact that breaches occurred but rather due to companies failing to reveal regional privacy disclosures because they were under no legal requirement to do so.

Industry: Self-Regulation

A strong desire to prevent government regulation and to protect the charter members of an industry has led to several aggressive self-regulation efforts—here we will highlight one successful and another not. These proactive-self-mandating organizations leverage their contractual agreements and operational dependencies to establish and enforce mandates throughout their industries. The most notable include the credit card industry's Payment Card Industry Data Security Standard (PCI DSS), which is required for all organizations that store, transmit, or process credit cards to varying degrees based on their type of business. The financial markets have the most mature set of government regulations but also a continued process of self-regulation and enhancement, such as through the newest publication of Basel II by the Swiss Bankers Association. Although the existence of any standard provides some level of assurance, many industries would benefit from a comprehensive single approach to prevent duplication, degradation of trust between operators, and inconsistency in controls by gaining efficiencies in a single secure system.

The energy transmission and storage companies in the United States have adopted IT control standards through the establishment of the North American Electric Reliability Corporation (NERC), a voluntary organization.

These industries, energy transmission and financial services, represent vital components of the market and lives of everyday citizens. The importance of the information contained within credit reports and financial assets is a critical impetus for ensuring that the companies overseeing, managing, trading, and safeguarding the data maintain proper control over their environments. It is estimated that nearly 159 million Americans had their identity or personally identifiable information records stolen between April 20, 2005 and August 27, 2007.[12] Nearly a third of the population in the United States and the United Kingdom have had personal information disclosed through a breach. Beyond the damage to consumer goodwill, the economic costs of these breaches are extremely harmful to companies.[13]

CREDIT CARD INDUSTRY

How Much Is That Credit Card Worth?

The availability of funds through the payment transaction network is vast— VISA Inc. alone processes over $4 trillion in card sales volume around the world.[14] As a result of the success of these organizations, continuous assaults occur at all points of the payment transaction cycle. In spite of the continued efforts within the industry to regulate and enforce safeguards, these attacks are periodically successful and fuel the continued debate for greater oversight and sanctions within the industry. The coordinated attacks against corporations are extremely profitable. The company liabilities resulting from a breach of such information have been shown to equal from $2 per record to nearly $300 per record depending on the source and amount of costs combined. Regardless, at even two dollars a breached account can result in a multi-million-dollar expense plus negative press.[15] These attacks are coordinated, sophisticated, and in most cases orchestrated by organized crime and terror networks.

Breaches of credit information or personally identifiable information that can be used for identity theft include organizations of all shapes and sizes. The most prominent breaches include those in the U.S and U.K governments, which have lost between 10 and 30 percent of the citizens' information. The largest retailers, service companies, and universities have been the victims of breaches of this nature. A study conducted by Phil Howard of the University of Washington suggests that electronic records in the United States are being compromised at a rate of nearly 6 million records a month, and the quantity and frequency are increasing year over year.[16]

PCI DSS: Clear, Strict, Enforced

The credit card industry has established the most defined and respected industry standard, known as the Payment Card Industry Data Security Standard. This standard is maintained by PCI Security Standards Council, which was formed in 2005.[17] The council was formed by the original five members that created PCI DSS, and includes VISA Inc., MasterCard, Discover, American Express, Diner's Club, and JCB Co. Together these organizations were able to leverage their operating contracts to include adherence to a specific security standard. This standard, developed over years of collaboration and from feedback by both customers and auditors, is recognized as thorough and sufficient considering the value of the data. PCI DSS established a phase-in process, set up a fine structure, and opened the effort of continuous maintenance and validation to any firm that is accredited by the PCI Security Standards Organization.

The PCI DSS, an international standard, is rapidly adding business efficiencies and providing greater confidence to consumers. In addition, businesses that once negotiated and required SAS 70 attestations are now asking for PCI DSS compliance certifications. This trend is timely and appropriate, given the nature of PCI DSS, its validation of proper payment processing technologies, and focus on strong IT controls.

To date, organizations that have violated the standard have been assessed millions in fines. Some, such as CardSystems, were completely disconnected from the card processing networks. This action, in effect, bankrupted the business and forced it to sell its assets. For the credit card industry, the standard's most important strength is enforcement. The fines are well defined; compliance is required without question based on a very simple risk approach test; compliance mandates are explicit and interpretation is swift and clear from both the auditing firm and the card companies; and penalties are levied on offending organizations. Should any of these facts change in the payment transaction industry to where subjectivity and inconsistency surrounding enforcement and control requirements exist, such actions will certainly lead to the introduction of future government legislation. As NERC chief executive Rick Sergel said regarding the need for imposing regulations on industries beyond voluntary mandates:

> The North American electricity industry has operated one of the world's most reliable electricity networks under voluntary guidelines for decades. . . .

Voluntary guidelines worked very well to a point, but they were not enough. The electricity industry is no stronger than its weakest link, and a mistake by one entity can affect customers hundreds of miles away, as we saw with the August 2003 blackout that affected 50 million people in the United States and Canada. To avoid future blackouts, everyone must follow all the rules, all the time. Mandatory standards are the next logical step toward achieving that.[18]

THE ENERGY SECTOR

We Only Notice It When It Is Gone

The terrible heat waves that hit Europe in August 2003 and June 2006 strained the power grid system. When it faltered, millions suffered and nearly 35,000 people died as a result, 14,800 in France, alone.[19] In the United States, transmission lines weave across the country. A mishap at a single location, such as in the northeastern blackout in 2005, can result in widespread blackouts, where many are without power across several states. These problems are documented as being self-inflicted or the result of bad timing, and not purposefully malicious. However, the power grids are controlled, in most cases, remotely. If they are attacked/compromised by a malicious party, even greater damage and loss of life may result if done in coordination with severe weather.

The energy sector in North America transmits, produces, and manages nearly 69.17 quadrillion Btu power a day. Through this interconnected industry, technology as old as power generation itself is connected with leading Internet technology. The blending of Internet technology and SCADA (Supervisory Control and Data Acquisition—these are the electronics systems that connect to the power production turbines and dams around the world) provides tremendous flexibility and agility to businesses, enabling them to respond to power-generation needs across the globe and region, but creates new risks to these systems by removing prior control assumptions. Prior to these connections, SCADA systems were secured by limiting physical access and direct communication lines. Today the connectivity removes the necessity to be physically onsite to manage these systems, and the public nature of the Internet allows for greater numbers of attackers. The threats to these systems, such as nuclear power plants, was highlighted as recently as August 2007 at Defcon, a hacking conference, and in the popular press, such as *Forbes*.[20]

Linking these nationally critical infrastructures and placing them on the public Internet is cause for concern. Technology safeguards have been developed and are promoted by NERC to secure these systems.[21] International standards have not yet been adopted, but those in the energy sector have self-imposed strict standards of security to ensure the availability and integrity of their systems. While the credit card industry has sustained greater financial losses and impacted more individuals, the energy sector's impact on society is far more severe and can mean life and death. The voluntary nature of the safeguards promoted by NERC has been elevated to mandatory after regulation was enacted to further require strong safeguards in the industry.

The security safeguards within the energy sector in the United States have been promulgated by two separate groups: NERC and FERC (Federal Energy Regulatory Comission). NERC members include any company that participates in managing the power grid system, from production to transmission.[22] FERC is the U.S. government oversight body for these companies. FERC has authorized NERC as an official Electric Reliability Organization (ERO), to develop and publish standards for the industry. With the passage of the Energy Act of 2006, FERC may enforce these mandates as it sees fit. NERC safeguards were established through voluntary peer evaluation, involved a review period, and required an overall positive response by the members.

FINANCIAL INDUSTRY

Additional Mandates

Financial markets around the world have very sophisticated and complex mandates that govern how business is conducted. These requirements were developed to protect the world markets and to ensure proper controls on the flow of money. Yet this industry, the most heavily regulated and monitored in the world, continues to introduce additional requirements and impose mandates, the most recent of which was published by the Swiss Bankers Association. It introduced Basel II, "International Convergence of Capital Measurement and Capital Standards: A Revised Framework" to accomplish several objectives, one of which was to improve the risk management of operations and enhance aspects of financial reserves and IT internal controls.[23]

While the standard was published in Switzerland, the impact is global in scale. Due to the interconnectedness of the financial systems and the nearly transparent movement of cash around the world, the requirements are being adopted by all organizations worldwide. Basel II is the first in what is expected to be many similar regulations of global impact. The insurance industry is likely to follow with its own regulations, due to the similarity and codependency of banking and insurance.

The stock markets around the world have mandates that apply to every company that participates in the exchanges. These mandates impact organizations that seek to have international listings or to participate in the public debt markets. As a result, organizations must recognize and adhere to the requirements set forth by these exchanges. Listing requirements that have impacts for IT internal controls and that have been updated recently include the Hong Kong listing requirements,[24] the Turnbull Report of the London Stock Exchange, the Netherlands listing requirements, which require a comply or explain process, and the New York Stock Exchange's 303A, "Corporate Governance Rules" in the United States.[25]

LONGEVITY OF MANDATES

Time will tell how long existing laws will survive as society struggles to establish an appropriate culture of control, safeguards, laws, and enforcement. The political environment is heavily influenced by consumers and business interests must cope with the power struggle that exists as control requirements veer from severe to nonexistent. While the current requirements are still fairly severe, the effort is under way to begin to relax some regulations. Regardless of the outcomes, the established controls, enhanced assurance provided to investors, and validation of service delivery between partners are in place and expected, and it will be many years before the market or companies completely forget about these mandates and can convince their stakeholders to operate without them.

ENDNOTES

1. COSO, Integrated Framework (1992), p. 1.
2. FSA, "Guidelines for the Basis of Assessment and Auditing over Financial Reporting (Public Draft)" (2007), translated from Japanese.
3. MI 52-109 is one of many government legislative efforts designed to enhance the integrity of the Canadian financial markets. "Certification of Disclosure in Issuers' Annual and Interim Filings," and updated with CSA Notice 52–313 (March 2006). URL: http://www.osc.gov.on.ca/Regulation/Rulemaking/Current/Part5/csa_20060310_52-313_status-52-111.pdf#search=%22CSA%20Notice%2052-313%20%22.
4. James L. Goodfellow, FCA and Alan Willis, CA Internal Control 2006, "The Next Wave of Certification Guidance for Management" (September 2006). URL: http://www.cica.ca/index.cfm/ci_id/33791/la_id/1.htm.
5. Autorité des marchés financiers, "2005 AMF Report on Information Published by Listed Companies on Corporate Governance and Internal Control Procedures." URL: www.amf-france.org/documents/general/6543_1.pdf.
6. PCAOB Release No. 2007-005A, "An Audit of Internal Control Over Financial Reporting That Is Integrated with an Audit of Financial Statements and Related Independence Rule and Conforming Amendments" (June 12, 2007). URL: http://www.pcaobus.org/Rules/Docket_021/2007-06-12_Release_No_2007-005A.pdf.

7. FEI 2006 Sarbanes-Oxley compliance survey of accelerated filers showed an improvement of 23% year over year in compliance costs related to SOX. URL: www.financialexecutives.org/404survey.

8. The Hackett Group, World Class Performance Research Reports based on *Hackett's 2005 Book of Numbers*™. URL: www.thehackettgroup.com.

9. W. Ge and S. McVay, "On the Disclosure of Material Weaknesses in Internal Control after the Sarbanes-Oxley Act," Working paper, University of Michigan and New York University (2004).

10. http://europa.eu/index_en.htm.

11. Several examples exist, but the highest-profile companies include ChoicePoint and TJMaxx.

12. Privacy Rights Clearinghouse/UCAN, "A Chronology of Data Breaches" (accessed on August 1, 2007). URL: www.privacyrights.org/ar/ChronDataBreaches.htm.

13. "2006 Annual Study: Cost of a Data Breach—Understanding Financial Impact, Customer Turnover, and Preventative Solutions" determined the cost per breach per account is approximately $182 per record, or $4.8 million per company. Study URL: www.pgp.com/downloads/research_reports/ponemon.html.

14. VISA Financial statistics published online state $4.8 trillion for the year in card sales volume for 12 months ended March 31, 2007. URL: http://corporate.visa.com/md/st/main.jsp.

15. TJMaxx quarterly report indicated that the cost of the breaches is estimated at approximately $2 per card when liability reserves are included. This did cause a material impact to the company's earnings report (April 14, 2007). URL: http://home.businesswire.com/portal/site/tjx/index.jsp?epi-content=GENERIC&newsId=20070814005701&ndmHsc=v2*A93877560 0000*B1188467802000*C4102491599000*DgroupByDate*J2*N1001148 &newsLang=en&beanID=1809476786&viewID=news_view.

Avivah Litan of Gartner has calculated the cost of breaches to be around $300 per exposed account. URL: www.cio.com/article/121207/Data_Breaches_Start_at_the_Gas_Station_Analyst_Says.

16. www.wiareport.org.

17. www.pcisecuritystandards.org/index.htm.

18. "New Era in United States Electricity Industry Starts June 18—Mandatory Reliability Standards Enforceable for First Time." URL: ftp://www.nerc.com/pub/sys/all_updl/docs/pressrel/06-01-07-Standards-PR.pdf.

19. Bhattacharya, Shaoni, "European Heat Wave Caused 35,000 Deaths" (October 10, 2003). URL: www.newscientist.com/article.ns?id=dn4259.

20. Andy Greenberg, "America's Hackable Backbone" (August 22, 2007). URL: http://www.forbes.com/2007/08/22/scada-hackers-infrastructure-tech-security-cx_ag_0822hack.html.

Ganesh Devarajan, "Unraveling SCADA Protocols: Using Sulley Fuzzer." URL: http://www.defcon.org/images/defcon-15/dc15-presentations/dc-15-devarajan.pdf.

21. NERC CIP safeguard standards. URL: www.nerc.com/~filez/standards/Reliability_Standards.html#Critical_Infrastructure_Protection.

22. NERC. URL: www.nerc.com/about.

23. Basel Committee on Banking Supervision, "Principle 1—Framework for Internal Control Systems in Banking Organisations"; Basel Committee on Banking Supervision, "International Convergence of Capital Measurement and Capital Standards" (June 2006). URL: www.bis.org/publ/bcbs107.htm. Basel Committee on Banking Supervision, "Sound Practices for the Management and Supervision of Operational Risk" (February 2003). URL: www.bis.org/publ/bcbs91.htm.

24. "Internal Control and Risk Management—A Basic Framework." URL: www.hkicpa.org.hk/publications/corporategovernanceguides/Guide_Eng_August.pdf.

25. www.nyse.com/pdfs/finalcorpgovrules.pdf.

6

The World Is Your Oyster of Resources and Guidance

A WORLD OF RESOURCES AND GUIDANCE

Implementer's Dilemma

Many myths and misconceptions exist regarding the adoption and selection of frameworks and standards. Simply stating that one is adopting a single framework causes other professionals to raise their eyebrows. These misconceptions are founded on the inability of a single program to address an entire enterprise's operations and control needs. Those who took the U.S. Sarbanes-Oxley (SOX) Act literally and endeavored to fully adopt one of the few named standards in the official documents completely experienced this situation, much to their regret. Likewise, if only a portion of a control is adopted, then it is believed that the organization may somehow miss out on important tenets and core risk management techniques.

The idea that an organization must adopt an entire framework fully or risk being vulnerable to cyberattacks, financial misrepresentations, or some other unfortunate event is inaccurate. An organization need not implement every control outlined in a single framework. However, it should at least consider every control and determine if it is appropriate for the organization to implement.

Unfortunately, governments that identify single frameworks and service organizations that promote specific standards perpetuate the illusion that one framework or standard is the solution to all compliance and control needs. Such proclamations steer organizations to adopt a separate control standard to address each set of mandates. The *use of blinders,* a phrase used by some auditors to describe the scope of an engagement, does not mitigate the risks to any organization; it mitigates only those risks that the engagement is meant to evaluate.

Absolute adherence to a regulation by adopting a basic framework without considering the entire organization and threats that affect it may make the organization compliant, but not secure or resilient to operational disruptions. Organizations may consider a compliant and industry-average posture when determining the appropriate operating range for their own control environment. Broadly, a compliant posture is considered a base or bare-minimum set of controls that address a regulation, but are not sufficiently resilient to disruptions. An industry score represents a better real-world control environment state that can withstand the attacks, errors, and faults of systems on a real-time basis. The organization as a whole depends on the integrity and consistency of its information technology controls, and therefore any implementation of a framework or standard must satisfy the enterprise's risks and needs.

The enterprise's goal is to realize the value of all the publications and, through a risk-based approach that respects the business, its processes, and future needs, compose an enterprise compliance-and-controls program by sharing the works of each publication. The result of such a program can enhance the organization's top line as it is focused on the business operations and on enhancing the ability to deliver and execute. The bottom line is improved through a reduction in the number of control failures, audit fees, fines, and carryover costs.

Risk of Reactive Control Environment

Organizations that fully adopt frameworks in reaction to legislation but without completely understanding their implications for the business are least likely to realize any net positive effects in the near term. Critics have stated that the mandated evaluation and attestation of internal controls lead to unsustainable costs for compliance programs.[1] Proponents of testing counter that such control programs will mature and, through improvements and clarifications, will allow organizations to apply a risk-based methodology whose cost is more aligned with the benefits.[2] According to annual filing reports, research, and open discussions at roundtable seminars with the Securities and Exchange Commission (SEC) and Public Company Accounting Oversight Board (PCAOB), organizations are reducing their key controls tested year over year and realizing minor savings with each newly refocused key control set. This trend of eliminating controls or simply unraveling the frameworks and oppressive unproductive controls is both global and expected to accelerate and continue. The greatest loss to these organizations is not the initial costs or the short-term operating costs associated with the fully adopted frameworks, but the loss to future earnings resulting from lack of integration with the frameworks and the business. Organizations that embraced an appropriate blend of controls and automation have been able to recover major cost savings and retain the necessary trust and assurances throughout the business processes.[3]

The more interesting result of these annual reductions in audited controls is that despite the fact that the corporations of the world are shifting away from specific frameworks and published standards as recorded by public disclosure and third-party audits, the actual controls are remaining in place without the documentation. This *stickiness* of controls can be explained in three ways:

1. Most organizations had instituted the controls, and their ethical and competent employees naturally continue to use these controls. This situation is most clearly demonstrated when we consider that most organizations have been in operation for decades (if not centuries) with their existing control environments; regardless of events, they have succeeded when others have failed.

2. Once instituted, controls provide statistics and computed analytics that business owners and managers come to rely on. These analytics and business intelligence components provide competitive advantages and predictive indicators that become as necessary as knowing the weather; if they are unavailable, their loss is noticeable.

3. Simply because they are not audited and publicly reported on does not mean that controls are removed from the operations. It is more than likely that the most positive and clearly beneficial controls remain. Corporations take a pragmatic approach to maintaining controls. They recognize that the regulations, mandates, and client requirements will evolve. Therefore, it is reasonable to expect some portions to reemerge in the near term.

The lesson learned from the massive effort to apply frameworks based on legislative mandate has been the need to implement a program that is self-sustaining, not one that is so costly that it alone materially impacts the bottom line more than the risks mitigated. The focus, which is being broadly supported by government institutions, has shifted to identifying tangible efficiencies in these environments.[4] Organizations must adopt these programs in a manner that reflects the nature of the business and the cost benefits to all stakeholders.

Programs for Many Purposes

A global effort to document and manage technology innovation has been in motion since the mid-1950s and is only gaining force regarding the implementation of technology, our dependence on technology for services and support, and a constant progression of legislative enactments (both private and publicly sponsored).[5] These events correspond to a universal effort to document and define the appropriate procedures, steps, and techniques to manage the new markets and virtual environments. While each legislative mandate is supported by narrow (in scope) publications of guidance, most can be leveraged toward control program efforts in any organization.

Programs may concern the business functions of handling sensitive data within an organization or simply a process for monitoring system activities for anomalies. An organization may operate with numerous programs throughout that are governed by a single division or strategic group. Organizations may adopt a program to govern a broad array of tactical programs. Stated another way, organizations may establish a strategic governance program, such as one inspired by the Turnbull Report, to manage the entire operational, compliance, and security needs. They may incorporate additional programs into the governance structure to provide tactical solutions for core safeguard requirements, such as The Center for Internet Security (CIS) benchmark guides.

Many publications around the world can be combined and adjusted to fit any organization. In fact, the historic trend of continuous efforts to establish regulatory structure and the relentless acceleration of technology throughout society and business operations ensures that there will be even more resources to take advantage of in the future. The key to adopting any program is determining the organization's goals and then reviewing available programs that support them. If a service-oriented approach is sought, a focus on such standards and guidelines as ITIL is appropriate. If an organization manages sensitive personal information, those publications that cater to defining and establishing safeguards sufficient to protect such valuable data are important. Key questions the organization should consider strategically include:

- Where are our current customers and where will they be in five years?
- What regulations in our home markets currently apply to us?
- Why are we duty-bound to these laws?
- How will these laws impact our expansion?
- How much can technology enhance our competitive advantage?
- What metrics are we meeting today, and what do we do need for tomorrow?

Once the organization's goals are defined, it can begin scouring the world for available resources to construct the most beneficial compliance program. You do this by first understanding the value of the available publications and then measuring their applicability to your organization's purposes. You must recognize that some brilliant control programs will be completely inappropriate for your purposes. The appendix provides a starting point for identifying available publications.

Discover and Adopt   To apply a control program, you must follow three general steps:

1. Identify publications that are applicable to the organization today and tomorrow.

2. Merge the data from these publications into a single superset of control information.

3. Score each merged control superset against a risk register for the business approach to give greater weight to business-identified core areas.

Most of the publications regarding control environments are free to use, download, and manipulate. Very few have fair-use restrictions for organizations that implement them internally, and an even smaller number charge for their usage.

Investigate the global library of publications focusing first on those depended on by your partners, vendors, and marketplace industry associations. Once you have vetted those publications, expand your research to include all the publications that are applicable to your domestic market legislative mandates, and then expand this list globally. For example, if your organization has healthcare legislation requirements—HIPAA in the United States—research should identify all global publications of control environments that address the same scope of concern. By taking this approach, you can keep the amount of data within reason and still apply it directly. Finally, expand into all areas that were identified as key to the success of the organization. Consider an organization that is governed by the Federal Financial Institutions Examination Council guidelines and is considering an expansion into the insurance markets. The insurance industry's publications regarding IT general controls would be valuable to adopt and would support the organization's strategic efforts over the next five years.

Once the global publications and their associated mandates have been identified, you need to merge the complete set of data together to form one whole compliance-and-controls program library. By doing so, you will be able to notice any duplications and similarities. You will end up with a single superset of control mandates that the entire business can consider based on risk, legal, and operational targets. This process of merging publications is discussed in further detail in Chapter 8.

Communities of experts debate and post their solutions to compliance challenges and operational improvements on public forums and at open roundtable discussions. These can be accessed online free of charge. Once you have isolated the control environment that is appropriate to your organization, you should participate in these forums to ensure you are kept up to speed and are aware of any changes moving forward.

Global Library of Control Guidance

As the world continues to integrate, and laws for industry, financial stability, national security, consumer protection, and others that place mandates on the management of information are enacted, the global wealth of documentation on controls, issuances of clarification, vetting of procedures, and open dialogues are growing at an unprecedented rate. We must embrace these global resources. The traditional modus operandi of business to develop internally in isolation is both dangerous and highly ineffective with regard to compliance and internal technology controls. To develop such programs without the available global resources ignores the experts of the world and means that you will have to adjust continually, as your business expands and grows and the world becomes more interconnected.

The world of resources on information technology controls and compliance should be considered to be a public library. There are many branches and each has a specific regional focus, but they are all available for perusal and learning. The sheer magnitude of available guidance published around the world grows daily.

Hundreds of documents have been published by institutions and government agencies. In addition, businesses are crafting their own market-space compliance programs. These programs may originate from your vendors, partners, or even competitors as the need for competitiveness and social contribution raises the bar for corporations. Globally these control programs are being developed by:

- Local and federal-level government branches, including
  ◦ Enforcement agencies
  ◦ Standards bodies (such as the National Institute of Standards and Technology, NIST)
  ◦ Working groups
  ◦ Open town-hall discussions
  ◦ Speeches from authoritative bodies
- Private industry groups

- ○ Voluntary members of self-organized groups (North American Electric Reliability Corporation, NERC; European Corporate Governance Institute, ECGI)

- ○ Nonvoluntary contractual enforced groups (Payment Card Industry, PCI)

- ○ Professional specialty groups (Institute of Internal Auditors, IIA; Association of Certified Fraud Examiners, ACFE)

The publications from these organizations vary in both their complexity and their applicability. Each publication may simply provide abstract terminology with principles on how an organization should strategically create or manage a control environment. At the other end of the spectrum is extreme prescriptive control information where authors illustrate precisely what should be implemented and managed and how. The entire spectrum is tremendously useful, and every organization should consider merging sections from the entire range to fit the needs of the organization.

Governance-level edicts, legislation, government-sponsored publications, and legal pronouncements provide the highest level of principles and direction an organization can embrace. Prime examples of this type of document include the Committee of Sponsoring Organizations of the Treadway Commission (COSO); the United Kingdom's Turnbull Report, which is officially called *Internal Control: Guidance for Directors on the Combined Code;* and Canada's *Combined Code on Corporate Governance.* There are also nongovernment publications that are internationally recognized and accepted in most countries. The most common include the International Standards Organization's 17799, *Information Technology—Code of Practice for Information Security Management,* and 27001, *Information Technology—Security Techniques—Information Security Management Systems—Requirements.* These publications represent the foundation for companies around the world as they seek to achieve a manageable balance between explosive technological growth and continuous international expansion.

Commonly a partner document or release of documents is provided to add clarity and direction for the organizations that are implementing or adopting these high-level control structures. These may include frameworks issued by independent organizations, such as the Information Systems Audit and Control Association's extremely popular *Control Objectives for Information and Related Technology* (COBIT). The enforcement branches of governments that are charged with validating compliance to legislation may also issue frameworks, such as the SEC and PCAOB issuances of Audit Standards 1 through 5, or by private industry. These types of documents range from explicit control requirements and guidance to general control structure requirements. The industry standard managed by the Payment Card

Industry Standards Organization, for example, is considered strongly prescriptive. The standard "PCI DSS v1.1" details specifics, from the type of access control devices to the number of characters in a password field. Other publications provide a more principles-based approach that is meant to be interpreted for each individual organization; NERC's Critical Infrastructure Protection initiatives fit in this category.

All publications are subject to wide-ranging criticism and debate. Implementation should be done according to the needs of an organization, not merely for the sake of edicts pronounced in the standards. Therefore, we do not initially have to be concerned with the degree of detail a document provides but rather how, where, and in what capacity we adopt such documents into our organization.

Published standards and guidance documents should be adopted only if they provide value and enhance the organization. If a single publication does not fully address your organization's needs, consider combining available publications from a range of regions, as translations are freely available.

There are clear advantages to seeking out completed and published works. Another entity has already absorbed the sunk cost of producing such a document; this can amount to tremendous savings, depending on the depth, complexity of legislation or industry it is meant to support, and sophistication of the toolset provided. In addition, such publications attract the attention of practitioners and experts in fields across the entire set of the publication's subject areas, and their complete works are available in a single coherent document. These published works run the gamut from those produced by world bodies such as ISACA, which publishes the COBIT standard through a massive coordinated effort by an international team of experts, to works commissioned by local governments.

It is important to recognize that these groups produce their publications for particular purposes. For example, a working group commissioned within the EU will focus on EU concerns and bounds. Likewise, a group commissioned in Japan focuses on its laws and culture. This specificity is also clear when works are produced and sponsored by specific industries or vendors. As cross-border and cross-industry consumers of these publications, we must always be cognizant of their origins, aim, and intended audiences. The tunnel vision of some publishers regarding these documents is not a negative; in fact, their narrowness of scope enables us to adopt those works without fear of duplication or excessive overlap. Their focus on individual requirements allows for a clearer understanding of what is necessary to meet a single concern (whether a legislative mandate or an industry voluntary performance metric). We are able to enhance these publications to meet our needs by expanding their mandates or reducing them, based on the nature of our business. Exhibit 6.1 highlights international and industry publications that could be used in any organization that manages information.

Exhibit 6.1 Key Resources

- **NIST Standard 800-53,** Recommended Security Controls for Federal Information Systems (URL:http://csrc.nist.gov/publications/nistpubs/800-53/SP 800-53.pdf)
- **NIST Standard 800-100,** Information Security Handbook: A Guide for Managers (URL: http://csrc.nist.gov/publications/nistpubs/800-100/SP800-100-Mar07-2007.pdf)
- **GAO/AIMD-12.19. 6,** Federal Information System Controls Audit Manual (URL: www.gao.gov/special.pubs/ail2.19.6.pdf)
- **CICA,** Internal Control 2006: The Next Wave of Certification—Guidance for Management (Canadian Institute of Chartered Accountants; released several publications, including Internal Control 2006: The Next Wave of Certification—Guidance for Directors, all of which may be found at URL: www.rmgb.ca/index.cfm/ci_id/3083/la_id/1.htm)
- **ISACA COBIT 4.1,** Control Objectives for Information and Related Technology (available for purchase or download to members of ISACA at URL: www.isaca.org/cobit)
- **HKICPA,** Internal Control and Risk Management—A Basic Framework (Hong Kong Institute of Certified Public Accountants published a framework that builds and references other widely accepted frameworks, such as COSO; available at URL: www.hkicpa.org.hk/)
- **AICPA SAS No. 109,** Understanding the Entity and Its Environment and Assessing the Risks of Material Misstatement (updated to reflect the need for a more risk-evaluative method for organizations; URL: www.aicpa.org/download/members/div/auditstd/SAS109.pdf)

SUMMARY

Executives and practitioners are challenged with the need to meet operational requirements of the business, including successful achievement of profit targets and positive delivery of services. This effort may be supported or hindered based on the organization's approach to regulations, vendor requirements, and pure operational improvements. This procession of adoption is impacted by the confusion that exists regarding standards, frameworks, and best practices. By using trusted business processes and verifiable controls available through standards and publications and adopting them to their own needs and style, organizations will realize the benefits of a return on investment while satisfying compulsory requirements.

ENDNOTES

1. Craig S. Lerner and Moin A. Yahya, "'Left Behind' after Sarbanes-Oxley," *American Criminal Law Review* (in press). URL: http://papers.ssrn.com/sol3/papers.cfm?abstract_id=981064.

2. Larry E. Rittenberg and Patricia K. Miller, "Sarbanes-Oxley Section 404 Work: Looking at the Benefits," IIA Research Foundation (January 2005).

3. Financial Executives International conducts an annual survey to determine the impacts of SOX auditing on organizations that are required to be compliant. The study published on May 16, 2007, indicated companies achieved a 35% savings since the first year of the survey on the total cost of compliance. URL: www.fei.org/404survey.

4. The Office of Government Commerce (OGC) has a reporting guidance on determining and maintaining efficiency in the data systems that promote assurance. URL: http://www.ogc.gov.uk/data_assurance_efficiency_data_systems_assurance.asp.

5. Jan R. Heier, Michael T. Dugan, and David L. Sayers, "A Century of Debate for Internal Controls and Their Assessment: A Study of Reactive Evolution,"*Accounting History* (November 2005).

7

Reality and Risks to IT Controls Being Effective

Key Topics Addressed in This Chapter

Perception bias

Chasing fires

Inherent control weaknesses

OVERVIEW

> It is of the highest degree of necessity that the Auditor, before commencing the investigation . . . should thoroughly acquaint himself with the general system upon which the books have been kept. . . . Having thoroughly made himself the *master of the system*, the Auditor should look for *its weakest points*.[1] [emphasis added]

A great debate has occurred over the past century in the audit and assurance profession with regard to the significance and importance of internal controls and their numerous interpretations.[2] Guidance relating to internal controls has been put forth by the accounting/audit professions for over a century. Beyond guidance, governments around the world, their regulatory branches, public and private companies, and industry-watch groups have established mandates supported by routine testing and financial penalties. The quote just cited was published in 1892, and its points are still salient in the current information technology economy. It has long been realized that without proper oversight, the systems designed to protect an organization and owners could become susceptible to error and fraud.

According to a banker quoted in 1956:

> Today it's gotten to a point where all employers should give careful study to internal controls, cash receipts and audit methods.[3]

The debate over internal control requirements centered on the necessity and value provided to business functions. Throughout the past century there were numerous instances of safeguards being outlined in the accounting and audit literature and then gradually introduced into practice. This increase in examination and attestation by third parties has grown as technology has developed, and partnerships flourish. The expansion of technology and automation throughout companies has shifted from a supportive to an operational role. The literature in the early 1900s emphasized the importance of controls; events in the 1930s, 1970s, 1990s, and the global boom–bust of 2000 have promoted the establishment of government regulations, industry standards within professions deemed responsible, and a business requirement to substantiate that information is safeguarded and controls are effective.

While most agree that controls are needed and legislation exists requiring them, not all organizations have effective controls in place. In fact, regulators contend that the market and businesses must work to achieve efficiencies and that the regulators' purview is effective legislation and controls.[4] Organizations with strong controls are able to manage the seesaw legislation storm that exists in the world today. Strong controls also help organizations detect frauds and identify deficiencies before they become material weaknesses. According to recent studies, organizations currently employing more robust control environments, such as those dictated by Sarbanes-Oxley (SOX) and the Canadian Institute of Chartered Accountants (CICA), were likely to uncover fraud. In fact, the recent emphasis on strong internal controls is attributed to fraud detection by auditors and fraud detection programs that accounted for over 50%—the first time since the figures have been tracked.[5]

PERCEPTION BIAS

Adopters of a single standard completely have the belief that the organization is sufficiently protected against threats. This belief is detrimental to the organization and puts at risk the credibility of standards and frameworks. In some cases, a framework may be very detailed to deal with a specific threat; it makes sense to adopt that framework, or a portion of it, only when that threat is being encountered by the organization. For instance, generic frameworks have a broader application across many industries (international insurance risk equations); prescriptive frameworks are very detailed in order to apply to a specific type of threat (e.g., credit card point-of-sale device networks).

To avoid this mistake, organizations should understand for what purpose a framework or standard is designed. The purpose defines the mission of the publication and communicates the applicability of the work itself. Together this information explains what types of systems, assets, risks, environments, industries, and regulations are addressed. Numerous publications regarding standards are available from all corners of the globe, created by government agencies and regional trade groups. The document may be official guidance from a government enforcement agency or simply a public memo meant to clarify a portion of a legislation.

In general, when you are seeking to demonstrate compliance with a law, you should ascribe greater authority to government publications than private-sector works. You need to understand the purpose of the document in order to assess its ability to mitigate risk. As an example, the Information Technology Infrastructure Library (ITIL) series is focused on the performance of information technology (IT) environments and is an excellent resource for establishing metrics. The COBIT (Control OBjectives for Information and related Technology) framework provides a robust set of IT-specific controls and the means of measuring their implementation, but on a much broader scale. The Turnbull Report provides principles on how an organization should instill confidence but does not focus only on a single division. The unique goal of each framework provides for precision in addressing divisional and unit needs.

An organization that experiences growth and stability over many years can have a complacency bias regarding the adequacy of its technology controls. As operations continue to satisfy service-level demands and routine checks reinforce confidence, an organization can believe that its control environment is addressing all risks. This perception develops as no significant events occur to highlight the fallacies in it. The lack of events does not imply a sufficient control environment; rather it highlights the statistical probability of an adverse event occurring. An organization that does not understand the threats to it is unable to plan risk mitigation and safeguard efforts. It is therefore important for executives and management to force the organization to challenge its viewpoints and assumptions on a regular basis. Status quo and stagnant controls are inadequate for safeguarding any business in today's competitive marketplace.

Organizations that blindly adopt a complete standard or create massive efforts to meet compliance are prone to falling victim to exhaustion. Exhaustion occurs when organizations expect the impact of security and compliance initiatives to last longer than they in fact do. An initial effort to meet a regulatory or market need generally involves strong oversight, executive participation, and the full dedication of the enterprise. However, in subsequent years, initiatives tend to be sourced to specific groups that are not as dedicated to the compliance initiatives as they were in year 1. In addition, the team is typically smaller and rotated year over year as divisions and staff play pass-the-hot-potato.

Shifting Focus

Organizations commit funds and resources to compliance issues with the understanding that although initial costs will be high, costs will be reduced in subsequent years. Specifically, savings should be found through technology and automation of controls or processes, reduction in manual internal resource efforts, and reductions in audit fees. These efficiencies are justified to an extent. The initial costs of establishing a program include creating controls that never existed, adding technology, bringing in temporary staff to support the surge in establishing the controls, and spending extended hours with the external auditing firm on advising on the control setup. In the case of SOX, recent data show that international companies that developed and instituted SOX experienced a 20 to 30% savings in the first few years after achieving compliance.[6] The life-cycle costs of maintaining the control environment, auditing and managing it, and adjusting as the organization develops will continually improve through experience and maturity of controls to a point where a floor will be reached in achievable cost reductions. These operational costs, like insurance premiums that the firm pays annually, must be expended to satisfy the organization's needs. Thus, after setup of the IT control environments, organizations can expect cost reductions. However, there will be a baseline set of expenses that must remain to ensure that the organization is operating effectively.

Establishing a method of maintaining focus on the control environment ensures that major risks do not impact the operational viability of the business. It also allows the organization to support the legislative requirements while still keeping up with projects that are critical to the organization's success. The constant shifting of business pressures, government actions, and media concerns of the hour challenges this focus. An organization must meet each new demand with vigor and resolve, but mechanisms must be instituted that allow for controls to be monitored. Chasing the everyday fires puts the unattended firehouse at risk. In its reactions, the organization must consider the impact and likelihood of each new risk.

INHERENT CONTROL WEAKNESSES

Complacency and a shifting of resources combine to cause a weaker control environment and one that can be less dependable, but there exist more basic risks to the organization and the enterprise control environment. These risks threaten the core of an organization, as they introduce the possibility of fraud and criminal actions, and can result in the insolvency of the entire enterprise. These inherent weaknesses include:

- The staff's subjective judgment of risks
- Communication breakdowns
- The ability of management and administrators to override safety protocols
- Collusion

No company is too large or too small to be immune from these weaknesses or their impacts, as is clear from recent major defaults in the United States (management overrides and collusion contributed to the collapse of Enron and near destruction of HealthSouth) and Japan from 2000 to 2003, and repeatedly throughout history.[7]

The major weaknesses that have significant impact on the organization focus on the people who make up the control environment. It is true that every business is a success because of its people and the management team. So too is it true that these same individuals can cause a business to fail. As in the game of chess, each decision made by representatives of the company is based on the situation, available information, time constraints, and the pressure to perform. These judgments allow for several outcomes. Without some form of guidance or safety nets, an organization cannot rely on employees to make decisions that might be right morally and also meet the company's legal obligations and the rights of the stakeholders. Nevertheless, on any given day, there is the possibility that the advice is misunderstood. A breakdown in communication can occur and cause errors throughout the system. Therefore, it is important to ensure that all parties understand what controls exist and the rationale behind each implementation.

Exceptions occur to every situation. This is to be expected and must be built into every organization. These exceptions may come from a new client or new legislation from an overseas market. The exceptions must be documented to demonstrate that the environment is still processing information properly. A technical override by a system administrator or an override by management must be documented and managed properly.

Managing collusion presents the most difficult and challenging basic risk for an organization. It is challenging for two reasons. First, collusion threatens the first tenet of a good company and strong control environment: competent and trustworthy employees. Second, these parties are capable of compromising multiple detective and preventive controls to mask any crimes they may commit. The use of background checks and full rotation of duties can help tremendously in reducing this risk.

PERSPECTIVES OF MANAGEMENT, AUDIT, AND IT

The focus on the control environment, technology, and controls in place has three functional stakeholders of an enterprise and an audit:

1. Management team and board

2. Auditor

3. Technologist

The management team and board commission the audit, as a result of regulatory or business needs, and rely on the results for competition and operational purposes. The auditor engaged—whether a team over several months or a single department within the corporation—seeks to present a report to communicate the organization's current status. The technologist at many levels in the organization maintains the environment and responds to the auditor's requests. Together these three make up the cycle of establishing a control environment, living within the controls for daily operations, and reporting these processes. While part of the same cycle, each party provides a unique perspective and has different objectives from the others. These differences create the balance that enables the system to trust the control environment.

The management team, including the board of directors, relies on systems throughout the organization to ensure delivery of services around the world. Organizations must be able to rely on both the quality and the integrity of services delivered. For example, in PayPal's case, electronic transactions must occur accurately and timely, and the performance of the business must be measured. These financial and nonfinancial metrics are the impetus for the management team's decisions for the entire organization; therefore, they must be accurate and correct. Finally management relies on these systems to report back to stakeholders and regulating bodies. In some countries, managers stake their personal livelihood and freedom on these figures. Management seeks not only the best efforts by the company and the technologists who implement and support the environment, but also a fair accounting from the auditor's perspective on what can be improved on to lower risks and enhance operations.

Auditors of any type—internal, external, accountant, or specialist in technology or fraud—seek to validate the trust an organization is placing in their systems and operations. Auditors assess and report the risk to management and the technologist using a trust-but-verify focus. Auditors come to engagements with no knowledge of the systems, their architecture, or how controls are deployed. They must acquire the knowledge of the systems and architectures that support and control the business functions. They also must develop an understanding and leverage the experience they have and develop an audit plan that is appropriate for the operations under review. Auditors seek to understand the environment by evaluating the controls in place, the people, and the processes connecting these together. The aim of these evaluations is the production of an objective accounting on what is occurring, both good and bad, to enable management and technologists alike to mitigate the chances of some negative event.

The task of the technologist is to continuously improve and operate within the technology controls. This team or individual possesses the knowledge of the environment, all the controls, and the interrelated processes that hold the business together. These individuals are tasked with and rewarded for ensuring the systems are maintained and are accurately delivering services. Technologists will have implemented controls and safeguards to ensure that operations are maintained. They must achieve a balance based on their knowledge of the systems and the requirements of the business. Consider consumer services and oil refinery technology environments. The systems cannot be taken offline, and the aim of all management activities is to ensure continuous operation. Often controls that are critical in one organization, such as timely patching of systems, are not necessary in others due to environment and separate controls. The risk of patching outweighs the risk of not patching in these organizations.[8] In order to ensure that the proper control environment exists, technologists must be able to assess the intent of the control requirements and the business model.

ENDNOTES

1. L. R. Dicksee (1892), *Auditing: A Practical Manual for Auditors* (New York: Arno Press, 1976).
2. Michael T. Heier, Jan R. Dugan, and David L. Sayers, "A Century of Debate for Internal Controls and Their Assessment: A Study of Reactive Evolution,"*Accounting History* (November 2005).
3. "Embezzlement Rises 400% in Ten Years,"*New York Times*, May 13, 1956.
4. Public Company Accounting Oversight Board, Standing Advisory Group meeting, February 22, 2007, SAG transcript: Participants presented the perspectives of the regulators and the auditors, and argued that efficiency is not the goal of regulators, but that of effectiveness. Efficiency should be ruled by the markets themselves. URL: http://www.pcaobus.org/Standards/Standing_Advisory_Group/Meetings/2007/02-22/SAG_Transcript.pdf.
5. Serious frauds discovered by those professionally responsible for doing so rose to 50%. Alexander L. Dyck, Adair Morse, and Luigi Zingales, "Who Blows the Whistle on Corporate Fraud" (January 2007), AFA 2007 Chicago Meetings Paper available at SSRN: http://ssrn.com/abstract=891482.
6. FEI 404 SOX Survey conducted annually and reported at URL: http://www.fei.org/404 survey.
7 Michael R. Young and Jack H. Nusbaum, *Accounting Irregularities and Financial Fraud: A Corporate Governance Guide*, 3rd ed. (Chicago: CCH, 2006).
8. Brad Martin of Chick-Fil-A quote: "Compliance, audits, internal control mandates, regulations, and auditor visits are all necessary in order to protect businesses in today's ever changing IT environment. Although compliance is necessary, I do believe that there can be no 'gold' standard that fits every business. In our experience. . . the risk of patching far outweighs the risk of not patching" (April 2007).

PART THREE

IMPLEMENTATION

It is not the strongest of the species that survives,
nor the most intelligent, but the one *most responsive*
to change.
—*Charles Darwin*

CHALLENGE

Organizations today face an international and domestic swarm of requirements and mandates that are thrust upon them with varying degrees of
necessity and impact. In an effort to equalize markets and maintain a fair
market, governments shift existing regulations or introduce new works to
establish consistency and assurance in operations, both public and private.
These efforts have accelerated as organizations have shifted from small
groups of owners to a wide variety of international stakeholders.

In parallel with the extension of ownership to stakeholders that may
include private equity funds, hedge funds, state-sponsored pension funds, or
even the central banks of countries, business supply chains and operations
are becoming more intertwined.[1] Nearly a half century after integrated supply chain and near-real-time supply efforts were introduced, organizations
today work in real time with dozens of companies supporting any number
of business functions. These business partners and affiliates demand, as they
should and so should you, respect for their intellectual property and the
integrity of their operations, and have established contractual protection to
ensure these leading practices are in place.

The challenge at hand is that leading organizations and a majority of
the firms that conduct business beyond their regional borders are audited to
ensure mandates are met on a regular basis. These audits may be performed
by third-party firms that are hired by the company itself. They may include
one of the top-tier accounting firms conducting a financial audit, an accredited International Standards Organization (ISO) firm that is determining
compliance with ISO 9000, or an authorized auditor commissioned by the
Payment Card Industry Standards Organization. Additional audits may
be those that are conducted by partners, such as service-level agreement
checks or vendor audit programs, customer satisfaction audits, and government audits. The many requirements and subsequent evaluations present a

sizable challenge for any organization when considered independently; we can get a greater appreciation of the challenges to which businesses today are exposed when we consider the unique attributes of each audit.

The scope of an engagement is defined by the legislation or auditing standards that require it. The scope is the business processes, assets, and areas of the organization that are evaluated based on the guidance documents that govern the attestation. Strict adherence to these documents tends to create many partially independently tested environments that are retested from different approaches but on similar principles. Of course, this matter of scope defines why businesses and security professionals say that being compliant is not good for business or sufficient for security. The overlap in testing increases waste and amplifies the negative perceptions of these activities. It is a fallacy to believe that an organization that is audited is compliant and/or secure simply as a result of more audits. Even though an organization may be audited more than its peers, the assets tested may not be material to the risks encountered by the organization.

All of the contractual, performance, and cultural agreements within an organization, whether originating from a business or a government, establish the specifications of the audit requirements at varying degrees of sophistication. These attributes become difficult to apply exclusively because organization information technology (IT) environments are horizontal and cater to all branches of an organization, despite the natural vertical nature of departments and regional branches. Thus single components of the technology infrastructure often are under the purview of several requirements. Businesses then must address the variance among control thresholds, risk acceptance, ownership, and budget implications. Ignoring other components that do not fall within the strict guidance of established engagements may blind an organization and make it unaware of security and compliance weaknesses.

OPPORTUNITY

Ironically, despite the fact that the organization may have a wide disbursement of technology, a plethora of control requirements, and numerous stakeholders, the actual implementation and validation falls to a single group. This single group is tasked with supporting the entire organization's technology validation needs and is exposed to the inefficiencies that exist. This team is able to observe the—usually great—amount of duplication that exists in most regulations around the world.

Organizations have many available options for addressing these mandates (such as routine SAS 70, vendor audits, European Union privacy validations) and responding to validation requests (queries by oversight bodies or government institutions for evidence of control activity and documentation). Professional organizations and government oversight bodies both state that a risk-based approach is the most effective way to address these mandates. However, such risk-based approaches are not always the most efficient method for the organization when addressing multiple regulations and assurance requirements at once. Therefore organizations must consider each together relative to an enterprise strategic governance program that tactically and through an evaluation based upon risk satisfies each instance completely. The *test-once and report-to-many* approach is ideal. The creation of a test repository maintained by the organization will allow organizations to be more able to respond to evidentiary requests.

The convergence together of legislations that are applicable to the organization positions them to embrace all requirements at once under a single umbrella. The blending of requirements, if averaged, has the dangerous effect of lowering the acceptable threshold for the attributes of each requirement. Therefore, when uniting these together a weighting system should be applied based on mandatory and optional goals, and then the most severe attribute should be depended on by the organization. Successful strategic management of all mandates by an organization through such a process results in a more refined and manageable control structure. As a result an organization may meet all its requirements, attack the aggregate enterprise compliancy needs, discover efficiencies that will bolster internal IT responsiveness, elevate the security posture of the business, and reduce *future fire drills* by a large degree. This blending of requirements also offers an opportunity to reduce reporting requirements for components that are evaluated multiple times; controls for them can be managed with a single report being created for all known audit and security checks.

By developing and embracing a strategic risk-based enterprise IT control environment program, a business can eliminate the seemingly continuous returns to the budget well. The discussion of an enterprise and an international program addresses the dynamic and competitive nature of the existing marketplace by establishing a business-appropriate level of agility and assurance throughout the control environment. Adoption of a flexible and globally inspired program allows businesses to expand and adjust to shifts while maintaining reasonable expenses. In addition, the embrace of a principles-based program allows an organization to manage the technology environment without becoming distracted by weaker tactical solutions. The elimination of reactive situations will even out technology projects and allow for greater dedication to internal projects.

ENDNOTE

1. Governments have more cash in reserves and are investing it in equity stakes around the world. The U.S. Treasury calculates that the global foreign exchange reserves total "roughly \$7.6 trillion," or 15% of global

gross domestic product, and such investments are being placed more into individual companies while transitioning from safe or liquid government bonds. Jason Singer et al., "Governments Get Bolder in Buying Equity Stakes," *Wall Street Journal,* July 24, 2007. URL: http://online.wsj.com/article/SB118523825903875664.html.

8

Enterprise Risk Analysis

Out of intense complexities intense simplicities
emerge.

—*Winston Churchill*

Key Topics Addressed in This Chapter

Identifying and mapping IT control safeguards

Risk measurement and reporting

Gap analysis and project management

IDENTIFYING RISK-BASED CONTROLS

Identify Strategic IT Controls

Understanding the pressures on an organization and the subsequent weighted-risk valuations requires recognition and consideration of the near- and long-term strategy of the business itself. Doing this requires sufficient management direction and communication to account for the firm's forward direction. Of course, plans change and markets shift, so the program must be somewhat flexible and reviewed regularly (quarterly). The short-term outlook should consider the fiscal year ahead; the long term covers up to five years beyond. The strategic direction of the organization affects how the control environment is defined, established, managed, and maintained by the entire enterprise. External influences must be taken into consideration both at the operational customer-delivery level and at the level of legal commitments.

A process of assigning a value to these influences that reflects the organization's strategic direction shall ensure that the control environment appropriately reflects and responds to the needs and requirements of the organization and all concerned parties. In an age when the entity itself is beholden to internal employees, external shareholders, international regulatory enforcement agencies, and service-delivery commitments to customers and partners, a thorough consideration must be reflected in the IT controls themselves.

Organizations should evaluate each influencer first separately and then together, considering the multiple time periods, as each influencer when paired with another affects the business differently.

Valuation: Industry and Regulators   The first step for an organization to determine what is required and necessary to operate in the future is to survey the laws currently applicable. Initially an organization should canvass the local markets of the entire organization and identify all laws that require information technology and controls over the data they manage. Such laws may focus on privacy of citizens and consumers or may deal with after-effects of an event, such as a hacker stealing credit bureau data. Other laws may speak to the integrity of the financial transactions that are occurring, and some may focus on the confidentiality of the data set itself.

The CIO or committee tasked should first work directly with the company's general counsel and request all laws that the organization currently is in compliance with or those that are applicable. If possible, a breakdown of those that have IT requirements or implications is useful. This is best provided in electronic format using a spreadsheet program, but printouts with comments would be sufficient also. Once this list is developed, the organization should conduct an internal exploratory exercise to identify business contracts and service-level agreements that have extended the company's control requirements. Once these internal efforts are complete, an investigation of external requirements should be conducted, and must include mandates that are pending votes and approvals. In addition, based on strategic direction of the company, a catalog of legislation that will be required based on growth and strategic initiatives is necessary. As the organization investigates more international regions, the team should seek the advice from a regional manager who is familiar with local laws and customs. Organizations with operations in Europe must consider the likelihood that the country they have facilities within may join the European Union (EU) and how EU directorates will affect the scope of IT internal controls. Besides having their own separate laws, EU member countries also implement laws required by directives from the EU governing body. This arrangement can be complex and the technology group should seek expertise when necessary. Although the EU is in the process of streamlining the laws and regional differences, a level of flux in the specific requirements for each region still exists.[1] It is necessary to be aware of political climates within operating countries to ensure the business can respond timely and consciously throughout any shift in parties or positions.

Staff members can research the laws through online resources found around the world that are maintained by governments or by oversight organizations. Practitioners should start with the appendix first prior to conducting online searches or bringing on third parties. The organization should secure a copy of every law and guidance document from these organizations to use as guidelines while designing or updating the control environment. Leading organizations meet the intent of legislation and avoid nonauthoritative interpretations.

Valuation: Contractual Obligations   Contrary to legislative mandates that are generally public in nature and accessible, requirements a business accepts through contracts with third parties are done in confidence and seldom widely disbursed.

Organizations establish contracts with partners, customers, and suppliers and each contract has the potential to include language that specifies a level of assurance regarding the IT control environments. The concept of requiring diligence and safeguards surrounding IT controls has existed for decades, but only recently have contracts begun specifying specific information safeguards and including legislative references, such as requiring both parties to adhere to the security safeguards of the Gramm-Leach-Bliley Act (GLBA). In addition, organizations are also agreeing in contracts to a defined vendor security program and the right of audit by a third party on a regular basis to provide attestation of these contractual provisions.

The stronger focus on IT controls has occurred naturally without the help of legislation as operations have become more virtual. While these business contracts may have been established originally to define the transaction relationship, now they specify very clearly the expected level of service, response time, and the safeguards required. These specifications will continue to grow as technology becomes more relied upon, services and infrastructure become more distributed, and with greater reliance of business functions on third-company providers. Just as a company would not simply ask for a toy doll to be created but instead would describe the color, feel, size, and shapes, companies today dictate the specifics of computing services.

Vendor audits are concerned with only the relevant applications, systems, and physical environments of the organization that is contractually protected. Typical vendor programs evaluate the technical and physical controls of an environment through an on-site visit prior to signing an agreement. Thereafter, annual spot checks occur and reports are provided to each party. A common error initially found is that the vendor audit programs are broad and abstract in their requirements and the resulting evaluations are also broad and abstract. A proper program is one that is fine-tuned to fit the purpose of the engagement, the type of information, and the intent of the safeguards. Companies responding to such programs must proactively work with all parties to ensure that the appropriate level of controls are required and validated. To the same point, your organization must design an equally fair vendor audit program, include the "right to audit" in all contracts, and establish an information validation program.

Organizations assume responsibilities and establish performance commitments with third parties through a multitude of explicit and implied contracts. All lines of business in an organization are likely to have accepted terms and conditions relating to IT technology safeguards. Storing, processing, and transmitting sensitive data can become an enormous and complex endeavor if careful review of these commitments does not occur. The ensuing responsibilities to abide by defined metrics and safeguards expose the organization if these are not met. Negative results may include fines or a breach in contract that can damage relationships and business partnerships.

Due to the numerous areas of the organization that may sign a contract, the best process to identifying such IT control mandates is through a survey effort. Canvassing a diverse group requires explicit queries that originate from the highest level of the organization. The surveys must identify all agreements where the organization, vendors, or clients rely on their IP and information technology. If either party depends on digital assets, a contract likely exists, and it must be located. The key areas for contracts that should be identified include:

- IT outsourced colocation contracts
- IT managed services contracts
- Vendor maintenance contracts that allow for callback features or remote connections
- Client contracts that state electronic access is granted

The contract should state the type of data that are protected and subject to evaluation, the level of safeguards mandated, and the implications of a breach in the contract (due to an organization not complying with the security safeguards outlined in the program). In some cases, external references (on partner Web sites or referencing government standards) are used in lieu of detailed security requirements in the signed contract, and should be monitored as they can be easily updated. Once the readily available contracts are reviewed, a report should be produced and sent to all the business and process owners outlining the findings, the affected systems, and business processes.

The vendor control requirements will be in line with most leading practice publications. This is true for most organizations, but especially those of the largest institutions. Once the contracts are identified, the organization should capture the specific requirements in a matrix of some form and include the scope of the requirements. While we are more concerned with the technology control mandates, the scoping detail allows for greater granularity and refinement in the future. Understanding these similarities and refining in the future allows an organization to cost effectively integrate any additional contracts.

Organic Practices and Controls   The culture of every organization is affected by, among other things, the business, the geography, and the tone at the top. These influences result in an organization naturally adopting and employing good practices. Many organizations have been in operation for decades or longer without any new standard or legislation necessary to save them. Many companies tell auditors and oversight boards that most of the compliance work is simply the documentation of current practices, not the development or implementation of new and original controls.

The organization itself organically determines what assurances are required in order to maintain satisfied clients and stakeholders. It is simple economics of supply and demand—companies must offer a product that is better than the competition, and in most cases that includes safer and more reliable operations. While many controls that develop and mature begin as informal best practice initiatives, these are put in place by teams or individuals who see a need and establish a safeguard. These organic control environments have existed since the dawn of an enterprise and are evident by the length of time certain companies survive compared to competitors that fall to scandal.

The further evolution of these controls from simply organic to integrated and optimized for the organization is sought as organizations implement safeguards to enhance the customer experience through better efficiency, more reliable transactions, a better overall experience for all parties involved, and general goodwill.

The discovery of what is being done across an enterprise should take place in a focused, collaborative fashion. The effort should identify the existing infrastructure and library of controls. An effort should be made to discover how the organization operates with the given controls and which of these controls coincide with documented legal mandates. A thorough evaluation of the current processes in place allows for expansion and adjustments to be made through an additive approach that builds on earlier successes.

Inherent Technology Risks

Technology itself introduces risks to an organization that, like operational risks, must be considered thoroughly and transparently. These risks may involve the hardware, operating systems, applications, databases, or the established procedures relied on throughout the organization. Human errors in configuring systems or a successful malicious code attack are key concerns of those who rely on technology.

A set of risks levied against the technology environments include:

- *Loss of connectivity.* Example: e-Commerce Web site is unavailable.

- *Alteration of data in transit.* Example: Theft of customer data.

- *Theft of sensitive information.* Example: Requiring public notification.

- *Modification/destruction of data.* Example: Oracle database is erased.

- *Unauthorized system change.* Example: Emergency change without approval or testing causes service interruption.

- *Fraud.* Example: System administrator hides wire transfer by erasing logs she manages.

Businesses and security professionals must work to develop a set of systems that when operating effectively provide adequate protection to known risks. In addition, safeguards must be defined to prevent problems that have yet to be known through broad mitigation strategies. Throughout this book we identify core areas of security that warrant investigation and inclusion in order to focus on the key IT control environment appropriate for your business. The American Institute of Certified Public Accountants (AICPA) released Statement of Accounting Standards (SAS) 94, which lists these additional risks that can arise or change:[2]

- *Changes in operating environment.* Changes in the regulatory or operating environment can result in changes in competitive pressures and significantly different risks.

- *New personnel.* New personnel may have a different focus on or understanding of internal control.

- *New or revamped information systems.* Significant and rapid changes in information systems can change the risk relating to internal control.

- *Rapid growth.* Significant and rapid expansion of operations can strain controls and increase the risk of a breakdown in controls.

- *New technology.* Incorporating new technologies into production processes or information systems may change the risk associated with internal control.

- *New business models, products, or activities.* Entering into business areas or transactions with which an entity has little experience may introduce new risks associated with internal control.

- *Corporate restructurings.* Restructurings may be accompanied by staff reductions and changes in supervision and segregation of duties that may change the risk associated with internal control.

- *Expanded foreign operations.* The expansion or acquisition of foreign operations carries new and often unique risks that may affect internal control.[3]

In order to identify and catalog the types of risks to the organization that exist, a discovery process must take place. Attacks and therefore threats to the organization may originate from inside or outside. These attacks may be either intentional or unintentional. In either case they can cause significant harm to the daily operations of the business. When compared to the other possible combinations of harm—external-intentional, external-unintentional, and internal-unintentional—that caused by internal-intentional attacks has by far the greatest impact on an organization.[4]

External Attacks   External attacks are those that originate beyond the physical or logical perimeter of the organization. These attacks must face the oldest, best-defined, and most clearly understood security defenses of the organization. This perimeter is referred to as the *hard outer shell* of an organization. The inside of an organization is referred to as the *soft-chewy center.* (This saying is used to describe organizations that secure *only* the perimeter while ignoring the interior and are unaware of their weaknesses.) It is important to recognize that nearly all organizations have established basic access control technologies in the logical space and added physical doors with locks to gaping entranceways, and in some cases they have placed a receptionist or security desk in the front. While the outer shell is the best defined and most noticeable, it gives a false sense of security to most organizations. This false sense of security does not arise due to weaknesses that exist within the perimeter safeguards but instead is the result of complacency concerning their effectiveness to deter external threats. These safeguards are totally ineffective when threats originate within (or past the security technology in) the organization and therefore wholly bypass the control. Using an example from medieval times: Having only a strong outer shell is like raising the drawbridge to defend against attackers who are already inside the castle, or who walked through a back door left open.

Internal Attacks   Internal attacks are caused by villains who already have bypassed the existing perimeter security of the organization and are given the same access and provided with the same trust as employees. Internal attacks have become an increasingly effective approach due to the level of data access provided to employees. The perimeter safeguards do not apply to this type of attack. Therefore, the organization's *layered security controls* are the next best line of defense, including technical access control safeguards by device and user and logical separation of duties. While the need to establish rules and accountability is not new to corporations, the new accessibility has introduced the need for a complete separation of duties and restrictive access to assets. The layering of defenses and refinement of access permissions are core to reducing the amount of damage caused by attackers on the inside.

Intentional Attacks   Intentional attacks, whether internal or externally based, are dangerous, as the attacker has a specific goal in mind (i.e., steal credit card information in order to sell on the Internet and pay off college/bookie/ego). These types of attacks typically involve individuals and locations that are known for such activities. (An internal intentional attacker is usually already considered a high risk to the organization based on such criteria as access privileges and domestic legal environments—an administrator/salesperson who knows he is going to be fired, or a region in Russia or Brazil that is identified as a hot spot for logical attacks.) The organization must rely on monitoring safeguards and layered technology to limit exposure to these attacks. In most cases it is not possible to wholly stop a determined attacker with unlimited resources, but it is possible to slow and increase the costs of the attack to the point where detection is highly probable. It is important to recognize that intentional attackers are funded or motivated by a certain incentive; that may be to resell sensitive information or to enhance their company's sales by damaging their competitors. Therefore, these organizations are constantly considering a cost-benefit analysis. The fact that attackers tend to search for organizations with weaker security instead of focusing on a specific organization further supports the need to raise the costs to attackers as a means of defense.

Unintentional Attacks   Unintentional attacks are those where the host computer committing the attack, internally or externally, has itself been exploited by some type of Trojan or malicious piece of code to become what is called a zombie node for a malicious individual. These hosts may be laptops used at employee homes or within client environments. Like people, they may catch a virus (malware) and bring these pieces of code into the soft-chewy center of their organization. Implementing segmented networks and trusted zones is an effective safeguard to limit the potential for exposure to infected and nontrusted systems.

CONVERGE MANDATES

Your organization is unique, its people are different from those of your competitors, and the technology and procedures within your organization, while similar to those of other firms, provide a competitive advantage against all other players in your market. It is illogical to assume that any one published standard will address the needs and wants of your organization in total without some form of customization.

There are strong similarities between international frameworks, industry guidance, and government mandates that have allowed ad-hoc alignments to be published. The publications themselves are not identical nor are they completely different. On average, there is about 40% duplication. At the time of this writing, there are dozens of mappings that have already been completed and published across industry and international mandates. These should be leveraged for your internal efforts, but not taken absolutely. The Center for Internet Security (CIS); the IT Governance Institute (ITGI), the authors of COBIT; and the Information Technology Infrastructure Library (ITIL) have all published documents that demonstrate similarities between controls and subsections of the organization. However, these published mappings should be taken in the context in which they were developed and awareness of these unique attributes considered.

An internal process of aligning publications down to controls, commonly referred to as a *crosswalk*, is a successful approach to developing a single set of key controls from multiple documents. This is done through an analysis of each level of the applicable standards or regulations. Through a crosswalk exercise, a matrix is constructed and regulation components are aligned; for each publication, an IT control team and committee can assign the control components to the organization's existing control-and-compliance structure to develop an organization-specific control framework. The crosswalk must be done in a way that is scalable (as you are looking to expand the organization's operations across the globe), is suitable (the controls and their implementations address the true risks of the organization), and is defensible (all parties are confident and assured of the competency and propriety of the control environment itself). The output of this effort is a reduction in duplication across requirements, a retasking of duties relating to managing controls, and a general consensus on where technology enables the business.

Place a Stick in the Sand

In every great challenge, the first step in identifying and executing a solution is finding a place to focus one's efforts. Determining such an anchor point is your first task in developing the organization's unique control environment framework.

There are two approaches to establishing the anchor point in creating the initial crosswalk for the organization. The first is to embrace existing key control documents that reflect the current safeguard environment or to work from a generic starting safeguard document that does not have the familiarity of the first. The second approach is more appropriate in working without any prior history within the company, where broader strokes are taken in building a framework and how additional control requirements are blended together. In each approach an iterative process should be employed. Instead of engaging in a Herculean effort to map every single control to the lowest level, an organization may shorten the cycles to provide rapid wins for the project. These rapid iterations are necessary to maintain a cadence in publishing and embedding this type of program. Steady cadence also allows for better development of controls and real-time adaptation as business-unique operations are encountered. As the team depends on business owners, executive management, and regular cooperation with technologists from around the business, constant progress and positive communication are important. By bringing these solutions quickly to reality, continued support from the organization is ensured and involved parties are encouraged by the timely achievement of milestones.

Small development and publication cycles ensure that the team is able to meet targets that allow for "business-as-usual" disruptions and shifts in the business operations and environment. An iterative method also integrates a feedback process where all stakeholders may provide input throughout development.

Focused-Linking Approach   This first approach allows an organization to select any single document (your beta superset), which may include using a published standard as a base to work from and linking other regulations and safeguard requirements to it. Additional sources may include the standard the organization has been certified under. A subject matter expert from the company has to be involved in the linking process.

The linking process entails breaking down every control mandate for every identified influencer (remember, influencers may be government regulatory requirements, partner contractual mandates, industry voluntary standards, or internal customer satisfaction and loyalty programs) of the organization and then determining which control safeguards are most like those found in the superset. This process, although laborious, is absolutely necessary and, fortunately, a onetime event. External sources and service resources may be leveraged during this process to help accelerate these mappings.

Some of the controls will not match any superset item directly, and these should be recorded and appended to the superset list. As the team progresses through each influencing document and guidance, the list of items appended will grow until all controls are represented. It is appropriate to place a degree of importance on applicability to allow for future enhancements and reductions of controls.

This approach is perfect for organizations that have been operating with a fairly well-defined control environment and are seeking operational efficiencies, more rapid alignment, and support for future expected legal mandates.

Scattered Approach   In the second approach, no specific document is your starting point. Instead, you establish an anchor point by working from the most robust guidance or framework. The framework chosen should be the one with the greatest level of granularity and clearest definitions. Note that simply selecting the most robust or the most comprehensive framework is not always the best choice; these may actually slow down the process due to their expansive requirements. Specifically, the starting framework should resonate with the organization's industry or the team's background. As an example, embracing the National Institute of Standards and Technology (NIST) 800-53 standard is great if your organization participates in the government sector, has a team with military or government experience, or is seeking to expand into this industry. The challenge with NIST 800-53 is that the controls are written in a language that is not meant for laypeople or those unfamiliar with government requirements or acronyms. In addition, the controls themselves are sometimes burdensome, and the control language requires a level of interpretation to ensure comprehension and proper adoption.

Working without a superset requires taking all the given controls of the first influencing document and lining up the subsequent requirements to the following documents. For all those that do not match, additional line items would be added to represent the additions. The process and subsequent repetitive steps of linking should occur as described in the first approach.

This approach is acceptable if there is no clear agreement regarding industry focus or an absence of any controls program. This is most common for conglomerates or holding companies with very diverse business lines that have historically operated independently with duplicate teams, technology, processes, or lack of connectivity.

Value and Importance

The appreciation and recognition for risk and value must be applied when architecting the organization's control program. The first part of this effort occurs by weighting the standards and guidance documents that are being mapped into the superset list for the organization. The values for each shall be different and are subject to the perspective of the business itself, but should follow a single measurement scale.

The organization should assign a high/low valuation to each document and subsequent control that is being mapped into the superset. This high/low rating should define whether the control is of high or low importance to the organization. This rating is truly a subjective gut check by the team and committee involved in the development of this program.

Ratings should be based on both qualitative and quantitative evaluations. The more extensive the criteria applied to these standards and articles, the greater the accuracy and the more holistic a view will be adopted by the organization, as these documents are absorbed into business operations. The longevity of any publication must be considered; an organization should not alter the control environment in response to requirements that are (or are soon to be) no longer applicable. (For example, there is no need to favor specified controls for regions or industries that are soon to be divested by the business.)

The strategic level of the organization must understand and accept the proposed control environment safeguards. Executive review ensures that future strategic shifts are accounted for in the program. Executive acknowledgment and acceptance ensures the organization establishes the capabilities to address all management directives in a timely and efficient manner. The decision to adhere may be a legal requirement to the organization or a (public-relations) goodwill effort deemed appropriate by the business. Decisions may also stem from these business measures, among others:

- Financial penalties or consequence costs to the entity

- Liability assigned to management or practitioners for failure to adhere to the mandate

- Legal precedents in place that establish a pathway for punitive damages

- Total amount of resources (time, finances, and personnel) distracted in handling inquiries or making rapid corrections

- Publicity and enhanced regulatory scrutiny[5]

- Competitive advantage in markets resulting from attestation

- Strategic growth into new markets requiring adherence to currently inapplicable mandates

It is important to recognize that this is only half of the risk-prioritization equation. In the next section we place the importance of the standard in the context of the business, industry, market drivers, and systems. We define specifics on risk and values of the controls.

Considerations and Contrarian Views

Certain points must be understood and certain truths accepted in order to fully appreciate the process of converging and customizing the organization's control environment. It is also necessary to highlight opposing views to such a program to ensure that your organization is at ease with these concerns and is able to prevent problems from occurring.

The fact is that the mandated legal requirements dictated around the world are mappable (again not 100%). When combined, the requirements create a finite list of mandates for the organization to manage. Companies have had to align themselves to legislative requirements for centuries. Recent requirements have addressed the heightened importance of information within an enterprise through information technology controls. A tremendous volume of references, sources, approaches, and alternative methods of varying specificity can evolve. The perception of a disconnected framework is common initially due to the incomplete mappings that result. These outliers, meaning the controls that have no immediate mapping partners or relationships, become great in number as the amounts of publications are mapped.

In fact, embracing these requirements and merging them together reduces the total number of safeguards the organization explicitly is addressing. The fact remains that the organization seeks to achieve an operational level of compliance and capability to service clients, and these safeguards exist regardless if they are mapped to reduce duplicates. Beyond the challenge of managing additional controls, duplicates create a multiplier effect that includes the number of controls times the number of assets times the number of tests and subsequent reports produced that a test-once, report-to-many system can address. The elimination of the multiplier effect and the general reduction in controls greatly reduces the number of control safeguards even as the number of regulations required may continue to increase. This efficiency trend exists after several mappings of regulations. Eventually an organization (depending on the type and breadth of the control mandates that are mapped together) will be able to address many regulations without a significant increase in control safeguard implementations.[6]

Not all control safeguards require the same level of scrutiny or attributes. For instance, the J-SOX, a nickname for Japan's Financial Instruments and Exchange Law, and the U.S. SOX requirements, while similar in nature and intent, require different levels of assurances to be made and therefore are not completely mappable. Another example is that the need to have a password is a universally consistent requirement, but the length of the password is not. The variances between control attributes result in some organizations, need to seek a balance.

The concept of merging all requirements together causes the strictest requirements to be applied across the entire organization, a process that many view as inefficient and a problem with the homogenization of control legislations. The committee and the project teams involved must understand and address the threat of raising the control standards to high, creating a burdensome environment. Therefore a review of each control attribute is desirable to determine where control attributes should be applied universally, and where selective applications should occur. This review process must look beyond initial change resistance, and determine why the control attribute is not necessary universally. Self-reflection should answer whether the risk defined by the legislation or other influencer is not present for the rest of the organization.

A remedy to the all-or-none debate exists where organizations can implement a segmentation effort for those unique safeguards that are burdensome when applied across the whole business. Excessive control attributes do not have to be applied to the business as a whole; the integrity of the highly sensitive areas can be maintained by isolating and segmenting them from the common areas on the network and the physical environments. The most immediate result of this converging effort includes reduction of controls (and the resulting costs of maintaining, auditing, reporting, and updating) and more efficient usage of management.

Progress through Iterations

"Don't try to boil the ocean" is a common warning when companies seek a centralized IT compliance program. Many companies become overwhelmed by the vastness of controls and lose the support of the business owners when progress deteriorates. Abandonment of IT strategies is the result. Software development teams manage this risk with defined iterative software development life cycles (SDLC), and international standards implement variations of Plan–Do–Check–Act life cycles.

The most effective approach is to apply this same logic to developing the technology control environment. Initially work at the top levels of all the safeguards and frameworks. Once they are identified and accepted throughout the enterprise, additional iterations may occur where each progressively addresses a greater number of controls and more granular attributes. Feedback on the necessity of the controls as well as their applicability and the reality of adoption is vital. The architects of the control environment need to understand where something does not make sense and where a certain environment needs better and more restrictive controls.

Developing and launching such a program provides business owners with feedback and visibility on what exists and what is needed throughout the process. Too often communication between business and technology breaks down, and accountability regarding specifics is lost. This process of involving all parties creates dialog, encourages debate, and bridges service centers.

RISK-BASED CONTROLS: FILTER AND PRIORITIZE

The need for assurance surrounding the systems security and integrity is paramount to a trusted computing environment. The AICPA's SAS 109 guidance states that as a result of management's reliance upon data for operations and decision management, such data must be "sufficiently precise" and provide a "reliable basis."[7]

Identifying all the obligations of an organization, describing the organic control safeguards, and detailing the metrics and benefits desired provide a strong baseline of where we are and what we hope to achieve.

At this point you must prioritize the gathered information to identify the value provided by the systems and consider the significance of the control safeguard requirements. In weighing and debating the identified influencers of the organization, you must consider all levels of management and perform a clear cost-benefit analysis. This process should result in a list of the organization's relevant and significant concerns and provide a framework to manage the organization.

Once the risks and control influencers are prioritized and filtered, the team must determine the organization's current state. (The current state is the equivalent of an organizational report card when compared against the final prioritized and filtered control influencers.) By noting the organization's current state, you are able to determine how far it is from a desired posture. Then you can develop remediation tools and initiate projects to enhance or reduce the sophistication of the controls in place for the identified areas.

Risk and Opportunity

Risk is defined in many ways to fit a given situation. *Webster's Dictionary* says that risk is the "possibility of loss or injury" while opportunity is defined as "a favorable juncture of circumstances." The Institute of Internal Auditors defines risk as "the possibility of an event occurring that will have an impact on the achievement of objectives."[8]

A favorite adage of the risk management world is an interpretation of John Shedd's "A ship in harbor is safe—but that is not what ships are for." To those in business and risk management, the act of being in business is dealing with risk, and it is the existence of risk that creates the opportunity for enterprises to profit. Interestingly, business gurus like Peter Drucker and others over the past century consistently emphasize that business professionals (from line managers up to executives and entrepreneurs and nonprofit teams) are in the business of risk management, and it is only through a balance of the risk and the opportunity that a business may succeed. This concept is succinctly illustrated in Jim Collins's book *Good to Great*, where he demonstrates the need for such environmental considerations.[9]

Conducting a realistic assessment of what may be gained or lost in all aspects of the business is key to ensuring that sufficient measures are taken to mitigate any identified threats or to seize on opportunities that arise. Determining risk and opportunity, capturing intelligence from both management and practitioners, and prioritizing these to ensure sufficient resources are available to engage in identified opportunities or withstand a negative event without depleting the capacity to address the regular business operations is the goal the governance and compliance program and the result of the evaluation process.

Identifying Your *Most Important* Assets

Every organization relies on a group of key individuals or has a core process that keeps the doors open, so to speak. These may simply be the phone lines that are relied on by the sales team, billing department, or the group that coordinates the shipments of the goods around the world. Of course, now an organization may depend on the Internet backbone or sourcing providers. The interdependencies may be the result of an interwoven supply chain where service-level agreements define contractually the accuracy and ability of services. Regardless of its sophistication and technological wizardry, every business has components that must be available for a certain period of time and must deliver reliable services in order for the enterprise to remain in operation. The concept of "most important" was highlighted recently in the United States Securities and Exchange Commission and Public Company Accounting Oversight Board updated guidance for SOX Section 404 and has been practiced throughout many nations within the EU and Australia.[10]

An organization must evaluate its operations and coordinate discussions with all levels of employees to uncover the critical aspects of the business. A group should be assigned responsibility for coordinating the identification of the most important assets, and be advocated by an executive with related job responsibilities—such as a chief risk officer or equivalent (CISO or CAE).

Identifying the most important aspects of the business will help the team to define types of assets and processes that should be the focus of the effort. A top-down approach, versus a bottom-up approach, delivers the best balance between resource commitment and mitigation of risks in the most concise time frame. To capture this information, the market forces, the business culture, and the existing threats must be identified, evaluated, and assigned a level of risk, and must determine the suitability of controls. As critical aspects of the business are uncovered, the information assets that support or make up the process are identified. IT implementations contribute to many areas of the business: sales, customer relationship management, running factory machines, releasing quarterly reports, and billing clients. A top-down approach provides a macro-view of the most critical business strategies and business functions that allows the team to drill down to identify the information technology assets. These information technology assets directly contribute to the organization, and provide a reference point for practitioners to determine the indirect critical assets.

Identification is the discovery process of what assets make up the material aspects of the business. This may include a review of key accounting systems and ledgers, an evaluation of client revenue contributions, or a focus on the production systems and a determination of which allow the business to function (e-mail, factory floor conveyer belts). The discovery process should leverage works produced by others, whether conducted under the auspices of an enterprise risk management program or a government-required evaluation, to expedite the effort. Heads of all departments and lines of business should perform this review. They and the project leader should then discuss what accounts, services, and activities each division relies on and assign each a weight (quantitative and qualitative measures—i.e., Level of Importance; Revenue Production; Public Relations Value). Discussions with business owners must focus on the business functions and delivery of services. Captured information on these business requirements may then be reviewed with managers and technologists to identify the underlying technology assets.

The values defined should at least be assigned general attributes (such as critical/not-critical, client facing/not–client facing). Discussions and research will provide greater specificity as conducted. Ideal attributes to start off the discussions include:

- *Availability importance.* How long can the business operate without that service or function (hours, days, weeks, months)?

- *Contribution.* Dollar value or percentage?

- *Sensitivity.* Are there business intellectual property, copyrighted works, employee or customer personally identifiable information, other sensitive data?

- *Dependency.* Is this function an input or output for another segment of the business? The function for one business owner may be of relatively low importance, but the output may be of paramount importance to another business and therefore may elevate the concerns for this function.

Once initial attributes are defined for the enterprise, an iterative process of evaluations should occur. During the evaluation, a value is placed on the identified assets, both actual dollars and soft costs. This evaluation should study existing transaction volumes through specified assets and business processes. The greater the specifics, the larger the cost savings and efficiencies that will be gained for the organization. All assets can be assigned a dollar value, but only a portion of total enterprise assets will have transactional values attributed to them depending on their role throughout business processes. Examples include:

- E-commerce Web site:
  - Identify the number of transactions that occur on the site.
  - Determine the amount of revenue accrued from the site.
  - Determine the functions supported beyond sales on the site, and assign a soft value, including:
    - ✓ Customer help desk
    - ✓ Customer feedback system
    - ✓ Vendor procurement and ordering processes (may reside on the same system)

- Internet connection from factory to office:
  - What type of traffic is transmitted?
  - Do any services require real-time connections (i.e., if the Internet is unavailable, will the factory stop operating)?
  - Determine the amount of revenue attributed to this connection.
  - Determine that secondary functions are supported beyond defined usage, and assign a soft value, including:
    - ✓ Research and development computer-assisted drawing approval process
    - ✓ E-mail communications
    - ✓ Centralized file storage for the factory

The specific attributes and possible value for each asset are unique to the individual organization and may be quite different between regions for the same corporation. Therefore, this evaluation process should be done in regional or divisional segments. Whenever possible, the hard values should be associated with the source data and permit dynamic updates. This will help ensure that real-time data are available and enable the proper accounting for business segments that improve or decline. If a dynamic live feed is not possible, then a regular asset valuation exercise should occur at least annually if not semiannually. The review cycle is widely dependent on the pace of the business climate: the number of acquisitions, increases of assets on a percentage basis, divestitures, or a shift in the marketplace and the products delivered.

The determination of the suitability of controls is both an additive and subtractive exercise. It is just as likely that technology will be deemed unnecessary or at least excessive given the risks and assets under discussion as the opposite.

RISK-BASED CONTROLS: CURRENT STATE

Context

At this point we have identified, assigned values, and debated with both management and technologists on the level of contribution an asset provides, and investigated the applicability of international, domestic, and industry control mandates. These weighted assets and legislative requirements paint a near-complete picture, but lack the context of organization's operating environment. The final part of this phase is to assign the proper weights to each individual control influencer according to the aggregate risk effect, and then determine the organization's current state. The aggregate risk effect is the potential for a chain reaction of negative events. This chaining effect is material when the events affect risks identified as low frequency and high impact. In general, such risks are accepted by management and not mitigated. Nassim Taleb in *Fooled by Randomness* discusses this situation.[11]

The operating situations of the company and its different divisions face a varied degree of risks that must be considered independently and collectively. The risks and the controls must take into consideration the context of these divisions. Understanding what influences the organization and being able to measure that influence ensures that the technology control environment is sufficient and appropriate given the unique business operating environment. For example, consider a baseball score without knowing who is playing: The scores themselves are meaningless without the context in which they are applied. (See Exhibit 8.1.)

Exhibit 8.1 Business Function Analysis Across Core Influencers.

Control Type	Asset	Location		Data Classification		Legislation		Supportive Business Processes		Asset Weighted Valuation:
		Weighted Value	Value	Weighted Value	Value	Weighted Value	Value	Weighted Value	Value	
Logical Access	ERP System	Low ~ 25%	5	High ~ 75%	10	High ~ 75%	15	Key Business Function ~ 100%	15	35

Maximum Value: 45
Lowest Value: 11.25

{ ERP System is in the high ranvge for assests at 78%

Formulas calculated as follows: (Location Weight × Location Value) + (Data Classification Weight × Classification Value) + (Processes Weight × Processes Value) = Weighted Value for that control

Evaluating the Current Posture

Once a complete accounting of the factors that influence the business is created, the organization must determine its current posture against such measures. This process involves a cross-functional team effort where heads of departments and specialists throughout the company contribute their domain expertise. This team may be made up of the initial identification team. The goal is to determine the type, level, and effectiveness of safeguards deployed throughout the company compared to what has been determined that the organization needs.

Thorough testing should reflect the structure of the organization to which it is being applied. An organization that has a single large physical location will proceed with a single testing plan and develop a comprehensive risk score for that facility. Organizations that have many locations, such as holding companies with many business units, will proceed in the same manner, but each location will have a single score, and the central holding company will maintain a comprehensive score. The process and actions are the same, but the manner of recording and recognizing safeguard implementations and the resulting scores varies. The variations represent that distinctiveness of the location, the significance of the control implementations, and the relevant weightings. (See Exhibit 8.2.)

The first task is to break down the framework and control safeguards into logical groupings that facilitate the distribution and response collections. Heads of departments should be given all groupings that they manage. These senior managers may then forward the appropriate sections to team

Exhibit 8.2   Enterprise Risk Valuations across Divisions

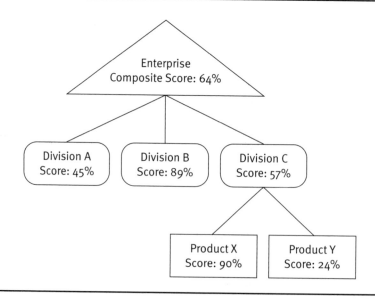

members, who may further pass along the questions. This method follows the current chain of responsibility and ensures accountability. These initial groups of tests typically involve simple survey questions seeking information about the controls and assets, identifying domain experts, and clarifying any initial unknowns. The objective is to request data from the authorities, who either will respond or will task it to the proper groups.

This reassignment process is the foundation of discovering the posture relative to the assets under examination and of making a reasonable number of requests to the subject matter experts. Allowing top-tier managers to either respond or reassign ensures that the efforts are given sufficient attention in the organization, and that those who have the authority, and knowledge of the areas in question are responsible for responding allows for highly confident results.

Upon completion of this first pass the team now has a full record of owners/subject matter experts, controls, and other safeguards. This level of detail is useful in future efforts when evidence and on-site validation assurance engagements are required. In addition, by pairing owners to assets and safeguards, the organization can determine the propriety of such assignments and recommend future changes. Thus, the survey activity itself is a control. The results provide immediate clarity into the disbursment of authority and accountability within the business.

Methods and Communication   It is necessary for a variety of discussions to occur in order to determine the true posture and state of the organization. Surveys are the cheapest, fastest, most frequently used tool for reaching the largest population in the organization. These are ideal for initial gathering of data and for addressing large populations of managers or those geographically dispersed.

Once a baseline of information is determined through analysis of survey results, the team should schedule interviews with key management. These meetings should focus on each manager's lines of business and how the current state of information technology supports the organization as a whole.

Questions should be presented to each manager and left open-ended, as these interviews are meant to explore the possibility of reducing and enhancing the IT internal controls within this manager's departments, and his or her feedback and buy-in is critical.

The interviews should explore:

- Revenue contributions

- Criticality of identified services within the manager's scope of concern

- Trends in the business that indicate the need for more or fewer technology controls

- Trends in the marketplace that may cause an increase in liability (new service-level agreements, expansion into a market, winning a new customer)

- Sensitivity of the data

- If the building were wiped out today, how long the business could continue to operate (Determine managers' maximum availability outage allowance.)

The purposeful sequencing of surveys to asset owners through the tiers of management provides the desired level of detail regarding the current state. Once all the data have been collected, the team analyzes the information using roundtable open discussions.

The aim of these discussions is to present all of the information collected and create a near-final set of corporate IT control measures for the organization that are prioritized, attributed to corporate viability (revenue, legal mandates, service-level agreements), and reduced to their key points (eliminating control measures should be achieved objectively using cost-benefit analysis, another form of financial weighting, or through a reasonable expectation for a compensating control to address a component). This succinct matrix presents the technology controls and the current score for each according to the responses from throughout the organization.

Once all parties have contributed and weighed in on the focused control measures, executive management, the board of directors, or an established executive committee must sign off on and accept the reduced and targeted grouping of control safeguards. This document should be presented to management for review and acceptance by the head of internal audit, the chief risk officer, or another equivalent person who oversaw the activities of the team and has accountability for the organization's risk and control state. In some organizations the senior risk manager, general counsel, or even the financial chief may oversee this process. As the process of reassessing criticality of the business occurs, future presentations and acceptances will be necessary and should therefore be included in future plans.

The purpose of buy-in at this level is to ensure the defined control measures and risks are appropriately communicated, allow for a final scrutiny on the work up to this point, and ensure that the control measures are in concert with the organization's forward-looking strategy. This strategy may not be published, but it is familiar to those at this level of management. Ultimately the senior management must also accept the proposed target states for all control measures. This refinement of target states will reflect management's risk tolerance in light of all the influencers and provide a risk register for future control measure reviews.

Once accepted, or after rework has been completed to meet the satisfaction of this group, the team will have a set of control measures that accurately reflect the businesses needs, risks, desires, and future projected performance requirements. The program at this point has been fully embraced by the organization and may be considered its IT control program. When combined with the responses provided during the surveys, interviews, and debates, these safeguards make up the entire current state of the organization.

Gap Analysis and Next Steps   At this point the project team has included all subject matter experts, business managers from across the enterprise, and senior management in the identification, prioritization, internal rating, and refinement of desired IT control measures. It has specified the necessary risk acceptance thresholds for each control measure in the context of the business processes associated with each. The organization has the two pieces necessary to perform a final evaluation: the target state and the current state of the organization.

The target state is made up of the aggregation (likely captured in an Excel matrix) and weighting assigned to the factors that influence the IT control environment. The merging of attributes for each control measure must be done individually to ensure that the importance of any given measure is not diluted or inflated beyond what is necessary and desired. Initially the target state will raise the bar of compliance and safeguards throughout the entire organization. Later iterations of analysis throughout the organization, once a more mature and integrated control environment has taken hold, correct this problem.

The current state of the organization is based on the feedback provided by all of the surveys, questionnaires, work groups, debates, and sidebar conversations. These efforts provide a current evaluation and accounting of the organization's current safeguards.

Finally, simple arithmetic is necessary, with the target state attributes being subtracted from the current state attributes for each control measure. The resulting values may be placed on a chart or listed on tables to show trends and values. The identified gaps represent potential areas of improvement in all facets of the business. Variances in the scores will indicate if too many or too few safeguards are in place. The identification of these differences represents areas of cost savings and efficiency that the organization can achieve. The performance impacts of a single gap discovered are magnified depending on the number of procedures processed through that given control, the time spent by internal technology teams maintaining the control, the effort to provide proper representations to management, internal audit, and external auditors, and technology costs. (See Exhibit 8.3.)

Prior to engaging in corrective actions, the organization must consider the means of measuring its performance relative to the identified control measures listed within the gap analysis matrix (sometimes called a *risk register*). Metrics for the organization should consider the business

Exhibit 8.3   Spider Gap Analysis of Enterprise Operations

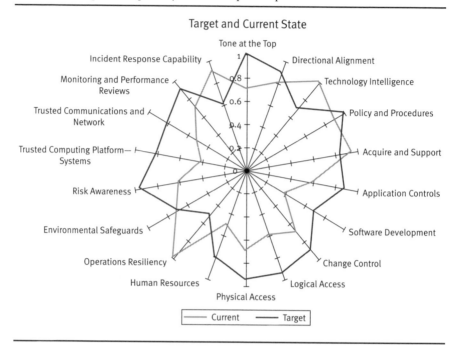

Target and Current State

objectives, the nature of the targeted control environment, the velocity of change desired/required by management, and the nature of the business. These indicators should be composed using data feeds from available assurance activities and any automated systems to capture the organization's real progress through the maturing of the control environment; the metrics should identify weaknesses and enhance their management by indicating where to apply resources.

The next effort is to review the remaining measures and define next steps based on the outputs. If the values are positive (the desired control is greater than the existing control), the organization should place these overly severe controls in a group that will be assigned remediation efforts to enhance them. For items that are negative (the desired control is less than the existing control), the organization must consider means of reducing the level of safeguards for the identified components. These items too should be placed in a separate group. The remaining items should constitute the controls that are operating at the ideal level for the organization's needs and future objectives. These should be separated and placed into a third grouping.

The project team must review the groups identified as having excessive or too few safeguards, and a project plan for developing a remediation plan should be drafted. The plan should consist of reengaging the owners of assets and processes for the identified control measures. These persons together with the team should evaluate the technical and procedural implications of adjusting the control structures. The parties should be aware of macro-effects on the rest of the control environment and verify that controls considered excessive or lacking in one control environment do not constitute a compensating control in another department.

The remediation plan should include technical and management-level buy-in and acceptance to adjust any controls already in operation. Once a control has been adjusted (enhanced or reduced), a period of diligent observation must occur. During this observation process, the team must ensure that operations continue to be effective and efficient. The controls should also be placed on a regular testing schedule over the first quarter to ensure that operations continue as expected and that shortcomings in the updated control environment are identified quickly.

The controls that were in line with the target state required by the organization should be placed in a monitor control group. Here the monitoring of acceptable controls should focus on enhancing the efficiency of the controls. These efforts are meant to streamline and add improvements that will help the business operate more effectively while continuing to meet requirements.

Organizational Benefits

At the outset of committing resources a realistic projection of benefits should be specified. These benefits must cross the chasm of what is theoretical and proposed by academics and what is promoted by snake-oil salesmen.[12] The benefits must be real, have a meaningful impact to the top and bottom line, contribute to a better client experience, and establish a sense of purpose and propriety in the core of the business soul regarding the integration of internal controls throughout the organization and information technology.

The objectives may be defined simply as efficiencies, cost savings, reduced outsourcing fees, or better realization and delivery of services. The types of benefits that should be expected vary somewhat based on the size of the organization and its current maturity regarding IT adoption. An organization may measure the benefits and progress of the governance and control program by these benefits:

- Decreased risk management values
- Efficiency and control of technology functions
- Effective management of information technology, fiscally and through full utilization of human and technological resources
- Defensible and repeatable leading practices throughout organization and through new acquisitions
- Better prioritization of high-impact projects

- Increased delivery of technology and therefore business services

- Shareholder contentment

- Agile organization[13]

The establishment of general benefits provides a scale to determine the effectiveness of the governance and control program and provide a path for the organization to follow. It will take at least a year for the organization to begin to realize the benefits; it may be nearly five years before they reach their peak delivery. This length of time is necessary to overcome previous inefficiencies, allow for true integration of the controls to the core of the organization, and realign resources throughout the organization due to the control and the process adjustment. The benefits realized raise the confidence level of investors and public institutions, align the priorities of technology internally, and contribute to the elimination of siloed divisions.

Credit agencies, such as Standard & Poor's in the United States, are seeking assurances that businesses have proper IT control environments that are aligned in a risk-conscious manner.[14] Organizations that have instituted such solid and integrated programs are rewarded with favorable ratings by credit-rating agencies and regulators. Governments around the world encourage companies to embrace control environments.

Establishing an enterprise IT control environment that spans all divisions aligns the business owners instead of pitting them against each other. The removal of competition for resources and the consistency provided by a common vernacular enhances the organization's ability to apply resources where they are most beneficial for the entire organization. This achievement ensures clearer roles and responsibilities and that all concerns are consistent with the enterprise's strategic direction and control mandates.[15]

The elimination of the vertical divisions within business units around technology introduces what Marshall calls "dependency models."[16] This concept is consistent with the elimination of silos or fiefdoms within enterprises and ensures that all businesses are effective internally and thus equally competitive and agile in the marketplace. A publication by Booz Allen Hamilton supports this case. "The problem with this stovepiped approach is that it not only ignores the interdependence of many business risks but also suboptimizes the financing of total risk for an enterprise."[17]

A Process, Not a Project

Engaging senior management and traveling to the far reaches of the organization is expensive for the company. Staff loses immediate productivity; some even must focus entirely on the IT control program. It is also a costly effort with a fairly long time horizon for return on investment (ROI) calculations. As mentioned, the ROI for programs of this nature can take up to five years for the largest corporations. One reason the program takes so long to institute is the slow-to-change culture of most organizations. We are working to change the entire culture of the organization and how it interacts with systems through processes. Many of these changes may be natural to some participants, but to others they are not.

The cost is not from heavy technology or outside resources, but in the mental capital required by management at all levels and the staff tasked with the execution of the new procedures. Once the learning curve hump is scaled, the business operations should be more effective and certainly more accurate. The organization does not have to consider hiring new staff to achieve operational efficiency. No new technology tools are needed; nor is an army of consultants. (This does not mean that such technology cannot enhance the organization's efforts, simply that it is not required.)

Technology is the support mechanism for our business and ensures that we can remain valuable to our consumers and effective in the marketplace. Therefore, the organization should consider where enhancements can be made to ensure the efforts conducted regularly are captured and kept alive throughout the organization. The terms *risk, control, safeguards,* and *business agility* should be common throughout the organization. These phrases should be made viable through tools that enable all departments to leverage the knowledge captured by the organization.

Managers commonly ask: "What can we do to expedite our IT control environment?" The answer is simple: Bring more people into the team that conducts these evaluations of the organization. This staff preferably should come from internal business departments. The additional personnel will contribute intelligence to the discussions and actually reduce the number of iterations the organization must make to reach a sufficient level of granularity to be operating at the optimal level of control. Temporary staff, such as consultants or contractors, help achieve the same task, but they lack the intimate knowledge of the organization's operations, and when they leave they take their knowledge with them. These indirect costs are very high and should be resorted to only when expediency is required.

ENDNOTES

1. In "Internal Control in Corporate Governance Codes: A Comparative Study" (Uppsala University, Faculty of Social Sciences, Department of Business Studies, 2005), Annika Jettingstad and Sara Kaver compared internal control requirements of Sweden, Belgium, Cyprus, the Czech Republic, Denmark, Finland, France (internal procedures), Greece, Hungary, Italy, Malta, Slovakia, Slovenia, the Netherlands, and the United Kingdom.

2. Statement on Auditing Standards 94 (SAS 94), "The Effect of Information Technology on the Auditor's Consideration of Internal Control in a Financial Statement Audit." American Institute of Certified Public Accountants Auditing Standards Board (2001).

3. AICPA SAS 94.

4. CSI/FBI survey published annually has historically identified internal threats to be the greatest risks to an organization. URL: www.gocsi.com/forms/fbi/csi_fbi_survey.jhtml.

5. The FTC enforced a 20-year period of third-party evaluations over ChoicePoint resulting from their data disclosure. The energy sector was given more oversight through FERC and NERC. The public accounting profession in the United States had the PCAOB introduced in SOX legislation.

6. Most recently these publications have been frequent and extensive in regard to technology general internal controls. Authorities within the United States that have released cross-referenced guidance include the Human Health Services (HHS), Department of Defense (DOD), Department of Energy (DOE), National Institute of Standards and Technology (NIST), Federal Financial Institutions Examination Council (FFIEC), Public Company Accounting Oversight Board (PCAOB), Securities and Exchange Commission (SEC), Department of Homeland Security (DHS). Private professional organizations such as the Institute of Internal Auditors (IIA), Association of Certified Fraud Examiners (ACFE), American Institute of Certified Public Accountants (AICPA), Information Systems Audit and Control Association (ISACA), IT Governance Institute (ITGI), Information Systems Security Association (ISSA), and International Information Systems Security Certification Consortium, Inc. (ISC2) have all published literature or support literature that links requirements of one regulation to another. Internationally, all corners of the globe have incorporated or referenced such standards as ISO 17799, COSO ERM, and other principles-based requirements. All countries that mandate internal controls advocate the use of appropriate requirements for their organizations and support the linkage of a single control to many regulations.

7. SAS 109, "Understanding the Entity and Its Environment and Assessing the Risks of Material Misstatement," AICPA. URL: http://www.aicpa.org/download/members/div/auditstd/SAS109.PDF.

8. Institute of Internal Auditors. Glossary URL: www.theiia.org/guidance/standards-and-practices/professional-practices-framework/standards/standards-for-the-professional-practice-of-internal-auditing/?i=2343.

9. *Good to Great: Why Some Companies Make the Leap . . . and Others Don't* (New York: HarperBusiness, 2001).

10. PCAOB, Auditing Standard No. 5, "An Audit of Internal Control Over Financial Reporting That Is Integrated with an Audit of Financial Statements." URL: www.pcaobus.org/Standards/Standards_and_Related_Rules/Auditing_Standard_No.5.aspx.

11. *Fooled by Randomness: The Hidden Role of Chance in the Markets and Life*, 2nd edition, paperback (Random house, 2005).

12. Brian Warren, "What Is Missing from the RMIS Design? Why Enterprise Risk Management Is Not Working,"*Risk Management* (October 2001).

13. Adapted from Johan Loggerenberg and Eugene Wessels, *IT Governance: Theory and Practice,* Expected Benefits of IT Governance table, (2006). URL: http://citte2006.cut.ac.za/res/wessels.pdf.

14. The financial rating agency S&P is extending its evaluation of companies to consider implementations of ERM within the organization across industries. As an example, S&P considerations within the insurance industry created greater activity and adoption of ERM. URL: www.insurancetech.com/news/showArticle.jhtml?articleID=181500402; URL: www.roughnotes.com/rnmagazine/2006/august06/08p040.htm.

15. Carolyn Kay Brancato et al., "The Role of U.S. Corporate Boards in Enterprise Risk Management," The Conference Board (2006). URL: www.conference-board.org.

16. Christopher Marshall, *Measuring and Managing Operational Risks in Financial Institutions* (Hoboken, NJ: John Wiley & Sons, 2001), 136.

17. Booz Allen Hamilton, *Convergence of Enterprise Security Organizations,* Alliance for Enterprise Security Risk Management (AESRM), USA (November 2005). URL: http://www.aesrm.org.

9

Principle 1: Strategy Orchestration

Key Topics Addressed in This Chapter

Tone at the top

Business and technology alignment

Documentation and communication

PRINCIPLES OVERVIEW: CONCEPT AND APPROACH

Operating a business in a consistent fashion that is mindful of the threats surrounding it daily around the globe is a challenge that entrepreneurs and managers have dealt with for centuries. While the sophistication and the media in which these threats present themselves have changed, the impacts to the business remain. One primary objective of business is to manage risk to a point that ensures the business is able to serve its customers the next day. It is impossible to avoid all risks. If this were medieval times, raising the drawbridge would have the same impact as locking the office doors and unplugging the enterprise from the Internet. The common folk and the village would surely starve, and the business would go bankrupt.

A general theme is common throughout the world's recommended and mandated controls. The consistency of intent and the commonality of control implementations introduce an opportunity for organizations to view their information technology (IT) assets as business assets that contribute to the business processes that directly impact profit and loss.

The principles that follow represent the culmination of analysis by leaders in controls testing and certification that spanned the globe's regulations, best practices, and general frameworks and dozens of corporate attestation reports. The data have been updated over the years and are supported by fieldwork involving organizations across industries and of varying sizes (e.g., Fortune 50, government institutions, and nonprofits) and researching the most influential legislation and standards around the world. The end result is a practical breakdown of the influencers (nearly 50 primary sources and 200 secondary sources) on organizations and an enterprise risk–based approach to embracing these operational necessities. Each organization and division is unique in some ways; however, these principles may be applied wholly or in part to structure the IT control program. The control principles discussed herein represent global concerns at the time of publication. While the principles are universal in application and interpretation, you must be prudent when applying them and consider the threats around the world and your firm's technology, unique nature, and business nature. Use these principles and their associated global core IT controls as a reference point and build your program on them.

GLOBAL PRINCIPLES

The starkest lesson the world has learned from aggressive control legislation is that organizations do not adopt the correct controls based on these laws but instead adopt the controls mandated by the legislation. In reality, most organizations operate without major failures for decades. Nevertheless, a structured control environment surrounding the technology of the business improves performance in the eyes of customers, satisfies the concerns of shareholders, and ensures the resiliency of the organization in the face of market and technology shifts. The adoption of controls and the validation of these controls through internal audit departments or independent third parties must be done in regard to the business, its own risks, and the need to satisfy private and public parties. The five principles identified through this multiyear effort include the following:

1. Technology strategy orchestration
2. Life cycle management
3. Access and authorization
4. Sustain operations
5. Security and assurance

These principles were developed by collecting the most referenced and enforced standards from around the world and comparing them to actual certified controls found in companies around the world. Sections of the mandates were broken down into their most elemental levels and assigned attributes that captured numerous data points. These publications were then linked together through rigorous expert analysis and weightings based on the identified data points. Finally the principles were tested against the original reference organizations to ensure no areas were overlooked or over-emphasized. Together these global principles allow for the specification of global core IT controls. These core controls are the direct result of the most prominent linkages identified and encompass the greatest returns to stake-holders and the necessary assurances mandated against the organization.

The sources consist of standards, frameworks, guidelines, and legislative documents from around the world. A statistically large set of the sources originated from the United States. The European Union (EU), Canada, Australia, Japan, the United Kingdom, and Switzerland represent the remaining primary contributors to the library. In addition, public and private expert professional organization sources were examined and include the Institute of Internal Auditors, the Information Systems Audit and Control Association (ISACA), IT Governance Institute (ITGI), and the Association of Certified Fraud Examiners (ACFE).

The nature of the global market and the consistency found within international IT systems ensures that the findings provided here are applicable and valuable to any organization. Certain cultural and societal adjustments shall always exist, but the core tenets of identifying and managing through risk will always be true. The principles range from the most abstract and strategic aspects of IT controls to the finer specifics of maintaining operations in the event of catastrophic incident.

PRINCIPLE 1: TECHNOLOGY STRATEGY ORCHESTRATION

The initial principle identified from analyzing the world's regulations is *technology strategy orchestration*. The formalization and management of an organization's IT and control environment is critical with regard to legislative compliance and fiscal responsibility to the stakeholders. While most businesses around the world have established a technical awareness and dependency on technology, most have not integrated the business functions to reflect this relationship. The more organizations have visibility into how business processes rely on technology and the subsequent dependent relationships, the more likely business values will be identified and leveraged.

The uppermost level of an organization must strike a balance between what is necessary and what is desired, in light of the costs of those activities. The establishment of policies and procedures for the organization provides top-down direction regarding short- and long-term goals. In addition, such communications within the organization, its staff, and at the management level set a tone at the top that is recognized throughout the entire organization. When the behaviors and proclamations of upper management are consistently communicated, the organization's culture becomes and remains stable.

The value of an organization's digital assets (intellectual property, capital, and data) is ever increasing as new models and markets expand to leverage this massive amount of information. Recognizing and managing these digital assets requires a thorough understanding, identification, and management approach.

The structure of reporting lines for personnel throughout an organization is critical for ensuring that the motivations and actions of everyone, staffers up through management, are in line with the strategic direction of the organization. Therefore, the job objectives, hierarchy, reporting structures, and compensation programs must be aligned properly.

This principle focuses on the macrostructures placed on an organization that ensure that the entire technology control challenge is addressed in a manner appropriate for the business, the risks it faces daily, the risks it expects in the future, the regulations it seeks to address, the best practices it hopes to achieve, and the financial balance that ensures that all components of the operation are complete and appropriate. The global core IT controls that are highlighted within this principle include:

- Tone at the top
- Directional alignment
- Technology governance
- Policy and procedures

Tone at the Top

The conduct of management within the business and in public must be consistent with the organization's core values, as the staff of a company is likely to follow the examples led by the leadership. The forms of communication, formal and informal, regarding expected behavior of personnel within a company are a key control for every organization and should start at the top and be integrated at all levels. Such entity-level controls protect the organization, both public and private, large and small. All organizations of every type and industry are susceptible to fraud, and as demonstrated in Japan and the United States in the early 2000s, all levels of leadership can be the source of such wrongdoing. If an organization does not have a properly instilled and managed culture, the costs can be extreme and even can damaging the broader economy. It is calculated, for example, that organizations in 2006 lost approximately $652 billion in the United States alone from fraud.[1] Extrapolating from these figures to reflect the global accumulated fraud damages, we can project costs to business worldwide of nearly $2.3 trillion a year.[2]

Management overrides of controls, the backdating of stock options, and the excessive use of perks to preferred employees affect the entire company's culture and operational posture. Management's actions can positively and negatively affect how business is conducted within the organization.[3]

Organizations that have and communicate clear ethical behavior from the top of the organization have a greater chance of discovering fraud and a reduced likelihood of its occurrence compared to those that do not.

The *tone at the top* of an organization is a phrase that has been commonly used for the past few decades.[4] It should be considered the ethics and behavior of the business's personnel—at all levels of the company and in all roles. An organization's tone is created by the actions and words of the management. Together these must ensure that the working environment fosters trust, camaraderie, ethical behavior, and a sense of purpose.

The "top" of the organization in this control does not refer just to those in the executive suite. There are many "tops" of an organization, and all must be considered when developing, updating, or reviewing such organizational environments. The direct supervisors of line workers are their "top"; the director of sales is the sales teams' "top." All managers, supervisors, directors, unofficial leaders (typically a founder or company thought leader), and of course the executive suite must foster an environment that is in concert with the ethical and responsible tone of the organization.

The tone of organization must encompass several specific attributes that support its vision and direction and are aligned with the commitments to the stakeholders (employees, shareholders, the community at large, the legal constraints placed on the organization by local and international governing bodies). These *soft controls* include intangibles like ethics and integrity. While regional differences may shift the center of ethics and integrity interpretations (for instance, gift giving in one region is frowned upon, but it is insulting to refuse a gift in others), globally there are recognized definitions and restrictions on how wide the margin of interpretation is acceptable. International treaties, governance bodies, and national laws, such as the U.S. Foreign Corrupt Practices Act, all establish a ground floor on what is acceptable practice.

The company's philosophy regarding compensation, recognition, and other material or nonmaterial rewards is important when compared against employee behavior and actions. Before evaluating or improving the existing control environment, management must consider the culture of the company. The reward systems should support the vision of management at all levels and reinforce the ethical tone of the business. Conversely, rules for dealing with inappropriate behavior must exist and be applied consistently. This structure will ensure that poor behavior does not spread to other people who would normally not commit such actions but do so because others have gotten ahead through unethical actions. The occurrence of fraudulent behavior within an organization creates a greater likelihood of fraud among more persons and the likelihood for collusion. These risks increase the size of the frauds and the impact on the organization. Consider the loan officer who *manages* the applications to meet the volume compensation metric; the company loses due to excessive and abusive loans or unqualified customers who have a high default rate.

The tone of an organization is a very organic and cultural reflection of how the business deals with its employees, customers, communities, and vendors. The participation of all levels of managers, including the board of directors and associated committees, is vital for reinforcing such cultural values. This commitment ensures the operational efficiency of the organization for the long term. Supplanting those who do not adhere to the organization's ethical tone enables greater delivery on the promises to all stakeholders to the company.

Application   Legislation and governance groups around the world recommend that organizations establish an appropriate control environment. Probably the most-referenced guidance is that from the Committee of Sponsoring Organizations (COSO), which includes integrity, management philosophy, and commitment to competence as core intangible safeguards. While this control specifically focuses on intangibles—integrity, ethics, and tone—it is best monitored and evaluated through formal activities. These include the use of communication systems and training programs, the establishment of fraud monitoring and prevention systems, and the institution of and adherence to policies and procedures. These formal controls act to support tone-at-the-top concerns and operate independently to assure operational activities are appropriate. Organizations as a whole should consider their control environment and evaluate both the effectiveness and efficiency through regular evaluations and daily reinforcements. A few activities to maintain clear communications include the following:

- Management presents and conducts operations ethically, as evidenced by a code of conduct or other verbal or written directive.

- The board of directors has established an audit committee or equivalent that is responsible for engaging the auditor, receiving all reports and communications from the auditor, and ensuring that audit findings and recommendations are adequately addressed.

- Proactive management participation in control scope and budget recommendations.

- Executive adherence to program compliance requirements.

- Management's commitment to competence ensures that staff members receive adequate training to perform their duties, and regular verification and incentive programs are established.

- Management establishes appropriate organizational reporting structures to avoid conflicts.

- Management institutes and supports a positive feedback program (to include a hotline and anonymous submission system).

In Practice

Management at all levels and degrees can enhance the organization's control environment through a few practical, personal actions. These cannot replace other formal efforts but certainly can provide immediate gains to the company:

- Communicate the importance of ethics, integrity, and company values through a publicly accessible standards policy and a code of conduct.
  - Codes of conduct can be as simple as "Do No Evil," as championed by Google, or can provide more industry-specific guidance.
- Practice strong values consistent with those stated by the company. Make a conscious effort to demonstrate to those around you how the ethics of the organization work in real life to enhance the reality of the codes of conduct.
- Be ethical. Organizations must set targets and goals for employees that are achievable. Placing employees in impossible situations and then demanding that they "make it happen" is counterintuitive to the decrees of the ethics policy.
  - Organizations that *manage* the numbers at the end of the quarter or ask sales teams to book undelivered items early (against generally accepted accounting principles) in order to recognize them in a given quarter have the makings of a financial house of cards like Enron.
- Establish accountability in the organization and those that report to you. Actively enforcing the standards of the organization when an ethics policy has been broken is critical to ensuring future adherence to the program. No matter the person or the situation: No exceptions should be granted for those who break these core company values.
- Communicate, communicate, communicate. Constantly update your teams and the organization on any pertinent events, the health of the organization, and any changes to the strategic short- or long-term directions, and reinforce your ethics policy.
- Understand the implications of someone's actions for the balance sheet and for the company's public image.

In Practice

Setting the tone of the organization requires a concerted effort from all managers to consistently apply the ethics policy and to establish a program that communicates and properly represents the importance of the established tone of the organization:

1. Hire the right people, or as appropriately stated by Jim Collins, "Get the right people on and off the bus."[5]

In Practice (continued)

---

2. Establish new hire and existing personnel checks. Perform:

   a. Past employment verification

   b. Criminal conviction checks

   c. Drug screening

   d. Reference checks

   e. Education and certification checks

3. Establish and communicate the corporation's tone:

   a. Establish training for all personnel.

   b. Test awareness regularly within the organization.

4. Monitor awareness.

   a. At least annually, require employees to complete an anonymous survey. It is best to use an independent third party in these cases.

   b. Measure human resources notices and cases that violate the tone of the organization.

   c. Establish an expectation of detection. Employees who are aware that they may get caught are less likely to commit an operational fraud. (Expectations of detection are possible through the full application of the controls listed in this section. They should focus especially on the existence of controls, awareness that controls are examined, and the presence of recording and logging.)

5. Enforce the expected behavior.

   a. Consistency in penalties must occur for all infractions. This enforces the tone of the organization and complies with several state laws on applying such penalties.

6. Establish a whistleblower system.

   a. Set up hotlines. (They are great when managed independently of the organization and by remote office personnel.)

   b. Set up a rewards system. (Establishing an atmosphere that promotes the correction of wrong behavior is consistent with successful organizations.)

   c. Prohibit retribution. (Formal and informal actions must be taken to ensure that all those who report fraud or ethical violations are not made vulnerable to the accused—a requirement defined and enforced through industry and legislation.)

Directional Alignment

Technology must be leveraged toward the goals of the business that consider both its near-term needs and its long-term strategic vision. By aligning the existing architecture and project portfolios with the business needs, the organization transforms technology into a business service function. The concept is promoted strongly by business performance management organizations and those international workgroups aimed at enhancing the efficiency of IT delivery of services.[6]

The alignment must consider all of the organization's business functions and the related importance of data and assets throughout the enterprise. The ability of an organization to transition technology processes and physical devices to tangible and manageable business items allows for better assignment of responsibility and accountability.

The lack of alignment causes the organization to incur costs that may not be necessary to the business needs. The simplest example is a major financial institution that had a technology deployment that was very sophisticated and required many specialists to maintain. After a thorough evaluation of the business needs of its technology projects and operations, the organization uncovered 40% excess in the organization. Specifically, the organization identified that the technology department had, following best practices in the technology industry, configured the majority of their servers and applications for five-nine availability. (This means that that the servers and applications had 99.999% uptime.) This introduced redundancy in software licenses, systems, and facilities. In addition, these systems also absorbed resources during upgrades, patching, power consumption, space, and environmental controls. According to the evaluation, only a portion of the services required such availability, and the staff was able to reduce the technology expenses considerably from a single identified business need.

Business Impacts   The cost to an organization for not having such directional alignment can be stated through business value items, as highlighted earlier, or through direct costs to the technology environment. Beyond the transparent fiscal impacts, the organization also will be susceptible to indirect costs that must be considered. To assess the true impact of any cost, you must consider both the obvious immediate risks and also the dependencies and long-term affects of shifts in the technology deployments of an organization. Through consideration of the interdependencies of technology processing systems and the business value they provide, it is possible to identify all primary and secondary cost impacts.

The organization faces direct financial costs resulting from a number of factors. These factors generally include:

- The expense of unnecessary projects ("necessary" in terms of strategic direction)

- The expense of incomplete or aborted projects (projects that were reprioritized down, lost a key staff member, or lost their sponsor)

- The focus of resources on maintaining a level of preparedness for a negative event

- Fines that result from missing compliance or service-delivery targets

Returning to the financial institution, after the technology projects for a given period were evaluated, it was discovered that nearly $650 million was expended on dropped or failed projects.

Hidden costs that may weigh down an organization include the loss of business due to poor performance for clients and customers, including those inside the organization. These costs can be so high that the business unit owner outsources the functions that were handled poorly internally. The risks and related costs can be identified through customer retention figures, customer service records, system usage (gradual reductions may be indicative of poor services), and shifts in client requests. Indirect costs are difficult to identify during an initial technology service analysis because they support or depend on unknown system components or because of to their long-term impacts.

Application Top-level support is required for developing, implementing, and maintaining an enterprise program to be successful and long lasting in an organization. Otherwise, after a great deal of energy is expended analyzing and disrupting the status quo from within the organization, the old habits will return, costing the organization even more. Ideally an organization will have a champion who is compensated to drive the technology innovations, support the business, and address all service requirements while managing profits and losses. This champion may be the chief information officer (CIO) or chief information security officer (CISO), who should report directly to the chief executive officer (CEO) to ensure that the strategic vision is captured and communicated. By sitting near the highest level in the organization, the champion is able to drive all units of the business without bias or constraint.

In order to achieve alignment, you must first determine what the business needs are. These needs should be structured as business values that IT can deliver on. Each should relate directly to an accounting line item or a specific line of business. Through this direct linkage to the contribution revenue a hard value may be attributed to that business value and subsequently used in a cost-benefit analysis by the technology group. This can be part of the risk assessment process, but also may be conducted more rapidly through a collaborative session with the business owners.

Following the business evaluation and determination of business value items for IT, the technology group must evaluate its active projects and the status of the services being delivered for each business value item. This process will identify areas of strength, excess in manpower expenses, weaknesses, or clear gaps. The results will allow the technology group to reset the service-delivery priorities against those stated by the business owners.

The technology group will reprioritize the services provided throughout the organization based on the input provided by the business owners. In order to ensure open communication, the reprioritized services linked to the business value items, their financial revenue figures, and the cost breakdowns provided by IT are made available to the executive management team for signoff.

This process ensures that there is a closed-loop process, business strategy is in alignment with costs, and budgets are sufficient to meet the demands of the organization. In case of a shift in the organization's direction due to a merger and acquisition or other opportunity, management–business owners (clients of the technology group) can turn the dials or flip the switches and reprioritize the technology services provided.

Not all organizations are able to fully realize the benefits from such alignments. Typically most require a major negative event or some form of significant culture shock to create an imperative for such a process. All organizations can benefit from such a program. The more strategic and in line with the business operations, the greater the returns that will result.

What type of organization is ready for such an alignment process?

- The champion of the process reports directly to the CEO.

- The culture is open to collaborating, and there is sufficient knowledge regarding the value of each service line.

- The business depends on the technology environment.

In Practice

DELIVERING SERVICES THAT THE BUSINESS REQUIRES

As the technology group continuously replaces, extends, and augments existing business process operations with more sophisticated technology, the interdependencies and their criticality to the operational integrity of the business increase. Most organizations know the depreciation value of every building, vehicle, desk, and chair as a result of routine insurance and tax calculations. Even though technology is much more important than a vehicle or desk, many organizations do not clearly understand the value that technology is adding to each business unit and to the company as a whole. To determine

In Practice (continued)

the business values provided by the technology group, follow this eight-step framework:

1. Determine the long-term business strategy of the organization, and articulate and promote it.

2. Identify business priorities by customer, service, and systems.

3. Correlate the business values of the company with the systems within the IT network.

4. Determine the dollar and goodwill provided by business functions and then attribute portions to the appropriate technology systems.

5. Establish a dynamic assignment of systems to business units, and create a means for management review of performance and controls.

6. Centralize projects and technology efforts and communicate any proposed or active projects to business owners who will be affected or benefited.

7. Allow for internal billing of services, so that business and technology work toward the same goal in a fiscal and pragmatic approach.

8. Conduct regular prioritization efforts of systems, projects, and business functions based on actual business valuations.

Technology Governance

It is vitally important that the organization controls and manages its digital property in a competent manner. In an age where the 1s and 0s stored on a single server represent billions of dollars in market capitalization, organizations must institute and demonstrate intelligence to safeguard the viability of the organization. The data may be the trial results from recent clinical tests, client sales figures, health and retirement records of current and past employees, the secret ingredient in your soda water, or simply drafts of patent-pending schematics. The information also may be not for public disclosure due to the negative implications that may follow such a release, from fraud or criminal activities; it may be protected by government laws or simply may be competitively damaging to the owner of the information.

Awareness of the value of the innovations and intellectual property (IP) captured on systems allows for stronger recognition of asset value. These values in addition to those derived from the directional alignment activity produce a stronger reflection of the organization's technology contributions and provide guidance on the level of safeguards necessary for such assets. It is important to realize the difference and relationship between directional alignment control activities and those of technology governance detailed in this section. Technology governance focuses on the actual data represented digitally on systems. Technology governance provides visibility into the strategic management of the data itself and provides guidance on the placement and implementation of controls. Directional alignment is the focus on the connection between business functions and technology services. These distinctions should be translated through the data classification policy and procedures.

Organizations that define a formal effort by creating a permanent team or by adding such duties to the job objectives of appropriate parties are able to manage the IP and sensitive data that are protected under the laws of various governments and maintain sufficient control over the allocation of resources.

Business Impacts   The value of a business's IP may be quantified based on the realized market return based on contribution accounting or through an analysis of the total costs that would be the result of an intentional or unintentional negative event. While the market returns may be calculated through transparent financial bookkeeping, the impacts that result from negative events require a bit of analysis and reflection by the organization to determine its own sensitivity to a variety of risks. Prominent high-level risk factors include the loss of secrecy, the negative impacts of exposure (data breaches), and physical losses.

The ability for a company to sustain and excel in the future may be attributed to its ability to innovate in a competitive environment. A company's innovation into the future and ability to compete is most clearly demonstrated by the secrecy that Steve Jobs and Apple employ regarding product releases and updates. The secrecy is legendary; a communication protocol has been established where all stakeholders expect announcements to coincide with sales returns and a stock that clearly tracks with public Apple events. The number of copycat solutions released in quick succession after product announcements makes the importance of such secrecy brutally clear. Through innovation and secrecy, companies are able to establish a market presence prior to any competitive product.

The value or market rate for the company's IP can be based on the amount a competitor or organization would pay to gain access to that information, and the internal costs associated with development and production that establish the value of IP within an organization. Information that is not proprietary but categorized as private and sensitive by certain parties should be valued equal to the total available market rate (black market) of the data when known, or based upon public recovery costs. "Personally sensitive information" is defined differently around the world, but there is sufficient consistency to allow us to propose a definition. Sensitive information is anything that can be sold or utilized to benefit another. The escalating occurrences of data theft are a stark example of threats to businesses and consumer confidence. Credit card data are considered sensitive within the payment card industry. In the event of a breach, fines are incurred. In addition to fines resulting from breaches of personal identifiable information including social security numbers or other protected information, organizations may be susceptible to civil lawsuits and in some states are liable for additional damages.

Losses to companies may be the result of a thousand different scenarios but can include hurricanes knocking out the only archival location for the pharmaceutical company or backup tapes containing millions of consumer identities getting lost in the mail.[7] Systems or sets of systems can physically lose the data stored on them. Losses can occur through the purposeful actions of a recently fired, disgruntled employee who had administrative privileges or simply due to an unusual set of hardware failures and a lapse in corporate backup procedures. Regardless of the cause of the incident, the loss is real and can impact the organization at multiple levels. The loss of resources invested into the projects and market competitive technologies can be calculated simply by the time spent in development. The cost to recover the IP through rebuilding and recovering must be considered. Of greater significance are the impacts to the organization as a competitor in the global marketplace. The loss of market capitalization that was already added into the stock by the market based on prior press releases is a measurable result. Many markets do not tolerate product misses or broken delivery promises, but the semiconductor market is one of the most brutal of them all. This is, in part, a result of the product dependencies and *just in time* manufacturing processes employed by many computer companies that sequence their own product releases with those of their partners. The delay of even a few days results in a ripple effect throughout the entire supply chain and business.

Application Ascertaining the value of intellectual property requires the participation of the business owners throughout the organization. Internal audit or another team within the organization skilled in evaluating risks should work through a top-down approach by first interviewing the executive management. Through these conversations and through subsequent discussions at the lower end of the upper management structure, the team should determine the organization's core IP areas.

The team should then facilitate the process of determining the values and the risks facing these IP centers, and then finally evaluate the effectiveness of the controls in place within the organization. By working through a top-down approach, the importance is captured and alignment is achieved with strategic initiatives. The team must ensure that it is the business owners and management who are determining and scoring the value and risks to the organization. This collaboration provides greater buy-in from management and ensures greater transparency throughout the process.

A classification system should be developed to reflect the type of sensitive information handled by the organization and the culture in which this information is managed. The labeling of information is a logical step after identifying the type of data and must be done in a manner to ensure sufficient controls and levels are defined for the organization. Measures of success should produce a data classification scale. The scale may be a simple two-tier scale or a complex adaptive scale of five levels or greater; regardless, it should reflect the security mentality of the organization, the systems involved, and the business processes in place. Awareness of the organizational culture is vital to avoid adopting an overly burdensome structure that may not last over the long term; nevertheless, the structure must be sufficient to address the needs of the organization. A functional approach is to define the desired classifications and then introduce a progression program that gradually includes technology and adjusts processes to achieve the data management requirements based on classification.

The work process and structure of the defined IP concerns become the groundwork for the formal creation of a permanent data custodian program. This program should follow a process that reflects the structure of the organization and may be leveraged as a reference for internal and external audit processes to avoid the duplication of work. The data custodian function is key to ensuring that organizations are fully aware of the nature of data entrusted to the organization, and ensures that controls are placed and executed properly.

Policy and Procedures

The process that defines how personnel throughout the company understand what action is appropriate for every unique situation requires clear executive support. This support is provided by establishing a formal structure that provides a life-cycle process for managing policies consistent with corporate goals. The objective of such a process is to allow for the development, acceptance, and implementation of policies. Policies are a key component to an effective governance process and represent the directors' and executive management's expectations regarding performance and activities. Given that such publications cannot account for every situation, it is the duty of policy owners to create documents that establish the tone and desired behaviors, and it is the responsibility of management to ensure that these are understood and embraced by all associates within the organization.

Management of the company must promote these policies, which must be consistent with and accurate regarding the direction of the company, the tone, and the culture. The organization must define owners of the policies who oversee their development and implementation. Such owners should be given sufficient authority to ensure that a single set structure of policies is communicated throughout the organization. Strategic policies can be supported by divisional policies created by each locale to fit the region's culture and language. It is difficult to expect a single policy to apply and provide clarity in various situations found on the factory floor without some form of expansion or adaptation. Also, in some instances company policies may conflict with regional cultures. Management supervising such areas must address these issues. Adjustments must respect the intention of the board and be translated, figuratively and literally in some instances, to embrace the traditions of the diverse divisions.

Many different types of policies and supporting documents exist within an organization. These policies and documents can be quite different from those of other organizations. The differences are rooted in the culture of the organization, the industry, and the mandates placed on the business as a whole.

The culture of an organization affects the number of policy documents and procedure documents published. Organizations made up of individuals who spend their entire career there and where a high degree of competency and trust exists are likely to have more strategic governance policies. This reliance on less prescriptive documents and more directional policies is the result of a greater trust established within the organization. It also reflects management's tone across the organization and the individual management philosophy applied by those throughout the organization. This trusting environment does not lack policies; it has the requisite policies to ensure proper actions throughout the organization based on a mutual acceptance and adherence by management and associates.

The opposite end of the spectrum is an organization with high turnover and a greater need to ensure specific behaviors. This type of organization is not necessarily untrusting per se, but it cannot establish a mutual reliance among the parties due to the short-term nature of their relationship. This is seen in top Fortune 500 companies, and a wonderful example is Starbucks. As a company, Starbucks is fantastic, and continually receives awards; one specifically is an award for "Fortune's 100 Best Companies to Work For," which Starbucks received in 2007. Starbucks has very strict policies and tomes of directional guidance for personnel throughout the organization.[8] This management focus on tactical situational issues ensures that employees abide by a clear code of practice every day at every location anywhere in the world. Culture affects an organization's institution of policies and the depth of the associated procedure publications. Factors such as regional differences, religion, correct translations, the length of time an employee remains with the company, the experience level of the specific persons within the organization, and the degree of variance that each employee must manage with every day for the company should be considered when developing and updating the company documentation.

The industry in which an organization operates dictates the level of detail found in the governance documentation regardless of the culture found within each. Participating in heavily regulated industries does not negate the effects of certain cultures, but it does play an equal part in the balance that management seeks to achieve. An organization that operates in a high-risk environment has more policies and greater specificity surrounding the guidelines than those in other environments. Consider organizations that provide healthcare or manage nuclear reactors. They have volumes of mandates and tactical procedures that are to be followed in any event and in any situation. This granularity ensures a consistent application of best practices by the organization and its agents. Highly mature organizations have more strategic policies for functions that require a specific sequence of previously validated operations. This granularity is common in disaster recovery preparations (DRPS), DRP events, and human services. DRPS are meticulously detailed to ensure that actions taken to prepare for an event, those taken during an event, and those during a recovery are complete, correct, and consistent with the goals of the organization. Human services granularity is necessary to ensure both consistency in the application of rules and conditions and that subjectivity is not introduced into operating practices.

Enterprises that operate in heavily regulated government industries are those considered to have the ability to impact the public that threatens the safety, security, or integrity of the country. Organizations must adhere to the mandates outlined within the laws that affect them. The variation among legal requirements surrounding defined policy and procedures across the globe for similar and dissimilar industries is minimal, and therefore conducive to merging and mapping the requirements of each industry into a single enterprise policy process. Similarities include the need for separation of duties, the institution of an ethics policy, the application and recognition of corrupt practices, the need to respect human rights, and the adherence to limits and restrictions in the practices of managing data and operations.

Policies focusing on the global technology environments of organizations are applicable to every individual in the organization, and therefore must consider the forces detailed above.

Business Impacts The lack of adherence to standards can expose the organization to a number of risks. Such risks may include:

- Legal damages
- Loss of valued employees
- Loss of charters to operate the business
- Loss of business to customers (the U.S. federal government has strict guidelines that, if violated, can result in an organization losing its ability to offer specific government programs)
- Public image damage
- Compliance fines
- Increased operating costs

Policies establish the expected behavior throughout the organization, depending on the constraints under which an organization operates. It is critical to ensure that the purpose of policies is made clear to all persons throughout the company. Such clarity of communications and policy ensures that as situations arise, the employee challenged with a scenario will take the appropriate action, both legally and in regard to the business.

It is rare that an organization will be excused from delivering services to the government or to customers because it lacks defined policies. In fact, most business relationships do not require production of these company guidelines. However, the lack of such policies and a process to manage such documents is clearly evident over time, as the organization is exposed to and impacted by negative events. Such negative events may be an ethics violation in the use of company expense accounts or incorrect disaster recovery plans. The U.S. courts have recently ruled against companies that have lost or otherwise misplaced backups of records for any reason and have imposed negative judgments and fines.

Application   The policy life-cycle process must include details on:

- Policy creation/updates
- Finalization of the document
- Acceptance and authorization by management
- A means for ensuring employee awareness

The process should include an annual cycle that incorporates direction from the board and upper management to confirm the alignment of policies and the business. Policy updates should incorporate shifts in the business, new technologies, and any changes in the world's risk contributions.

Current policies and procedures should be assessed annually to determine if additional publications or a reduction/consolidation of policies or procedures is prudent. It is critical to capture the human capital knowledge through documentation and the development of procedures. Policies and procedures may be developed from templates and then customized through work sessions with human resources, business managers, and the IT groups. This process will ensure that accurate and viable policies are developed and implemented. These policies should provide sufficient guidance in all areas, from acceptable use of systems, to the duties of personnel within certain roles (i.e., separation-of-duty rationales), and should define reactions to any inappropriate activities.

Once management signs off on and accepts these new policies, the organization must ensure that they are promulgated throughout the company. This may be achieved through use of intranets, e-mail communications, posters throughout the enterprise, pop-up messages upon login by every user (typically a short excerpt is appropriate with some form of question to ensure the user acknowledged the message and comprehended the text), formal training, and informal management highlights of the policies. Organizations can instill a proper tone regarding adherence to policies by establishing a formal process through new hire orientation that includes a segment on policies, periodic yearly training, and the need to ensure comprehension of the published policies.

Organizations must also take measures to ensure broad awareness and acceptance of the policies. It is not enough to have policies; they must be comprehended and built into the culture. Mini-audit efforts should be exercised throughout the year to confirm awareness of the policies. Often managers performing these efforts do not recognize their importance. This attitude should be strongly controlled by upper management and HR. Simple evaluations may include online web surveys where employees can demonstrate their understanding of the policy. These can be simple two-minute exercises spread across a year or two 30-minute sessions. These evaluations demonstrate individual employee comprehension and understanding, and therefore must not be completed anonymously. Upon completion of the surveys, results can be analyzed to determine the level of understanding by region, division, role, and other demographics to ensure that the policies are communicated clearly for all parties. Continuous improvement of training, testing, and policies is critical to ensuring that an organization is able to manage the risks and requirements it faces.

The focus of policies varies but generally they should include:

- IT strategic planning: directional alignment
- Budgeting
- Personnel roles and responsibilities
- Segregation of duties: access control
- Resource management
- Third-party providers
- Human resources
- Information security
- Acceptable use policies

In Practice

Policies and procedures throughout an organization must reflect the organization's goals and provide sufficient guidance to everyone on the necessary behavior expected. When evaluating the organization, consider whether:

- Operating policies and procedures are clearly written and communicated.

In Practice (continued)

- Procedures are in place to reflect changes in laws, regulations, guidance, business operations, and customer service-level agreements.

- Management is prohibited from intervening or overriding established controls.

- Penalties and corrective actions for all infractions, regardless of the individual, are applied clearly and consistently.

- Adequate segregation of duties is provided among performance, monitoring, and recording of a task.

- The system policy and program controls include:

  ○ Data entry controls

  ○ Exception reporting

  ○ Access controls

  ○ Reviews of input and output data

  ○ Computer general controls and security controls

Compliance

Demonstrating executive-level support of an environment that is positive toward compliance and aware of necessary controls is recommended by industry groups around the world, mandated by many government legislative acts, and attested by auditors. The need to establish and communicate a proper control environment goes beyond simple ethics policies and today encompasses the technology environments and the controls surrounding them. A form of trust is placed on entity-level controls, such as ethics and training, in order to have confidence in the associates acting as controls. This is similar to the trust established by auditors with technology controls: If the systems are trusted, then the auditor may test the processes at a greater level, but if the systems are untrustworthy, then the auditor cannot rely upon the controls managed by these systems. This is the same as computer forensic teams not trusting a system that was hacked, and how leading practices require that the hacked environment be built from backups.

Organizations that are fiscally responsible through both appropriate allocation of resources and the protection of those resources are well regarded. Such fiscal control also lends to an organization's ability to manage cash flow and adhere to financial viability standards. While these controls play a small part in the greater context of a global enterprise, they do provide a stronger bottom line due to lower general costs and better margins on services and goods provided.

The actual business value alignment to technology processes and the leveraging of controls to increase efficiency, effectiveness, and perceived value to internal and external clients are valuable processes for businesses around the globe; they are not mandated. In fact, globally the requirements—meaning the legal bounds organizations must adhere to in order to operate within a region or industry—are minimal concerning the linkages between business revenue and controls.

These management controls apply universally. Every organization must consider and implement the necessary safeguards to protect itself from control failures and to ensure compliance with domestic requirements. As described throughout this book, the inspiration for the provided structure and principles was the product of fieldwork and research. Exhibit 9.1 provides a collection of publications that were a part of that research. The exhibit highlights each global core control and is followed by publications that either wholly or partially are supportive of the control. Given the broad nature of many publications, publications in the sense here to include government legislation, industry guidance, professional publications, and guidlyance documents, each is not exclusively a single control or principle. The collection of publications provided under each global core control includes sources from around the world to provide a full reference guide for organizations. While there are numerous references, this list is not complete and practitioners must seek out the latest resources to fit today's and tomorrow's needs.

Exhibit 9.1   Principle 1 Matrix

Principle 1: Strategy Orchestration[a]

Highlighted Global Core IT Controls:

- Tone at the Top

- Directional Alignment

- Technology Governance

- Policy and Procedures

Tone at the Top: Relevant and Complementary Publications

Basel Capital Accord Basel II
Canada, Combined Code on Corporate Governance
Corporate Governance in The Netherlands 2002: The State of Affairs
COSO, ERM Framework
COSO, Integrated Framework
FFIEC, Audit
FFIEC, Business Continuity Planning
FFIEC, Information Security

Exhibit 9.1   *(Continued)*

FFIEC, Management
FFIEC, Operations
GLBA, Privacy of Financial Information
HIPAA
HKICPA, Internal Control and Risk Management—A Basic Framework
IIA, GTAG, Guide 3: Continuous Auditing: Implications for Assurance, Monitoring, and Risk Assessment
Internal Control 2006: The Next Wave of Certification—Guidance for Management
J-Sox, Financial Instruments and Exchange Law
NERC, CIP-003-1, Security Management Controls
NFPA 1600, "Standard on Disaster/Emergency Management and Business Continuity Programs, 2007 Edition"
SP800-100, Information Security Handbook: A Guide for Managers
UK & Wales, Internal Control: Guidance for Directors on the Combined Code (Turnbull Report)

Directional Alignment: Relevant and Complementary Publications

BS 15000-2, 2003 IT Service Management, Code of Practice for Service Management
Canada, Combined Code on Corporate Governance
CERT, OCTAVE
Clinger Cohen Act
CMS, Integrated IT Investment & System Life Cycle Framework
COBIT 4.1, Control Objectives, Management Guidelines, Maturity Models, IT Governance Institute
Corporate Governance in The Netherlands 2002: The State of Affairs
COSO, ERM Framework
COSO, Integrated Framework
FFIEC, Information Security
HKICPA, Internal Control and Risk Management—A Basic Framework
IIA, GTAG, Guide 1: Information Technology Controls
IIA, GTAG, Guide 3: Continuous Auditing: Implications for Assurance, Monitoring, and Risk Assessment
IIA, GTAG, Guide 5: Managing and Auditing Privacy Risks
ISACA, IS Standards, Guidelines, and Procedures for Auditing and Control
ISO/IEC 13335-1:2004, Information Technology—Security Techniques—Management of Information and Communications Technology Security"
ISO/IEC TR 15443:2005, Information Technology—Security Techniques—A Framework for IT Security Assurance—Part 1: Overview and Framework, 2005
ITIL, Security Management
ITSEM Version 1.0, Commission of the European Communities, Information Technology Security Evaluation Manual
MAGERIT Version 2.0, 2005
OECD, Guidelines for the Security of Information Systems and Networks: Towards a Culture of Security
SP800-100, Information Security Handbook: A Guide for Managers

Technology Governance: Relevant and Complementary Publications

AICPA, SAS 94, (AU Section 319), Effect of Information Technology on the Auditor's Consideration of Internal Control in a Financial Statement Audit
Basel II
Bill 198, Ontario, Canada, Keeping the Promise for a Strong Economy Act (Budget Measures)
CERT, OCTAVE
Clinger Cohen Act
CMS, Information Security ARS, Version 2.0
CMS, Information Security Business Risk Assessment Methodology, Version 2.1
CMS, Integrated IT Investment & System Life Cycle Framework
CMS, Policy for the Information Security Program
NFPA 1600, Disaster/Emergency Management and Business Continuity
EU 2002/58/EC, Directive on Privacy and Electronic Communications, Articles 4, 6
EU 95/46, Data Privacy Directive, Article 17
FFIEC, Operations
FIPS 199, Security Categorization of Federal Information
FISMA
GAO/AIMD-12.19.6, Federal Information System Controls Audit Manual
GLBA, Privacy of Financial Information
HIPAA
IIA, GTAG, Guide 1: Information Technology Controls
IIA, GTAG, Guide 3: Continuous Auditing: Implications for Assurance, Monitoring, and Risk Assessment
IIA, GTAG, Guide 5: Managing and Auditing Privacy Risks
IIA, GTAG, Guide 7: Information Technology Outsourcing
IIA, GTAG, Guide 8: Auditing Application Controls
Internal Control 2006: The Next Wave of Certification—Guidance for Management
ISO 15489-1:2001, Information and Documentation—Records Management—Part 1
ISO/IEC 13335-1:2004, Information Technology—Security Techniques—Management of Information and Communications Technology Security
ISO/IEC TR 15443:2005, Information Technology—Security Techniques—A Framework for IT Security Assurance—Part 1: Overview and Framework, 2005
ISSA, GAISP
J-Sox, Financial Instruments and Exchange Law
MAGERIT Version 2.0, 2005
NERC, CIP-002-1, Critical Cyber Asset Identification
NERC, CIP-003-1, Security Management Controls
OCC 12, CFR 30, Safety and Soundness Standards
OECD, Guidelines for the Security of Information Systems and Networks: Towards a Culture of Security
PCI DSS v1.1, Payment Card Industry Data Security Standard Security Audit Procedures
SP800-100, Information Security Handbook: A Guide for Managers
SP800-30, Risk Management Guide for Information Technology Systems
SP800-33, Underlying Technical Models for Information Technology Security
SP800-53, Recommended Security Controls for Federal Information Systems

Exhibit 9.1   *(Continued)*

SP800-66, Resource Guide for Implementing the Health Insurance Portability and Accountability Act (HIPAA) Security Rule

Texas Department of Information Resources, Practices for Protecting Information Resources Assets

U.S. Department of Commerce, EU Safe Harbor Privacy Principles

Policy and Procedures: Relevant and Complementary Publications

12 CFR Part 30, Appendix A, II (Operational and Managerial Standards), B

AICPA, SAS 94 (AU Section 319), Effect of Information Technology on the Auditor's Consideration of Internal Control in a Financial Statement Audit

Basel II

BCI, Good Practice Guidelines

Bill 198, Ontario, Canada, Keeping the Promise for a Strong Economy Act (Budget Measures)

CERT, OCTAVE

Clinger Cohen Act

CMS, CSR

CMS, Information Security ARS, Version 2.0

CMS, Integrated IT Investment & System Life Cycle Framework

CMS, Policy for the Information Security Program

CMS, SSP Methodology, 2003

COBIT 4.1, Control Objectives, Management Guidelines, Maturity Models, IT Governance Institute

COSO, ERM Framework

COSO, Integrated Framework

DoD Policy 8500

DCID 6/3

EU Directive on Privacy and Electronic Communications 2002/58/EC (Article 4, 6)

FFIEC, Operations

FIPS 199, Security Categorization of Federal Information

FISMA

GAO/AIMD-12.19.6, Federal Information System Controls Audit Manual

GLBA, Privacy of Financial Information

HIPAA

HKICPA, Internal Control and Risk Management—A Basic Framework

IIA, GTAG, Guide 1: Information Technology Controls

IIA, GTAG, Guide 2: Change and Patch Management Controls: Critical for Organizational Success

Internal Control 2006: The Next Wave of Certification—Guidance for Management

ISO 15489.2-2002, Records Management—Part 2: Guidelines

ISO 15489-1:2001, Information and Documentation—Records Management—Part 1

ISO 17799:2000, Information Technology—Security Techniques—Code of Practice for Information Security Management ISO 27001:2005, Information

Technology—Security Techniques—Information Security Management
Systems—Requirements
ISO/IEC 13335-1:2004, Information Technology—Security Techniques—
Management of Information and Communications Technology Security
ISO/IEC 18028-4:2005, Information Technology—Security Techniques—IT
Network Security—Part 4: Securing Remote Access, 2005
ISSA, GAISP
ITIL, Security Management
J-Sox, Financial Instruments and Exchange Law
MAGERIT Version 2.0, 2005
NASD 3110
NERC, CIP-003-1, Security Management Controls
NERC, CIP-005-1, Electronic Security Perimeter(s)
NERC, CIP-006-1, Physical Security of Critical Cyber Assets
NERC, CIP-007-1, Systems Security Management
NERC, CIP-008-1, Incident Reporting and Response Planning
NERC, CIP-009-1, Recovery Plans for Critical Cyber Assets
NFPA 1600, Disaster/Emergency Management and Business Continuity
OCC 12 CFR 30, Safety and Soundness Standards
OECD, Guidelines for the Security of Information Systems and Networks: Towards
a Culture of Security
PCI DSS v1.1, Payment Card Industry Data Security Standard Security Audit
Procedures
Sedona Principles, Best Practices Recommendations & Principles for Addressing
Electronic Document Production, 2005, 2007
SP800-100, Information Security Handbook: A Guide for Managers
SP800-53, Recommended Security Controls for Federal Information Systems
SP800-61, Computer Security Incident Handling Guide
SP800-66, Resource Guide for Implementing the Health Insurance Portability and
Accountability Act (HIPAA) Security Rule
Texas Department of Information Resources, Practices for Protecting Information
Resources Assets
US. Department of Commerce, EU Safe Harbor Privacy Principles

---

[a]See the acronym list for explanations of all acronyms.

ENDNOTES

1. ACFE Report to the Nation on Occupational Fraud and Abuse
2006. URL: http://www.acfe.com/fraud/report.asp.
2. Calculation based on ACFE 5% fraud rate against the world GDP
figure, World Development Indicators database, World Bank (April 3, 2007).
URL: http://siteresources.worldbank.org/DATASTATISTICS/Resources/
GDP.pdf.
3. Wesley Cragg, ed., *Ethics Codes, Corporations, and the Challenge of
Globalization* (Cheltenham, UK: Edgar Elgar Publishing, 2005).

4. AICPA, "Codification of Statements on Auditing Standards; Numbers 1 to 111" (2006).

5. Jim Collins, *Good to Great* (New York: HarperCollins, 2001), 41–42.

6. Office of Government Commerce, IT Infrastructure Library. URL: www.itil.co.uk.

7. Backup tapes in transit are lost, potentially exposing millions of customers. Bank of America in 2005 (1.2 million): URL: http://news.com.com/Bank+of+America+loses+a+million+customer+records/2100-1029_3-5590989.html. CitiGroup 2005 (3.9 million): URL: http://money.cnn.com/2005/06/06/news/fortune500/security_citigroup.

8. Special thanks to the kind team at the Starbucks locations in Dunwoody for all of their caffeine and comments.

10

Principle 2: Life-Cycle Management

Key Topics Addressed in This Chapter

Application control environments

Application software development

Change control safeguards

OVERVIEW

Life-cycle management addresses an organization's need to embrace technology to manage the short-and long-term fiscal and strategic directions. This is necessary as organizations accrue more technology that is both more complex and designed for distributed interactions with all levels of participants. Increasingly the development of customized software platforms and modules to fit the organization's unique business requirements is occurring and through greatly increasing number of third parties. The establishment of a program that provides assurances regarding the manner of development, acquisition, and maintenance with a view toward reliability and trust within the systems allows for both aggressive production deadlines and confidence in the results these systems produce.

The software employed, whether purchased or developed in house, ultimately ensures and maintains the integrity of the data throughout the system. This fact impacts the techniques used throughout the development process and those used for validating software effectiveness and efficiency.

Operational systems require management and changes to reflect the ever-growing organization that they support. These changes may reflect the addition of a new division or the introduction of a new enterprise collaboration site. Vendor patching, software enhancements, or other code modifications

139

must all be thoroughly analyzed. In fact, all changes to an organization may impact the ability of the systems and company to deliver on customer requests in a timely manner. Therefore, full change control architecture must encompass all aspects of an organization.

Life-cycle management focuses on software that operates enterprise processes and the establishment of controls to ensure operational consistency and integrity. While remaining strategic in the establishment of programs and controls, managers must consider the outlined concerns and approaches below completely to manage the full life cycle of technology. The global core IT controls highlighted in this principle include:

- Acquire and support
- Application controls
- Software development
- Change control

ACQUIRE AND SUPPORT

A foundation must exist within an organization that provides support and direction to the acquisition and maintenance of the information technology (IT) environment. Organizations of all sizes must continually manage the introduction of new technology and the evolution of existing systems. Establishing and communicating such a program throughout the organization, of any size or scale, allows the technology to be acquired in a purposeful and prudent manner. Technology may include the applications operating on the hardware within the organization or via remote service providers. Infrastructure, operations, and general IT resources also make up the technology within the organization.

The acquisition strategy of the company must maintain a balance of current needs and future requirements based on the strategic direction and guidance from management. In addition to these demands, the organization must consciously monitor the capacity of the technology environment, as power, staff, and support resources become strained with unequal expansion of technology and not processes. Monitoring allows the organization to achieve a balance between excess and bottlenecks within the enterprise.

The evaluation and deployment of technology should follow similar procedures across all types throughout the organization. A defined set of requirements for all technology acquisitions should exist. The requirements should outline what is acceptable to the organization. These procedures should reflect the organization's needs and ensure that all new technologies meet the business objectives. Specific requirements may include fiscal viability of the vendor or technical capabilities, such as the speeds and feeds of the device. A formal vendor management program may manage these responsibilities centrally in any organization. Such a program is beneficial in that it reduces duplication of products purchased. Savings can result from reduction of existing license costs, reduction of maintenance and labor to support unique solutions, reduction of additional equipment to support solutions, and through bulk purchase agreements.

Management and evaluation of vendor solutions represent only part of the business imperative. Organizations also must ensure that follow-up and monitoring processes are in place for the acquired technologies. This provides a closed-loop process that ensures that the chosen technology is providing the expected results. Application performance metrics should be monitored internally throughout the year with annual reviews by independent parties. The review process should consider current and future needs of the organization. Such an evaluation should also include a review of the marketplace for alternative and improved solutions. This ensures that the technology environment of the organization addresses the business needs and operates at the efficiency and effectiveness required.

Business Impacts

Organizations were deluged by vendors and products in the late 1990s as a result of no visibility into technology acquisitions, a lack of formal structures to manage this emerging business system, and a disconnect between actual business demands and the cost of solutions. In a time where organizations were expanding and adopting new technologies, excess and waste abounded. This became clear during the early 2000s as companies tightened budgets and insisted on business cases for new purchases. The result has been the growth of vendor management programs in most companies. These programs provide insight into the need, confirm alignment with the business's long-term objectives, and establish a method of placing accountability on the vendor and the technology.

The implosion of many technology companies during the early 2000s highlighted the need for both technical and business evaluations prior to purchase. While businesses and technologies come and go, the institution of a vetting process prevents a business from making risky purchases from fly-by-night vendors. Organizations must work in technology environments that are supported. Vendors must be financially viable and available for technical support and ongoing product development improvements.

The cost to an organization of adopting an untested technology includes the time and resources to identify, vet, and purchase hardware. It also includes the expense of removing unsupported hardware and purchasing new hardware for the same purpose. These expenses may include the need to retrain staff and redesign the technology infrastructure.

Application

Every organization should establish a formal group that manages all technology purchases. This group may rotate over time, but the parties involved must be representative of the business and able to consider any conflicts of interest that may arise. For instance, it would not be an effective control to have the technology team acting as the oversight group. (This situation would be akin to the fox watching the henhouse.) The group's approval should be required for all technology initiatives and purchases. The mandate for the group should be to acquire technology that enhances business operations and protects the organization fiscally and operationally.

The vendor management group should document and make available procedures for budgeting, identifying, evaluating, maintaining, and monitoring all technology. These procedures should provide simple mechanisms that enrich, not hinder, the acquisition process. Enabling the process may be achieved by communicating the process to all managers and taking advantage of online collaborative tools that provide access to information, forms, and inventory. In addition, the requirements detailed by the vendor management group should be reasonable, given the projects and the expediency required. A thorough process that is respectful of the business and technology requirements of the organization ensures a collaborative and compliant environment.

The vendor management group is a key actor in the organization for ensuring return on investment for technology purchases. Working in cooperation with internal audit, it should establish metrics and routine testing of acquired and developed systems. This process ensures that technology solutions deliver as expected to address the needs of the business. Such evaluation metrics should be based on the business purchasing decisions formed by the original purchase requestor. Such an evaluation should consider the changes in technology, including improvements and shifts in corporate needs related to the technology.

A reliable technology environment must support the technology post-acquisition. It is necessary to establish a regular update and maintenance program that defines appropriate methods of patch notifications, establishes business-appropriate update cycles, and ensures that sufficient technical expertise exists within the organization. Management of these acquired and maintained systems may be accomplished through a central asset repository, such as a configuration management database (CMDB). Such a system facilitates the tracking and inventory management. Notifications on updates to the software should be configured to occur centrally and through push technologies provided by the vendor. Upon receiving a notification from these services, the organization must ensure that action is taken where software updates are tested on secondary systems, and, after approval by management, are deployed in a timely fashion consistent with the organization's policies and procedures.

In some situations, updating systems may not allow for immediate deployment. These systems may operate machinery or interface with other systems that do not support newer versions. In other cases, downtime may not be permitted, as it may cause millions in lost revenue. In such situations, applying patches that require system restarts may be unacceptable. In all cases, the organization must define what is appropriate and when existing updates may be applied. To assure the integrity of the system during times of exposure, the organization should rely on compensating controls to safeguard from known threats.

Business Case

BUSINESS SITUATION

A company operating an oil refinery in the Gulf of Mexico has key systems that are regulated using Microsoft server operating systems. These systems are necessary to manage the pressure within the pipelines. The organization refines approximately 2.5 million barrels a day. The loss of these Microsoft Windows systems would shut down the facility for a number of hours, as a sequence of shut-offs must occur prior to the servers going offline and then a reverse sequence is required to bring the systems and pipeline back in operation. The cost is in the millions of dollars in revenues.

ANALYSIS

Through a risk analysis, the organization would highlight these assets as critical at the initial deployment of the servers. An architecture centered on availability and fault-tolerant hardware is required, in addition to operational performance metric monitors to identify early signs of processing errors.

SOLUTION

The oil refinery company initially architected a fully redundant set of systems both locally and remotely to manage the flows of the systems. As full redundancy was required in the event of a system failure or simply an operational need to upgrade equipment, the organization leveraged distributed computing systems with multiple points of connection. This web approach allows for regular system hardware upgrades and patches without interfering with the flow of oil through the plant.

The organization must ensure that the corporation possesses the necessary skills to manage the systems deployed within it. The upkeep of talent may be achieved through contractually requiring transfer of knowledge for all product installations, regular training, and other activities that maintain the technical capacities of the in-house team. Setting these requirements at the product introduction phase ensures that issues may be resolved more quickly and that any exceptions are handled promptly by knowledgeable internal teams.

In Practice

These general procedures should exist to ensure the integrity of the technology systems and operations:

- A vendor management program exists and is made up of a diverse business and technology team.

- Business cases and budget approvals are managed by the vendor management group.

- Technology vendors must pass a business and technical evaluation that considers the viability of the business, the "bleeding edge" factor of the technology, the amount of expertise in the market that may support the technology, and other such factors.

- Metrics for technology evaluations must be defined prior to purchase and implementation. The business or group that benefits from the technology must accept it. If the technology will be applied business-wide, an appropriate executive should be involved.

- Business process valuations should indicate the net effect of the purchase to the top and bottom line.

- Management requires an independent third party to evaluate the adequacy of the security controls.

- Management records, measures, and reviews service provider performance routinely to ensure compliance with the contractual service-level agreement.

- A central repository is maintained and updated that contains all technology assets and their respective patch levels, versions, descriptions regarding associated business processes, and any associated evaluations.

- Systems, operating systems, databases, applications, communication infrastructure, and resource requirements should be reviewed annually against defined business objectives. Adjustments to resources and projects should be made to reflect strategic direction.

- Technical evaluation of the organization's assets (hardware, operating systems, databases, applications, communication infrastructure) should occur routinely to determine the posture of security and operational configurations against company-recognized best practices. (Best practices should be adopted generally and be reflected in the policies of the organization and the corporate system standard configurations.)

- An executive report or dashboard shows management the adherence of the information assets and business processes to corporate policies, status of changes to the configuration of systems, and any exceptions identified during evaluations throughout the year.

In Practice

Establish an application performance metric program that provides a closed-loop review process for all existing and acquired technology. To do so, follow these five steps.

1. Define technology objectives and required features for the organization.

2. Create a baseline of requirements and actual delivery of features by technology:

   a. Map these business objectives to existing and acquired technology throughout the environment, and demonstrate that all business needs are addressed.

   b. Document and address gaps or deficits in addressing business objectives with new technology, upgrades, or replacement of legacy systems.

3. Establish a monitoring and regular testing process to verify achievement of business needs by technology.

4. Tie job responsibilities to the achievement of these objectives and specific metrics. Define and consistently apply rewards and penalties.

5. Always review business current and long-term needs, and adjust business metric requirements as necessary.

APPLICATION CONTROLS: CORRECT PROCESSING

The correct processing of data within a computing environment may be measured by several factors, including functionality, accuracy, and integrity. Together these factors provide a set of concepts that allow an organization to implement and govern its processing environment. Processing within any organization can be broken down into three components: input, process, and output. No matter the service being provided, the application completes each of these steps in a regular fashion.

The functionality of an application is its ability to deliver timely results of the output to the recipient. The success and use of every application depends on its ability to function within an organization to a point that is in line with the culture. The greater the integration of the application within the organization, the more natural its use and controls become, to the point where circumventing the application is not necessary or easy.

The successful processing of information is dependent on the integrity and accuracy of the information that is provided to the system. Accuracy relates to the structure of the data received by the application and the capability of interpreting and importing the information correctly. The accuracy of the processing and output are key to ensuring that a repeatable, reliable computing environment exists.

The integrity of the data provided, processed, and outputted provides assurances to system users that the information was delivered, processed, and reported on without modification. This assurance is key, as the organization must be sure that the channels of communication that deliver both input and output are free from intrusion or unauthorized processing requests.

Application controls should be applied to the inputs and outputs for each critical application. These application controls should at least include how the data are prepared, where they originate, and how the data are entered into the system. Once the data are in the application, the system should have safeguards during the processing and storage of the original data, the processing information, and the results prior to retrieval. The application makes the final output available either through another system or directly to the user.

Blending reasonable assurance throughout the delivery, process, and output phases of the application assures management and third parties that the system is reliable.

Business Impacts

Improper billing, failing to meet customer expectations, unmanaged cash levels, and false accounting records are risks to every organization that is not confident in its application computing systems. The business costs to organizations with applications that improperly process everything from cash balances to determining the height of the drill in manufacturing centers are related to the activity managed by the application. This direct relationship allows organizations to calculate the costs and therefore determine the impacts to the operational capability of the business. Monitoring and regular testing to the highest impacted applications should be applied by level of importance for the application and its controls.

Beyond the cash flow impact due to accidents and inaccurate accounting data, manufacturing defects may damage consumer perception of the organization. Should any fault be discovered in a product, critics are ready to attack. The Internet, the speed of communications, and consumer-generated content are particularly damaging. Today, once-isolated complaints and situations now have worldwide reach. The damage may result in massive recalls of products or cause immediate software patches after the software is officially launched. The damage resulting from a small manufacturing or processing error can have long-term and costly effects.

Application

Reasonable controls can be implemented throughout the computing environment for applications. Fortunately, most applications developed commercially recognize the importance of assuring data are inputted accurately, processed, and delivered as required. This certainly does not eliminate the need for such application-level tests, but it does simplify regular evaluations.

The application must provide methods for ensuring that user-inputted data are correct and appropriate.[1] Restricting user input is achieved through limiting the types of data elements that may be entered into a given field, using postentry error checking and user validation windows. In addition, the application should allow entered data to be reviewed prior to processing. Applications can do this by requiring separation of duties to be established or requiring two peers to sign off on a set of data.

With batched data, the application and the company must expect that the data provided will be of the same structure and type every time. This is achievable by adopting strong application output controls on the originating system. The application should process any data delivered to it promptly to limit loss or modification by third parties. Wherever possible the application should archive the inputted data for review and evaluation at a later date. Such archives provide strong forensic evidence should problems occur, and such information should be protected and when necessary disposed of properly to ensure confidentiality.

To rely on the results of any system, the application must perform accurate processing. Both custom-built systems and off-the-shelf purchases should be tested to ensure that processing occurs as expected. This discovery process is important in order to establish reliability of systems-processing capabilities. The simplest approach is to manually step through a process or do it with the legacy system, then provide the same input to the new system and compare the results. The outputs should be identical in substance, not form. Perform similar tests of all processing requirements. This type of testing ensures that unexpected processing errors are detected, such as those that resulted from a hardware component that caused rounding errors.[2]

Applications controls must be tested and conform to the policies and procedures of the organization within the context of the type of information handled by these systems. General application control objectives include:

- Input data are accurate, complete, authorized, and correct.

- Data are processed as intended in an acceptable period of time based on the business owner requirements.

- Data stored are accurate and complete.

- Outputs and reports are correct and complete, and delivered to the appropriate parties in the necessary time frame.

- Process map records are maintained and track the process of data from introduction to reporting.[3]

***

In Practice

***

Common application processing controls that should be considered for the organization:

- An established set of core methods and procedures provides reasonable assurance regarding:[4]

  - Authority of data origination

  - Accuracy of data input

  - Integrity of processing

  - Verification and distribution of output

- Determine if software meets needs of organization:

  - Senior management has reviewed and approved technology objectives and guiding policies.

  - Verify that software features address documented requirements defined and authorized by management.

  - Confirm that application performance metrics are identified and documented for regular future evaluations.

- Determine that system maintenance and monitoring is established:

  - Confirm that documentation surrounding application procedures is updated and available.

  - Verify that end-user training and application administrator training is available and attended.

  - Ensure that job responsibilities are assigned and that awareness and acceptance exists.

  - Validate that a maintenance schedule exists and includes all stake-holders.

  - Identify application performance review results and confirm that another review is scheduled.

- Determine that procedures exist to ensure that only authorized, correct, and complete transactions are processed:

  - Confirm that policies and procedures establish that only authorized and correct transactions are processed.

  - Verify that such policies and procedures are communicated and available to all end users.

  - Confirm that uniquely referenced origination data are unique or sequential.

- ○ Verify that input checks are incorporated into all systems.

- ○ Confirm that input checks are active and sufficient to prevent unauthorized, erroneous, or incomplete entries from being processed by the application.

- Confirm that only authorized processing occurs in a timely, complete, and accurate manner.

- Confirm that procedures clearly define activities and that standards are enforced.

- Verify that output (e.g., control totals) checks for completeness are tested and reported.

SOFTWARE DEVELOPMENT

Every organization purchases software and/or develops it in house. We are using the term *develop* broadly to mean customizing prebuilt software, creating widgets or modules for applications, developing custom reports and interfaces, or simply creating triggers and filters that help remove information noise. In addition to these situations, end users may also create software or tools that contribute to the operations of the business; these include, for example, custom Excel equations and vbscripts in Microsoft Office applications.

Given the options available for leveraging software internally and the incredible efficiencies gained by customizing applications, organizations should establish a method of overseeing these critical installations and customizations. The institution of a software development process throughout the company ensures that all software that is utilized operates in accordance with stated policies. In addition to assisting in compliance with policies, a software development process allows for the centralization and management of development activities, and can provide a number of benefits. These benefits include:

- Quality checking may be introduced into end-user computing tools to ensure the application operates according to specifications.

- Scaling of software purchased or developed is possible only when the application and the business value provided are understood, communicated, documented, and made available.

- A formal control program overseeing the application operations within the organization is instituted.

- Centralizing the software development activities provides necessary documentation and evidence in the case of compliance audits, application scaling pursuits, and maintenance for future user requirements.

Business Impacts

The negative impacts of a failure of an application or its associated application controls to an organization can include a lack of trust in the technology environment as a whole. The predictable nature of technology allows for controls to be automated and depended upon for accurate and complete transactions. If the operating environment itself is called into question, management and auditors cannot trust the reports, data, and evidence produced by the system.

Another significant impact that can occur beyond the complete failure of trust on applications are the susceptibility for cost overruns and financial waste (e.g. - redundant systems; absorb power, carry licensing costs, physical rack space, maintenance, technical support, and human capital to manage and maintain). Failed projects and financial waste may result from a lack of management support and oversight, inadequate project management, scope creep within the organization, or simply inappropriate application of resources for a project. Other risks include a lack of quality in the existing infrastructure to support the project—a risk that can be addressed through a feasibility study. Other damages include:

- Service levels are not met, causing breach of contract with customers.

- Inadequate documentation in the actual programming code, creating a very difficult application to manage and update once the original team is off the project.

- Inadequate end user documentation, resulting in a lack of adoption and waste.

- Cascading failures occur in environments where systems provide or rely on data from an array of devices. Interruption of one device has the potential to impact numerous applications and business functions.

- Disruption in the business resulting from failed deployment.

Application

Business owners must define the nature of the information that is processed, stored, or transmitted by the software and classify the level of appropriate security safeguards.

Organizations that have a creative environment where applications are updated, modified, purchased, or developed should conduct a strategic direction audit of the software development process. This audit should include a project inventory that provides awareness of projects, their stage of development, current cost to the organization versus project costs, and updates of any details surrounding sponsors or application purpose.

Numerous software development processes are widely available. Depending on the sophistication and needs of your organization, any number of these may be appropriate. Some of the more popular processes include the Waterfall, Iterative, Spiral, Agile, Rapid Prototyping, and Extreme Programming. Each published software development life cycle (SDLC) aims to be consistent with the widely adopted frameworks. No matter which method your organization embraces, it should include five main process groups:[5]

1. Initiation

2. Acquisition/development

3. Implementation

4. Operate and maintain

5. Retire

The initiation phase typically compares projects to business objectives to determine if the proposed purchase or development request is in line with the organization's strategic direction. End users provide a general user specification on the business value of the project and outline the requirements. A review should occur at this phase to examine existing technology applications and deployed projects in order to identify similar initiatives. At the completion of this phase, the software development board, or equivalent, must review the business value and current technology portfolio and make a go/no-go determination.

The second phase focuses on gathering details regarding the project, the market, the required effort, and the development work effort. End user requirements are captured through a requirements analysis, and a conceptual design is produced. A discovery team, generally including a product manager and a developer, evaluates the current project portfolio applications that were flagged in the initiation phase and evaluates the work effort to enhance the functionality.[6] The discovery team's efforts and the findings from a market research effort are consolidated into an alternatives analysis report. At this point the team has ascertained several options that are possible for achieving the end-user requirements. A final report is put together that includes a cost-benefit analysis for all of the options and the necessary work effort and projected impacts on other projects resulting from the upgrade or new technology. A final request of the business owners is made regarding the type and sensitivity of the data involved in the project, and any necessary security controls are added to the application specifications and cost reports. Midway through this phase, management makes another go/no-go decision based on the business value and the full life-cycle projected costs of the solution. Upon approval, the development process begins and a new version is made available.

The implementation phase encompasses development, testing of the approved project, and formal transition from a development project to a production product. This should include a final acceptance sign-off by the user, management, the security-risk representative, and the technology teams tasked with maintenance. Upon acceptance from end-user testing, the code is submitted to the software development board for approval. Once the software is authorized, the code is migrated from the development network to a preproduction environment. There additional testing occurs prior to a final authorization and rollout into the production environment. At this stage enterprise user training is made available and all necessary documentation regarding the code, updates, maintenance, deployment, and management is created and made available.

Ongoing maintenance must continue for all deployed applications and should be monitored using performance metrics to ensure that services are delivered as required. Regular third-party evaluations should occur at this phase to ensure that no threats to the code base can expose the organization.

Retiring an application requires review of the dependencies and usage patterns to ensure no disruption of service occurs. Modules and applications must be removed in a manner that considers the sensitivity of the data and the interfaces established to other systems. Access permissions, data stores, backup procedures, disaster recovery preparations, and maintenance processes must be updated to reflect the retirement of the system.

The exact flow of the SDLC adopted for an organization is not mandated, nor is there a specific correct approach. An organization should examine the optimal means of introducing checks and balances in the system. Beyond the benefits of applications that are created based on business needs and in accordance with defined best practices and company policy, an SDLC in fact becomes a control for the organization. The action of evaluating options, receiving feedback, and having management acceptance and user acceptance and a defined process is itself a control that can be relied on. The organization can deploy such a control by creating a repository for all SDLC projects, approved and unapproved, as a demonstration of the process in action.

A process of application operations and security certification is appropriate and necessary to establish confidence in all new applications. The process should involve a comprehensive assessment of the management, operational, and technical security controls in an information system, to determine the extent to which the controls are implemented correctly, operating as intended, and producing the desired outcome. Management sign-off of all certification processes should be recorded and available for subsequent evaluations or troubleshooting situations.[7]

The certification and assessment process should not be reserved for software developed in-house but include any purchased software. Purchase departments and business managers should consider the development process, the source code documentation, and the history and reputation of the developers or vendor. Evaluating vendors must extend to include small third-party organizations, outsourced groups, and shrinkwrapped software. While the organization itself may not conduct full certification assessments on all applications, a process for determining the level and type of testing required must exist. Within the payment card industry applications that handle sensitive data are required to be certified against a published standard.[8] Vendor-provided attestations regarding the software should supplement any packages that are not fully evaluated. The amount of testing conducted by the corporation can vary for:

- *Software development procedures.* Check whether development adheres to a formal software development life cycle, receiving quality certifications (International Standards Organization [ISO], Payment Card Industry Data Security Standard—Payment Application Best Practices [PABP]), and testing procedures for secure coding validation.

- *History and reputation.* Code reviews are not always possible with shrinkwrapped software, so vulnerability history, timeliness of patches, and quality of support and maintenance should be weighed in place of code reviews.[9]

In Practice

Results of risk assessments performed on projects throughout the development process indicate the alignment and success of the organization's development efforts. The software board, change management board, and the security board should assign risk weights. The individual items should also be assigned a risk score, as defined by the evaluator.

Risk factors can be divided into four categories:[10]

PROJECT RISK MANAGEMENT RISKS

- Project requirements definition and business value
- Requirements complexity
- Complexity of work effort
- Confidence in project estimation of effort
- Scale of deployment
- Scope constraints
- Schedule constraints
- Budget constraints
- Monetary, reputation, and productivity risk
- Prior-period project management risk variation

In Practice (continued)

TECHNICAL RISKS

- Infrastructure and hardware
- New technology required
- Required skills
- Shifts in technology standards
- Number and complexity of interfaces to other systems
- Data conversion effort
- Contingency, performance, availability, and security requirements
- Prior-period technical risk variation

ORGANIZATIONAL RISKS

- Project sponsorship (executive, director, field)
- Alignment with business objectives
- Stakeholders/business owners
- Availability of staff
- Degree of internal modifications for deployment
- Use of third parties/outsourcing
- Dependencies on other projects/businesses
- Degree of impact on subsidiaries
- Prior-period organizational risk variation

NATURE OF BUSINESS RISKS

- Materiality of processes involved
- Compliance implications
- Sensitive nature of data involved
- Prior-period nature of business risk variation

In Practice

Additional verifications around the software development process should include:

- Systems perform intended functions.

- Systems function is unimpaired.

- All software development projects are developed and maintained as secure applications that reflect the sensitive nature of the data processing that is occurring.

- Established process ensures the incorporation into all projects of:

  - Correct processing in applications (input/output checks)

  - Cryptographic controls

  - Security of system files

  - Technical vulnerability testing

  - Safeguards for software libraries

In Practice

The software development program should reflect the business objectives and adhere to the policies defined by management. The process of ensuring appropriate acquisition and implementation of software should be ongoing and consider many aspects of risk to the operations of the organization.

- A software development board should exist that oversees and approves the development of all projects within the organization. A portion of this board or a separate set of individuals should act as a security board. Members of the board should be aware of business objectives and budget, and should manage the development process. These duties may be addressed with a project management office (PMO).

- Management has accepted a formal SDLC process submitted by the technology group that will oversee and evaluate the acquisition, internal development, deployment, and required future upgrades.

- Adaptive safeguards are applied for each project depending on the nature of the application and the sensitivity of the data. These safeguards ensure that sufficient controls (such as built-in monitoring or encryption) are incorporated at the initiation phase.

In Practice (continued)

- The security board reviews the data-sensitivity classification and the proposed security safeguards, determines their adequacy, and approves or denies the design.

- Newly designed or acquired software must be configured securely and adhere to defined policies and procedures.

- Acquired applications and designed software must support the segregation of duties and role structures that have been adopted in the organization.

- Third-party evaluations should occur on all acquired and developed technologies on a regular basis. Such testing should validate adherence to defined procedures and demonstrate best practice with regard to the organization's security posture.

CHANGE CONTROL

The wonderful fact of technology and computing environments specifically is that they will run forever, continuously processing whatever is passed along in the same way, every single time. This fact is the very reason that computers in general were created and have propagated, as it has been discovered that machines are more efficient and consistent at repetitive tasks than humans. This statement is true until we introduce today's dynamic organization that is navigating a massively competitive world with its torrent of rapid movements of customers and technology innovation that require these very systems to regularly adapt. We make changes to improve the application's features, correct a coding error that exposed the system to vulnerability, or simply to reconfigure a system due to a newly acquired division. Because changes are necessary and because we rely on the technology control environment for its repetitive nature, it is important to manage the changes that occur in every organization.[11]

Organizations must establish a formal group—the change control board—that is tasked with overseeing changes to the entire organization's technology environment. The charter should include all changes, including routine patches or emergency requests, to all production environment systems. Members of the change control board should possess sufficient independence within the organization to objectively evaluate each change request; at least one business manager and a technologist should sit on the board. The board should work in cooperation with the software development teams, the technology security group, the business development managers, and the network and communications group to develop a process that suits the organization's systems and deployment architecture.

A formal program should exist that communicates clearly the steps that must be taken for a change to be considered. Corporate policies should reflect the necessity of adhering to the change control process and define penalties for violation of the process.[12] The change control board must establish a tone that encourages all requests, from both users and technologists, to be submitted and be reviewed fairly. In addition to the institution of a formal program and its inclusion into the corporate policies, the board should establish planned maintenance windows and blackout periods (periods of time where no changes are made in an environment). The change control board should determine maintenance windows with business owners. Typically the maintenance windows and blackout periods include quarterly closings of accounting books, peak delivery seasons, and reduced staff periods, such as holidays and seasonal trends in vacation requests.

In addition to the initiation process established by change control, the board should define a postchange procedure. While a feedback reporting component is part of the formal change control process, the board will need to work with executive management to determine the type of reports and metrics that will be desired. Once this information is collected, the board should develop or acquire the means to capture-publish such information about the change control environment. The change control process typically includes:

- A request from the user
- A technical analysis stating the need and the impact
- A vote on the change request
- Implementation
- Postreview

The change control request should include a documented breakdown of the business need for the change, the technical specifications, the impacted systems, the backout plan, and the expected business benefits resulting from the effort. This documentation should provide clarity into the business need for such a modification and sufficient information to allow for another individual to complete the deployment. A review of the propriety of the technical details and the impacts should occur, and the affected business owners should be permitted a comment period to consider business operations.

If the change is necessary and must occur in the near term, it would be approved by the board and scheduled to occur during a defined maintenance window. Once the implementation is complete, a postimplementation review must occur to determine any surprises or unexpected results. A final report of the success and amount of resources expended for the change is recorded by the change sponsor and communicated to management. The reports, technical data, and all information should be archived to an online knowledge system that can be leveraged in the future. (A wiki would be a simple example.)

Business Impacts

Companies around the world weigh the risks of making and not making changes. If a patch is applied, systems may experience an unexpected stoppage in services or a massive failure of the technology infrastructure.[13] Technology groups tasked with implementing changes to systems on weekends incur greater risks; making the wrong changes or none at all can cause vulnerabilities.

Organizations must consider not only the direct risk that is identified under the change control request but the mitigating controls that may address the threat until a more appropriate upgrade period arrives. The requirement to maintain consistent operations is strongly reflected in organizations that require constant uptime due to customer (e.g., e-commerce sites during the holidays, air traffic control computers) or regulation standards.

Application

Organizations that apply a change control program both are compliant with widely applied regulations, and have better ability to manage their computing services. Once a change control process is applied, analytics are produced and delivered to executive management. Executive support is key to enforcing such a program, and it is management's responsibility to ensure that services are delivered as expected.

Organizations should be able to produce data that verify the effectiveness and efficiency of the implementations occurring. The report should highlight the root cause of any exceptions and present detailed corrections that occurred as a result. Every control and every risk has an associated cost. Normally the company absorbs these costs without recognizing the amounts or what part of the business benefits from the modifications. Organizations should determine the cost of every change prior to implementation and present this figure to the business owners who are benefiting. This review process allows the technology group to have visibility into long-term goals. A major cellular company followed this process. In many situations, the technology group submitted a costly upgrade process (a new software version had been released that was far better than previous ones). After discussing the costs with the business owners, it was discovered that other systems needed to be replaced and the business need required a different technology deployment. Instead of spending the money twice—on the new licenses and then again when the business shifted markets—the organization was able to capitalize on the change control process.

In Practice

Oversight of the system modifications must be done in a formal manner that enables business agility while maintaining committed technology services. Oversight should include:

- The enterprise has established a change control board that meets routinely (defined by the nature of the organization's change needs) and is made up of at least a business owner, a technical specialist, and a security-risk individual.

- All modifications to the system and the applications are performed in accordance with a formal change control program.

- All modifications to systems receive a priority-based ranking that ensures that priority is given to high-value systems and critical safeguards.

- Capturing and recording business requests for updates or modifications to systems, and establishing a feedback loop to the requestors.

- Modifications are requested, approved, and implemented by separate individuals in accordance with management's division of roles through separation of duties. (Developers should not be capable of promoting code to production. The approver and implementer roles may be combined in a single individual.)

- Modifications are tested in a development environment that mirrors the production environment.

- Requests for modification must be detailed with a change request specification that includes at least:
  - Reason for modification
  - Criticality of modification
  - Proposed change window
  - Business impact analysis (detail dependencies)
  - Approval from business owners who will be negatively impacted
  - Documentation of full change (e.g., proposed SQL statement)
  - Evidence and sign-off of testing and error-free trial
  - Confirmation that testing occurred in development environment without error
  - Testing standards adhered to completely (end user, stability, security, business strategy)

- System modifications are applied to production systems after backups of the impacted systems are complete and an accompanying backout plan is in place with defined triggers.

In Practice (continued)

- Modifications made without adhering to the defined process and recorded as emergency modifications must be thoroughly reviewed by the change control board to determine the situation and the impact of the modifications, and review evidence to support the necessity of the change. A post-change process should be established to develop procedures to prevent the same emergency change in the future.

COMPLIANCE

Globally the mandate for companies to vouch for the integrity and accuracy of financial information is highly regarded by stakeholders. Computing applications play a vital role in every organization in every industry. Technology application systems monitor the chemical content of drugs produced by pharmaceutical companies, create vehicles and planes, and test the integrity and safety. Trust is placed upon software and the software designed to monitor the operations of applications to ensure transactional integrity and consistency.

An airplane has software that measures wind speed and fuel levels; other systems monitor these systems to ensure responsiveness and integrity of processing. The world truly relies on software to both create and monitor. Therefore, organizations must thoroughly establish accreditation processes internally to ensure accuracy of operations for both business and compliance necessity. This process must also embrace the monitoring solutions that are deployed to ensure that these same applications are operating as required.

The control environment is the core of an organization's compliance program. Therefore, any changes to that environment must be done cleanly and with full transparency. Through the application of a formal change control process, the organization can demonstrate full control over the computing environment and confidence in the processing functions.

In addition to being able to demonstrate accuracy and integrity in the systems, both the United States and the European Union require that organizations manage and control changes to their technology environment. Exhibit 10.1 was developed similarly to the table at the end of Chapter 9. An interesting difference is the amount of supportive and complementary publications that focus on the life cycle of technology within organizations. Given the large amount of publications organizations should initially seek out those that cater to the region and industry of the business first. Only then should practitioners begin incorporating additional publications.

Exhibit 10.1   Principle 2 Matrix

Principle 2: Life-Cycle Management[a]

Highlighted Global Core IT Controls:

- Acquire and Support
- Application Controls: Correct Processing
- Software Development
- Change Control

Acquire and Support: Relevant and Complementary Publications

12 CFR Part 30, Appendix A, II (Operational and Managerial Standards), B
CMS, Information Security ARS, Version 2.0
CMS, Policy for the Information Security Program
CMS, SSP Methodology, 2003
COBIT 4.1, Control Objectives, Management Guidelines, Maturity Models, IT Governance Institute
FFIEC, Development Acquisition
FFIEC, Management
FISMA
GAO/AIMD-12.19.6, Federal Information System Controls Audit Manual
HIPAA
ISACA, IS Standards, Guidelines, and Procedures for Auditing and Control
ISO 17799:2000, Information Technology—Security Techniques—Code of Practice for Information Security Management
ISO 27001:2005, Information Technology—Security Techniques—Information Security Management Systems—Requirements
ISO/IEC 15288:2002, Systems Engineering—System Life Cycle Processes
ISO/IEC 18405, Common Criteria for Information Technology Security Evaluation Version 3.1
ISO/IEC 9126-1:2001, Software Engineering—Product Quality—Part 1: Quality Model
ISSA, GAISP
MAGERIT, Version 2.0, 2005
PCI DSS v1.1, Payment Card Industry Data Security Standard Security Audit Procedures
SP800-100, Information Security Handbook: A Guide for Managers
SP800-53, Recommended Security Controls for Federal Information Systems
Texas Department of Information Resources, Practices for Protecting Information Resources Assets

Application Controls: Correct Processing: Relevant and Complementary Publications

Bill 198, Ontario, Canada, Keeping the Promise for a Strong Economy Act (Budget Measures)

Exhibit 10.1 *(Continued)*

CMS, Policy for the Information Security Program
COBIT 4.1, Control Objectives, Management Guidelines, Maturity Models, IT Governance Institute
Corporate Governance in the Netherlands 2002: The State of Affairs
COSO, Integrated Framework
FFIEC Management
FISMA, Federal Information Security Management Act
GAO/AIMD-12.19.6, Federal Information System Controls Audit Manual
HIPAA
HKICPA, Internal Control and Risk Management—A Basic Framework
IIA, GTAG, Guide 1: Information Technology Controls
IIA, GTAG, Guide 8: Auditing Application Controls
ISACA, IS Standards, Guidelines, and Procedures for Auditing and Control
ISO 17799:2000, Information Technology—Security Techniques—Code of Practice for Information Security Management
ISO 27001:2005, Information Technology—Security Techniques—Information Security Management Systems—Requirements
ISO/IEC 15288:2002, Systems Engineering—System Life Cycle Processes
ISO/IEC 18405, Common Criteria for Information Technology Security Evaluation Version 3.1
MAGERIT, Version 2.0, 2005
SP800-100, Information Security Handbook: A Guide for Managers
SP800-33, Underlying Technical Models for Information Technology Security
SP800-53, Recommended Security Controls for Federal Information Systems
Texas Department of Information Resources, Practices for Protecting Information Resources Assets

Software Development: Relevant and Complementary Publications

12 CFR Part 30, Appendix A, II (Operational and Managerial Standards), B
BS 15000-1: 2002, IT Service Management—Part 1: Specification
BS 15000-2: 2003, IT Service Management, Code of Practice for Service Management
CMS, Information Security ARS, Version 2.0
CMS Information Security C&A Methodology, Version 1.0
CMS, Information Security Risk Assessment Methodology, Version 2.1
CMS, Integrated IT Investment & System Life Cycle Framework
CMS, Policy for the Information Security Program
CMS, SSP Methodology, 2003
COBIT 4.1, Control Objectives, Management Guidelines, Maturity Models, IT Governance Institute
COSO, Integrated Framework
FFIEC, Development Acquisition
FFIEC, Management
FISMA
GAO/AIMD-12.19.6, Federal Information System Controls Audit Manual

HIPAA
HKICPA, Internal Control and Risk Management—A Basic Framework
IIA, GTAG, Guide 1: Information Technology Controls
IIA, GTAG, Guide 2: Change and Patch Management Controls: Critical for Organizational Success
ISACA, IS Standards, Guidelines, and Procedures for Auditing and Control
ISO 17799:2000, Information Technology—Security Techniques—Code of Practice for Information Security Management
ISO 27001:2005, Information Technology—Security Techniques—Information Security Management Systems—Requirements
ISO/IEC 9126-1:2001, Software Engineering—Product Quality—Part 1: Quality Model
ISO/IEC 18405, Common Criteria for Information Technology Security Evaluation Version 3.1
ISSA, GAISP
Commission of the European Communities ITSEM, Version 1.0, MAGERIT Version 2.0, 2005
OECD, Guidelines for the Security of Information Systems and Networks: Towards a Culture of Security
PCI DSS v1.1, Payment Card Industry Data Security Standard Security Audit Procedures
SP800-53, Recommended Security Controls for Federal Information Systems
SP800-100, Information Security Handbook: A Guide for Managers
Texas Department of Information Resources, Practices for Protecting Information Resources Assets

Change Control: Relevant and Complementary Publications

12 CFR Part 30—Appendix A, II (Operational and Managerial Standards), B
BS 15000-1: 2002, IT Service Management—Part 1: Specification
BS 15000-2: 2003, IT Service Management, Code of Practice for Service Management
CMS, Information Security ARS, Version 2.0
CMS, Information Security C&A Methodology, Version 1.0
CMS, Policy for the Information Security Program
CMS, SSP Methodology, 2003
COBIT 4.1, Control Objectives, Management Guidelines, Maturity Models, IT Governance Institute
COSO, Integrated Framework
FFIEC, Management
FISMA
GAO/AIMD-12.19.6, Federal Information System Controls Audit Manual
HIPAA
HKICPA, Internal Control and Risk Management—A Basic Framework
IIA, GTAG, Guide 2: Change and Patch Management Controls: Critical for Organizational Success
IIA, GTAG, Guide 6: Managing and Auditing IT Vulnerabilities
IIA, GTAG, Guide 8: Auditing Application Controls

Exhibit 10.1   *(Continued)*

ISACA, IS Standards, Guidelines, and Procedures for Auditing and Control

ISO 17799:2000, Information Technology—Security Techniques—Code of Practice for Information Security Management

ISO 27001:2005, Information Technology—Security Techniques—Information Security Management Systems—Requirements

ISO/IEC 18028-1:2006, Information Technology—Security Techniques—IT Network Security—Part 1: Network Security Management, 2006

MAGERIT Version 2.0, 2005

NERC, CIP-003-1 Security Management Controls

PCI DSS v1.1, Payment Card Industry Data Security Standard Security Audit Procedures

SP800-53, Recommended Security Controls for Federal Information Systems

SP800-58, Security Considerations for Voice Over IP

SP800-100, Information Security Handbook: A Guide for Managers

Texas Department of Information Resources, Practices for Protecting Information Resources Assets

---

^aSee the acronym list for explanations of all acronyms.

ENDNOTES

1. Examples of application auditing: K. H. Spencer Pickett, *The Internal Auditing Handbook* (New York: John Wiley & Sons, 1997), 480.

2. Alexander Wolfe, "Intel Fixes a Pentium FPU Glitch," *Electronic Engineering Times*, November 7, 1994: "To correct an anomaly that caused inaccurate results on some high-precision calculations, Intel Corp. last week confirmed that it had updated the floating-point unit (FPU) in the Pentium microprocessor."

3. Institute of Internal Auditors, GTAG 8, "Auditing Application Controls." URL: http://www.theiia.org/guidance/technology/gtag/gtag8/.

4. Ibid.

5. Adapted from the U.S. NIST SP800-64 REV.1, "Security Considerations in the Information System Development Life Cycle" (2004). URL: http://csrc.nist.gov/publications/nistpubs/800-64/NIST-SP800-64.pdf

6. FFIEC, *"Development and Acquisition, Project Management"* (accessed on August 1, 2007). URL: www.ffiec.gov/ffiecinfobase/booklets/d_a/02.html.

7. NIST, *Information Security Handbook: A Guide for Managers*, NIST-SP800-100 (March 2007). URL: http://csrc.nist.gov/publications/nistpubs/800-100/SP800-100-Mar07-2007.pdf.

8. VISA has established a standard known as PABP, and under recent review is the release of a mandate by the Payment Card Industry Security Council (the body that manages PCI DSS) that will apply to all applications that store, process, or transmit card holder data.

9. FFIEC, *Information Technology Examination Handbook* (July 2006) (accessed on August 1, 2007). URL: http://www.fdic.gov/regulations/information/information/FFIEC.html.

10. Inspired by the Federal Reserve Bank of Philadelphia's April 24–25, 2007, presentation, Slides 25–31, by Ron Lavish, Audit Manager.

11. The IIA has produced a GTAG series that is focused on the testing of controls. The global technology audit guide, "Change and Patch Management Controls: Critical for Organizational Success" (GTAG2) is a great reference resource for anyone starting to establish such a program. URL: http://www.theiia.org/guidance/technology/gtag/gtag2/.

12. Thomas R. Peltier, Justin. Peltier, and John A. Blackley, *Information Security Fundamentals* (Boca Raton, FL: CRC Press, 2004).

13. As was experienced by major operators such as BlackBerry, Skype, Netflix, and Salesforce.com in 2007.

11

Principle 3: Access and Authorization

Key Topics Addressed in This Chapter

Technical controls

Physical controls

People, people, people

OVERVIEW

Access and authorization of physical and digital assets for an organization make up the third principle. Universally acknowledged as a necessity in every part of the world, the actual placement and implementation of these types of safeguards can vary greatly, depending on the environment and value of the assets. The restriction of assets, which may include physical or digital items, may be accomplished through the introduction of a hierarchy. Hierarchies may consist of a dozen varying levels with crossover between authorized users or may simply consist of two levels: public and private. The establishment of a defined and purposeful authorization process for any asset should be done in a manner that enhances the value of the asset.

As organizations continually expand their environments and leverage business process outsourcing (BPO) opportunities, the preservation of system integrity becomes ever more important. Beyond protecting the organization from partners accessing corporate data, an accidental disclosure threat exists in situations where clients accidentally gain access to others. This is especially a problem where a BPO provides services to the airline industry and all major airlines use the same provider. This situation is common in vertical niche and specialized industries. It can become dangerous if competitors accidentally gain access to each other's systems.

In the past, when the organization's data centers were buried in the basement and weighed two tons, there was hardly a threat of the systems being taken out the front door or being inadvertently accessed by a visitor. Today systems that weigh less than three pounds contain more processing power than the first shuttles that went into space, and can carry all of an enterprise's intellectual property, customer lists, product design specs, computer-assisted drawings, and entire music collection.[1] The accessibility of these systems within the confines of the corporate offices, and the mobility of the data, extend the requirements of physical and digital safeguards.

Role assignment is a key exercise and one that requires the participation of business managers, human resources, and the technology teams. Together a structure of user profiles must be developed that reflects the organization's structure, the unique subsystems throughout the system, and the corporate culture. Once incorporated into the job descriptions of every employee, these assignments ensure that as the organization grows, adherence to privilege separation is maintained.

Together the safeguards within the access and authorization principle are designed to ensure that the right level of access is provided and that the assets that are not intended to be acquired are sufficiently secured. Many of these aspects focus on the personnel within the company and their behaviors, but they also are heavily supported by technology and long-term planning. The global core information technology (IT) controls that are highlighted within this principle include:

- Logical access
- Physical access
- Human resources

LOGICAL ACCESS

The reasonable assurance that digital assets and resources are protected against unauthorized modification, disclosure, loss, and impairment fairly captures the intentions put forth by professional associations and government legislation. The ability to provide users with only the necessary access based on their job functions and further to limit access to sensitive systems and data is necessary in an intellectual property world. The value of digital data is too great to leave unrestricted. The limitations placed upon associate access privilege not only protect the individuals, but also limit the damage attackers may cause using valid accounts. By restricting access, organizations are able to fairly and honestly abide by a separation-of-duties and a checks-and-balance system that would be impossible without adequate privilege controls.

Employees should be granted access to systems and data based on their job objectives and necessary functions.[2] A great example is that the chief executive of a company should not need access to the data center or gain immediate technical access to the security systems.

Logical access should be overseen by the technology group or the security group, if one exists. The business owners for each identified system should be responsible for supervising and authorizing credentials. This ensures that only access that has been explicitly granted is permitted, while providing management transparency. Logical access may be enforced at the operating system, database, or application level of the computing environment.

Access to environments should follow rules developed from approved groups to ensure that appropriate access is granted throughout the organization.[3] The organization should consider the sensitivity of the data within the organization, and assign a level of criticality to them (high, medium, low), and then determine the necessary roles and functions within the organization. These roles should be referenced to job functions and operational systems. This activity will help identify what permissions a given role requires and allow for the elimination of excess access. Based on these two measures, the organization should grant access and any necessary additional authentication methods to the assigned user base.

The organization may institute the use of tokens (small devices that fit on keyrings that present specific numbers that a user enters along with a password to provide additional authentication) or simply alphanumeric passwords. Regardless of the means of authentication, the methods implemented must reflect the importance of the data and consider the fact that the logical access ingress points are more likely to be attacked than the lobby door. In fact, a system online today using an Internet address that has never been live will be attacked nearly three dozen times within the first three minutes.[4] The online attack vector is very active. Therefore, anything sensitive to the organization should be adequately protected with sufficient authentication methods.[5]

Organizations should use a two-factor authentication method when accessing the organization remotely or when accessing systems that contain sensitive information. In this approach, only those with administrator access, who work remotely, or who have access to sensitive information are provided additional authentication measures, such as a token or a biometric (i.e. fingerprint) reader.

Access controls should also include a reporting and monitoring function that provides intelligence of the activity toward the assets under protection. This information should indicate the account activity, any failed authentication attempts, and the areas in which failures occurred. (Contextual information is best here; for example, the unauthorized user attempted to change an employee's social security number.) Access controls should include all ingress points for the organization, including the virtual private network (VPN), modem dialup lines, wireless connections, and any cellular linkups.

Business Impacts

Access restrictions protect the sensitive information within the organization and are the primary defense against attackers. The most damaging attacks are done through authorized accounts, so the institution of role separation and enhanced security precautions helps mitigate these threats. Beyond preventing attackers from stealing or damaging systems that a user has legitimate access to within the company, the organization is safeguarding the possibility of collusion within the organization.

Ensuring that systems are not modified and data are not manipulated within a system helps ensure the system's integrity and availability. This prevents downtime due to unauthorized changes and enables management to trust the systems. Annual surveys and studies show that most successful attacks originate from within an organization's own computing environment and typically with authorized user accounts. These accounts are usually stolen or discovered by attackers, and this has led to huge damages to companies around the world.

Application

In order to operate an environment where access to data is restricted and users do not have conflicts surrounding their roles, the organization must fully review the data to determine classification types and points of access to the data within the organization.

If they have not done so already, organizations should bring together management and business owners and define the importance of the data held within the organization. This process should introduce any classification information found concerning regulatory requirements and contractual obligations to clients (i.e., contractual obligations for a hosting company may restrict the firm from allowing customers to access each other's data: Coke should not have access to PepsiCo's data). As this process progresses, the organization should capture an accounting of the data, the owner's criticality rating, and any supporting documentation. Based on this effort, the organization may need to rearchitect its infrastructure and data stores to redistribute the data based on usage.

Upon completion of these efforts, the organization has an established data-sensitivity scale that has been applied to systems and data that are segmented, and simplifies the establishment of restrictions for access to data. In addition, the user roles do not contain natural conflicts of interest, and it is easier to handle allocating and transferring individuals throughout the organization and managing different functions.

An evaluation of data access control restrictions and effectiveness should focus on all levels and manners of access, to include the network and operating system, remotely and on-site.[6] This evaluation effort should be applied to both purchased and developed systems to ensure similar functionality exists. Due to the numerous systems deployed within an organization and the wide range of ownership possibilities, an organization should consolidate the user databases as much as possible. This may be accomplished by leveraging an LDAP or active directory (AD) configuration that allows for multiple types of systems to pull access information from a single managed environment. The usage of a central identity management system, such as LDAP, allows for transfers and terminations to be done in a timely fashion and completely across the organization.

Access should require a strong user password that is unique to the individual. End users should understand that they are responsible for that account and that monitoring devices will review the activity under that account. Through this type of communication, the company is better able to enforce its documented policies.

The monitoring of access to systems and activities on systems should be captured and centrally aggregated. These data should be reviewed regularly by a security group, and all violations should be followed up by human resources. Administrative-level accounts should be subject to additional monitoring; all account activity, commands, and results should be captured in a secure system that is inaccessible to any personnel who are monitored by the system. This provides a document trail should any incident occur that requires validation of events or activities of employees within the company.

Access from locations outside the organization or wireless access should be subject to stronger authentication. Anyone accessing the organization's data via cellular, wireless 802.11, or remotely (coffeeshop, home) should be required to use a second username and password that is different from the primary corporate ID or use a token-type device. In addition, these types of connections should be fully encrypted; only systems that carry the organization's corporate encryption certificate should be able to connect to the network. The use of corporate certificates should be deployed in a manner to exclude personal computing assets.

In all areas where use privileges are defined, the practice of least privilege should be employed. Job responsibilities are given sufficient access to complete duties without excessive permissions throughout the environment. The most likely area of violation for this type of approach is around the administrator privileges. It can be mitigated through clear job descriptions, oversight, and job rotation. The routine switching of duties among a team allows members of the unit to have a transparent view into the activities of each member. This action does not merely prevent and detect fraudulent or policy-violating activities; it enables teams to function during vacations and transitions.

In Practice

Common logical access controls include:

- Business requirement for access control:
  - Access policy is defined and published, detailing the authorized usage and responsibilities for the users of the system.
  - Regular review of all individuals with access by management.
  - Management approves and authorizes users for systems.
  - User access and privileges are defined by job responsibilities.
- User access management:
  - Establish access controls to enforce segregation of duties.
  - Ensure individual user identifiers are managed and distributed for all users of the system.
  - User accounts should not be shared.
- User responsibilities:
  - Accountable for all access attempts done through user account information.
  - Responsible regardless whether account information was shared or stolen, as the safeguarding of the information is their duty.
  - Users are responsible for their own actions and should not take actions against the law or codes of conduct.
  - Users should ensure controls are sufficient for information they are responsible for.
  - Passwords should be kept secret by the user, be complex, and be of reasonable length (seven characters or more).
- Network access control:
  - Firewalls and access devices are deployed and configured to prevent unauthorized access and log all connection attempts.
  - Extraneous services and network ports are disabled or blocked for all servers and networks based on business owner requirements and the technology group's recommendations.
- Operation system access control:
  - Limit access to system software.
  - Restrict access to administrator privileges to limited group and establish real-time account usage monitoring.

- Application and information access control:
  - ○ Information classification (public and private) and privileges should define user permissions.
  - ○ Business owner sign-off and quarterly reviews.
- Mobile computing and teleworking:
  - ○ Device authentication is required at boot and may not be circumvented.
  - ○ Remote access requires two-factor authentication.
  - ○ Remote access provides limited access to sensitive data.

PHYSICAL ACCESS

An organization must control all physical access points for the corporate building, remote locations, computing centers, systems positioned in open areas, and media devices. The control required is dependent on the sensitive nature of data stored within the organization. All organizations are at risk to some form of physical breach regardless of geographical location, office culture, or nature of business. The degree of safeguards should be risk based, consistent with the other control safeguards deployed throughout the organization.[7]

Physical access is most clearly understood to include the building or facility of an organization. The four walls, doors with locks, and a possible fence or barrier separating the building property typify the basic access controls for many organizations. Additional layers of security may be added to the traditional organization, or existing safeguards may be enhanced. For instance, the entryways into the organization may be reduced to a few manned entrance points that require visible identification to pass through. The complexity and degree of physical security can be escalated to address the nature of the assets being protected to include high-powered surveillance cameras or simple electronic ID badges.

Beyond the exterior walls, physical facility access must include the inner areas of the building. It is appropriate to have layers of security where each one requires a different authorization than the one before it. This ensures that casual visitors do not stumble into the data center or walk into the research and development lab creating the greatest new widget in top secret—until now. Depending on its resources and its need, an organization may have only two layers of physical security: one for the exterior entrances and another for the data center.

Additional safeguards that enhance the awareness of personnel within the organization and provide a means of detection and investigation include a visitor policy and video surveillance. A visitor policy dictates how users are greeted, what information is required when they sign in, whether they are provided a badge, an escort policy, and any penalties for violating the policy. Surveillance should monitor access or attempts at access in sensitive areas in the organization.

Systems and hardware that are not protected by the physical perimeter or that reside in the common areas also require some form of security to ensure that theft or unauthorized usage does not occur. Workstations or other terminals accessible to persons in the common area must be secured physically, and the systems should be digitally locked when unattended. If laptops are used in these accessible areas, they should be tethered to the desk. Such precautions are good practice, as they instill a habit of security within users once they bring these remote computing devices outside the organization. The greatest example of this risk is seen when walking into a coffeeshop and observing the number of laptops being used. Eventually someone will order a drink, catch a call outside, or simply get up and stretch his legs, leaving his computing device alone. Providing secure cables and instilling a practice of locking the device limits the exposure to threats while the individuals are traveling.

Physical safeguards are in place solely for the protection of the assets, and by "assets" we mean the technology and the people who make the organization hum. The regular backup procedures and shipments of systems around the globe introduce a third focus of physical security: the media. Data custodians, business owners, and executives must assess what data the organization ships and the manner in which they are prepared, received, and restored to production in the case of a situation. Organizations typically will back up the most important databases and then ship them overnight via FedEx to a storage facility in a mountain someplace. Such activities are normal and safe, so long as the organization takes care as to how these transfers take place. The use of split-disk backups, encryption, proper key management practices, and having signing authority provides assurances that the information is safeguarded from all but the most serious of targeted attacks. The use of signatures ensures that only authorized persons have access to the data.

Business Impacts

In physical attacks, a complete stranger can attempt to enter the facility to steal hardware or connect to the network internally. As employees consider the interior of a building secure, they generally do not practice all of the security policies mandated within the organization. Beyond a complete stranger wandering through the facility, we must consider an employee or a contractor having access to the organization after-hours and the type of information that may be exposed as a result.

Information on mobile devices and media can be lost or acquired on purpose by individuals or organizations looking to profit from the data. The value of the hardware alone makes a theft worthwhile, but the treasure trove of sensitive information (credit records, credit cards, bank account information, secret-sauce recipes, or merger-and-acquisition information) found on systems can equate to millions of dollars.

An organization that is victim to a physical theft must question what safeguards were in place, whether they were operating effectively, and whether the employee overrode any of these controls. In an recent example, a company employed multiple authentications of user access challenges to a database containing alumni information. Four sets of usernames and passwords were required before accessing the data. Unfortunately, the user created a script that autocompleted all of the fields, and the system automatically loaded the database on boot, thereby defeating all four levels of controls and exposing millions of alumni. This example demonstrates the clear need for management to ensure that sufficient controls are in place and that they are effective. The cost of a breach, such as the one previously described, to the organization is that of time and confidence regarding the true threat to it and to those customers who entrust information to the organization. In the example provided, if the organization knew that encryption was in place there would be no threat of a breach of information: no lawsuits, no press release nightmares, no escalating audit costs to double-check every other safeguard, and no federal penalties. That is, if encryption is in place, it may be understood that criminals will not gain access to the sensitive information prior to the organization instituting countermeasures, such as activating creditwatch reports or modifying the passwords on SCADA electricity systems. With validation and assurance, the company is not making assumptions around the privacy or security of the information.

Application

Establish a policy that defines the protocol for visitors to the facility and ensure that all personnel are aware of the practices for safeguarding physical assets.[8] This policy should be clearly communicated and enforced for all company offices. It is important that consistent application occurs, regardless of the size of each office, to ensure that the entire organization is secured. The policy and safeguards should address the physical locations of the enterprise, the systems, and any media archives.

The organization should provide badges for all employees with unique colors and placement of information to be recognizable from a reasonable distance.[9] The color or layout should represent the type of badge and individual (i.e., green background is an employee; yellow is a visitor; orange is a service contractor with minor access privileges). The badges should not indicate the company or the person's last name, but instead have the first name in large letters with a photo and color background.

Depending on the layers of security employed within the facility, a mandatory escort policy may be required for visitors. The organization should ensure that personnel and visitors acknowledge this policy and agree to adhere to it while on premises. It is the responsibility of all persons to ensure that visitors, who should be clearly identifiable by their identification badges, are always escorted. If they get lost, they should be escorted to their sponsor.

The facility entranceways should be limited wherever possible and have a surveillance camera stationed to record all activity.[10] The installation of electronic locks for entranceways will help restrict traffic to public areas and allow recording for forensic investigations. Utilizing additional keypad locks throughout the facility ensures a limited exposure to wayward visitors.

The oldest attack to physical locks on doors is the action of an individual tailgating into an area by following closely behind an authorized entrant. The second individual does not badge in and uses the authorized person's initial swipe to pass through the door. The simplest safeguard to this threat is to instill a culture that requires every employee to badge in and prohibits tailgating. This can be supported by activating the audio on badge readers to provide an audible notice for each user swiping into an area. Two tones should be used to indicate a positive or negative authentication.

Systems that are set up in common areas or heavy-traffic areas of the organization require special attention. A simple policy of locking workstations (both physically tethered to the desk structure and digitally with Ctrl+Alt+Delete) ensures that unauthorized persons do not use another person's terminal and that equipment is not moved around the organization without management knowledge. This policy should also apply to the organization's portable computing devices, including laptops and PDAs, especially when these devices are used in the field.

Additional safeguards are needed for data that travel: a formal media handling/disposal process. Data that are traveling may be found on laptops, PDAs, BlackBerry devices, backup tapes, CD copies of data, iPods, and thumb drives. Organizations may institute several measures to protect such data. First, the organization must ensure that its data-handling policy includes such devices and that all personnel who have access and the means to transport data (mobile workers, sales teams, and technologists) accept this policy. The policy should dictate the level of encryption based on the type of information being transported and the procedures required. For instance, if the organization needs to ship backup customer files, the best practice would be to encrypt the data on two separate tapes and ship them separately to the destination. All data that are transported should be encrypted to limit the impact of theft or other incidents. The disposal, retirement, or reuse of systems requires similar precautionary steps to ensure that any data that were processed or stored on the device are no longer accessible. This may be addressed using any number of secure wiping techniques.

A classic attack on an organization is called *dumpster diving*. Here individuals literally go through the office trash looking for account information, hardware, and tossed disks to discover user account information or sensitive information that may remain on old storage devices. The new-age dumpster diving does not require shuffling through trash; instead decommissioned hardware is purchased from the company or ex-employees through online auction sites such as eBay. Even though such sales may be authorized by the company, sometimes systems are not sufficiently sanitized. In these cases, where the storage media were not completely erased, the hard drives and the data still may be readable and contain corporate information. A best practice is to shred all disks and papers whenever possible and destroy all hard drives if they are unusable. If the hard drives are usable, the technology group should securely sanitize them using a multi-erase format encryption process.

In Practice

Oversight and procedures should exist to restrict physical access to all local, remote, service provider, and storage facility environments. Necessary controls include:

- Only authorized individuals have access to the organization's physical data facilities.
- Access and activity are captured via surveillance monitoring systems and secured access log repository.
- Security locks are centrally managed and credentials are distributed through a physical security group.
- Access activity is reviewed, and violations are addressed by the physical security group.
- Authorization to the physical data facilities is granted by the technology manager based on role responsibilities.
- Authorization is required for physical access to the organization's data center or communication centers (separate from access permissions to the building and common areas).
- Security policies and procedures detail required actions in the event of a physical security breach.
- Remote storage facilities are secured from nonauthorized personnel, and access is granted by the technology manager.
- Access privileges are revoked immediately once an individual no longer requires access to the facility (due to termination or project completion).

In Practice

Physical access controls may include:[11]

- Manual door or numbered keypad cipher lock
- Magnetic door locks that require the use of electronic keycards

In Practice (continued)

- Biometrics (handprint, fingerprint) authentication
- Security guards or receptionist visually inspecting identifications
- Photo IDs with color identifiers
- Entry logs (required for visitors, optional for staff)
- Logs and authorization for removal and return of tapes and other storage
- Electronic and visual surveillance systems
- Perimeter fences around sensitive buildings
- Perimeter intrusion alarms
- Computer terminal locks
- Laptop and computer secure cable locks

HUMAN RESOURCES

The people of every organization represent its best and primary line of defense from numerous threats. Technology can provide only so many assurances before the team that manages, operates, and monitors it becomes the deciding factor. The castle with the drawbridge drawn is no more protected than one with the drawbridge down if the citizens trapped inside are the ones storming the castle.

In addition to reliance on staff to support and promote the control environment, the company relies on the human factor to bridge any gap that may exist in the controls. The implementation of controls cannot be done without the human component providing oversight and providing controls that were proven to be expensive and operationally burdensome to the organization. Therefore, organizations must rely on their staff at all levels and must establish and bolster the human factor within the control environment through a companywide program.

A companywide program should both address the human resources life cycle and instill a structure that encourages and supports the control environment. The human resources life cycle follows every employee from becoming a part of the business to transitioning to another career. The structure of the organization provides clarity in job responsibilities, establishes reporting structures, and ensures capable staff is supported throughout the business.

The ongoing training of end users within the organization must include security, business focus and principles, ethics, and procedures. Training provides valuable updates for all employees and assures the organization that the staff competency and capabilities are adequately enriched.

Business Impacts

Collusion between employees is the most significant threat to a control environment as it not only circumvents key controls but also leads to a poisonous atmosphere. Such an atmosphere is likely to breed further ethical and control violations, as it is considered the normal status quo. Therefore, organizations must consistently monitor and enable positive change in the organization.

The existence of such environments can create an atmosphere where civil and criminal charges may be filed. The mere existence of such charges is damaging to the organization, as the poor press and potential for increased associative exposure to clients and vendors grows. The trickledown effect is real, and organizations must expect collateral damage for every type of situation. For example, an organization that is exposed by charges of money laundering may find it hard to acquire new lines of credit. In addition, a firm found guilty or perceived of criminal activities shall cast a shadow on any associates of the firm that is likely to cause an early exodus of clients, as was the case with Arthur Andersen while it was being investigated over Enron.[12]

The financial impacts from lawsuits, collateral damage from lost sales, and the difficulty of acquiring talent all contribute to the likely impact an organization will face when the management and associates are untrustworthy.

Application

Enhancing the control environment within every business requires a blend of technology and people. Together the resulting process provides the competitive edge to sustain operations in the global marketplace. The capacity to engage, leverage, and enable the staff of the organization is essential to meeting the challenges of business and compliance pressures. A program should be developed that embraces the organization's culture, the needs of the control environment, and the management structure. The program described next should be embraced as a way to achieve a more effective and efficient technology environment by leveraging the human factor found within every organization.

The logical place to start is the organizational structure and reporting responsibilities. As organizations grow and shift due to mergers and the like, functional job descriptions and associated responsibilities become inconsistent with actual daily tasks. Therefore, the organization should thoroughly evaluate the established job descriptions and responsibilities associated with all end users. This exercise should first seek to identify what already exists, what is desired given the culture of the organization, and what is expected for these descriptions. Once a baseline is established on what is required for job descriptions, the organization may work with all levels of staff and management to develop, approve, and maintain these descriptions moving forward.

The establishment of clear job descriptions has two benefits. First, the organization can now set user access privileges based on clear job duties. This supports least-privilege and separation-of-duty requirements. Second, clear accountability and ownership for systems and data throughout the environment results from clear job descriptions. This level of clarity of ownership ensures that the right individuals are accountable and that those familiar with and responsible for the data become more vigilant and focused in protecting the environment.

While granting privileges based on user responsibilities clearly establishes proper access and control at the logical system level, the organization must verify that the actual reporting structure is similarly supportive. The human resources department should make this determination, or it should be done from an outsider's perspective in order to ensure that reporting structures are evaluated objectively. The management structure is not under scrutiny; instead, the evaluation and improvements should ensure that no manager has conflicting interests.

Every organization must ensure that it supports and encourages the right culture and ethical environment, and defining roles and improving organizational reporting contribute to this effort. The structure and efforts to sustain an ethical organization requires a mature process that identifies, acclimates, sustains, and manages the normal personnel changes and transitions. Organizations may sustain a mature process through defined and appropriate policies and procedures and active involvement of management.

New staff should be hired through a meticulous process that starts with the creation of clear job responsibilities and objectives. The role identification ensures that the business acquires the correct resources for needed tasks. Candidates should undergo background and security checks if they will have access to any sensitive environments, systems, or data. Finally, the selected candidates must agree to conditions of employment that include ethical and job function responsibilities, which sets a precedent for the organization's culture, ethics, and clear accountability for actions taken.

All new hires must undergo an immersive new-employee process to ensure the entities' expectations are known. The initiation of new employees should include training that addresses system usage, compliance, security, ethics, avenues of reporting concerns, company culture, and job training. This process of developing, delivering, and monitoring progress should occur continuously throughout the staffer's employment with the company. Ongoing and regular training is necessary to ensure that staff is capable of delivering expected work, and to inform all employees regarding corporate direction and perspectives.

In Practice

Human resource controls should include:

- Published human resource policy on acceptable behavior, use of technology, ethics, and hotline (whistleblower) protections

- Candidate conditional employment based on background security screening

- Regular training and suitable verification methods to ensure that ethics, business vision, culture, and system updates are communicated

- Established security management structure and clearly assigned security responsibilities

- Organizational reporting structures that do not present a conflict of interest

- Management identification and assessment of complex operations, programs, or projects

- Management knowledge of results of monitoring and audits, to enable review and consideration of related risk of noncompliance and operational needs of the business

---

COMPLIANCE

Preventing unauthorized persons from accessing sensitive data within an organization is mandated by industry and government legislation. The ability to prevent unauthorized access requires knowledge of who requires access and to what extent. Therefore, organizations must continually support the human resources of the organization and ensure that the entire company is of the same mind and principles with regard to security, compliance, and ethical operations.

The ability to limit access through physical and technical controls enables organizations to realize the level of assurance desired in an interconnected business. The granularity of restrictions is dependent on the sensitivity of the data, the operations of the business, the competitive environment, and the corporation's own standards. However, the requirements do expect sufficient controls given the nature of the data, so it is important to leverage management review of data. This ensures that as data become more or less sensitive, controls are adjusted appropriately. Further building on the exhibits found in Chapters 9 and 10, Exhibit 11.1 provides a robust archive of resources for any organization and demonstrates the importance and maturity of controls surrounding Principle 3.

Exhibit 11.1   Principle 3 Matrix

Principle 3: Access and Authorization[a]

Highlighted Global Core IT Controls

- Logical Access
- Physical Access
- Human Resources

Logical Access: Relevant and Complementary Publications

12 CFR Part 30, Appendix A, II (Operational and Managerial Standards), B
CERT, OCTAVE
CMS, CSR
CMS, Information Security ARS, Version 2.0
CMS, Policy for the Information Security Program
COBIT 4.1, Control Objectives, Management Guidelines, Maturity Models, IT Governance Institute
COSO, ERM Framework
COSO, Integrated Framework
DCID, 6/3DISA Field Security Operations V6R4.4, Network Checklist
DoD, Policy 8500
FFIEC, Development Acquisition
FIPS 191, Guidelines for the Analysis of LAN Security
FISMA
GAO/AIMD-12.19.6, Federal Information System Controls Audit Manual
GLBA, Privacy of Financial Information
HIPAA
HKICPA, Internal Control and Risk Management—A Basic Framework
IIA, GTAG, Guide 1: Information Technology Controls
IIA GTAG, Guide 8: Auditing Application Controls
ISACA, IS Standards, Guidelines, and Procedures for Auditing and Control
ISO 15489-1:2001, Information and Documentation—Records Management—Part 1
ISO 17799:2000, Information Technology—Security Techniques—Code of Practice for Information Security Management
ISO 27001:2005, Information Technology—Security Techniques—Information Security Management Systems—Requirements
ISO/IEC 18028-4:2005, Information Technology—Security Techniques—IT Network Security—Part 4: Securing Remote Access, 2005
ISSA, GAISP
ITIL, Security Management
MAGERIT, Version 2.0, 2005
NERC, CIP-003-1, Security Management Controls
NERC, CIP-005-1, Electronic Security Perimeter(s)
OCC, 12 CFR 30, Safety and Soundness Standards
PCI DSS, v1.1, Payment Card Industry Data Security Standard Security Audit Procedures

SP800-100, Information Security Handbook: A Guide for Managers
SP800-14, Generally Accepted Principles and Practices for Securing Information Technology Systems
SP800-53, Recommended Security Controls for Federal Information Systems
SP800-58, Security Considerations for Voice Over IP Systems
SP800-66, Resource Guide for Implementing the Health Insurance Portability and Accountability Act Security Rule
Texas Department of Information Resources, Practices for Protecting Information Resources Assets
U.S. Department of Commerce, EU Safe Harbor Privacy Principles

Physical Access: Relevant and Complementary Publications

12 CFR, Part 30, Appendix A, II (Operational and Managerial Standards), B
CMS, Information Security ARS, Version 2.0
CMS, Policy for the Information Security Program
COBIT 4.1, Control Objectives, Management Guidelines, Maturity Models, IT Goverance Institute
DISA, Field Security Operations V6R4.4, Network Checklist
FIPS 191, Guidelines for the Analysis of LAN Security
FISMA
GAO/AIMD-12.19.6, Federal Information System Controls Audit Manual
GLBA, Privacy of Financial Information
HIPAA
ISACA, IS Standards, Guidelines, and Procedures for Auditing and Control
ISO 17799:2000, Information Technology—Security Techniques—Code of Practice for Information Security Management
ISO 27001:2005, Information Technology—Security Techniques—Information Security Management Systems—Requirements
ISSA, GAISP
ITIL, Security Management
MAGERIT Version 2.0, 2005
NERC, CIP-006-1, Physical Security of Critical Cyber Assets
OCC, 12 CFR 30, Safety and Soundness Standards
PCI DSS, v1.1, Payment Card Industry Data Security Standard Security Audit Procedures
SP800-100, Information Security Handbook: A Guide for Managers
SP800-14, Generally Accepted Principles and Practices for Securing Information Technology Systems
SP800-26, Security Self-Assessment Guide
SP800-53, Recommended Security Controls for Federal Information Systems
Texas Department of Information Resources, Practices for Protecting Information Resources Assets
U.S. Department of Commerce EU Safe Harbor Privacy Principles

Human Resources: Relevant and Complementary Publications

CMS, Information Security ARS, Version 2.0
CMS, Policy for the Information Security Program

Exhibit 11.1   *(Continued)*

COBIT 4.1, Control Objectives, Management Guidelines, Maturity Models, IT Governance Institute
COSO, Integrated Framework
FISMA
GAO/AIMD-12.19.6, Federal Information System Controls Audit Manual
HIPAA
HKICPA, Internal Control and Risk Management—A Basic Framework
IIA, GTAG, Guide 1: Information Technology Controls
ISSA, GAISP
ITIL, Security Management
NERC, CIP-004-1 Personnel & Training
OECD, Guidelines for the Security of Information Systems and Networks: Towards a Culture of Security
SP800-100, Information Security Handbook: A Guide for Managers
SP800-53, Recommended Security Controls for Federal Information Systems

---

ªSee the acronym list for explanations of all acronyms.

ENDNOTES

1. The U.S. space shuttles have been slowly upgraded over the past 30 years, but many components bring back memories of older technologies and slower processors. As John Schwartz wrote in "High Tech in the 70's, Shuttles Feel Their Age," an article highlighting problems with the aging ships: "Some of the computers used in testing the shuttle's boosters still contained Intel 8086 microprocessors, which are from the family that powered the first I.B.M. personal computers in the early 1980's. That microprocessor has 29,000 transistors and operates at a speed of 10 million cycles per second. Today's microprocessors tend to have 55 million transistors and run at a speed of 3.4 billion cycles per second." *New York Times*, July 25, 2005.

2. U.S. General Accounting Office (GAO), Accounting and Information Management Division (AIMD), *Federal Information System Controls Audit Manual—Volume I: Financial Statement Audits 12.19.6, 115.* URL: http://www.gao.gov/special.pubs/ai12.19.6.pdf.

3. Denis Trček, *Managing Information Systems Security and Privacy* (Berlin: Springer-Verlag, 2006).

4. "Live" refers to an Internet address that was not previously available on the Internet being assigned to a host that responds to traffic on a network.

5. NIST Special Publication 800-63, *Electronic Authentication Guideline* (April 2006). URL: http://csrc.nist.gov/publications/nistpubs/800-63/SP800-63V1_0_2.pdf.

6. U.S. Department of Defense (DOD), *Security Technical Implementation Guide: Access Control, STIG V1R1, 21.* URL: http://iase.disa.mil/stigs/stig/index.html.

7. Richard E. Cascarino, *Auditor's Guide to Information Systems Auditing* (Hoboken, NJ: John Wiley & Sons, 2007), 330.

8. International Organization for Standization, "ISO/IEC FDIS 27001-2005(E), Information Security Management Systems: Physical and Environmental Security." URL: http://www.iso.org/iso/catalogue_detail?csnumber=42103.

9. U.S. DOD, Security Technical Implementation Guide, 16, 30.

10. Ibid., 36.

11. U.S. GAO/AIMD, 12.19.6, 55.

12. Enron grand jury charges: URL: http://news.findlaw.com/hdocs/docs/enron/usandersen030702ind.html. Article outlines concern from clients of Andersen and the stigma of association: "After Andersen, Accounting Worries Stick": URL: http://news.com.com/After+Andersen,+accounting+worries+stick/2100-1017_3-936813.html.

12

Principle 4: Sustain Operations

Key Topics Addressed in This Chapter

Business continuity

Environmental Safeguards

OVERVIEW

The fourth principle, sustaining operations, is emphasized primarily by both private- and public-sector trade groups and professional authorities. Interestingly enough, the need to ensure continuity of operations is not a major concern of governments around the world. Despite the fact that most laws focus on information protection and financial integrity through internal controls within the marketplace, governments rarely require that organizations validate their ability to survive a disaster or digital loss. These types of concerns are raised by customers and partners. Such resiliency of operations is an imperative that cannot be ignored by any organization.

The physical ability of an organization to resume operations after a disaster should reflect the expectations and requirements of its external and internal customers. This control's flexibility allows for all organizations of all sizes to both prioritize and identify systems that should be restored, and in what fashion. Resiliency must consider all possible events: a digital failure, a virus destroying the mail server, or a flood in the data center.

When establishing safeguards, the organization must consider the types of environmental impacts that may occur. These may include natural disasters, such as hurricanes, or man-made disasters, such as train derailments or chemical spills. Organizations should perform risk management analyses to consider the impact of these types of threats and to determine the most appropriate mitigation responses.

The ability of the organization to recover operations and provide predictable services should be developed and maintained based on the requirements put forth by business pressures, which include internal delivery requirements, customer requirements (market forces), partner demands, and legislative mandates. While not consistently globally mandated, an *always-online world* demands that businesses have continuous operations—without exception. The only caveat to such a grand proclamation is that these demands for return to operations vary for each organization, business division, and even product lines within the same organization. The global core IT controls that are highlighted within this principle include:

- Operations resiliency
- Environmental safeguards

OPERATIONS RESILIENCY

An organization's ability to provide continuous services has become an imperative. Individual concepts of *continuous* may vary across organizations, as most define their need for available services by contractual agreements and consideration of the whole process. The ability to ensure accessibility of both data and the delivery of services is addressed through the application of a formal process within every organization. *Operations resiliency* is used in this text to include the general disaster recovery plans (DRPs) and business continuity plans (BCPs) required by the organization.

The degree of availability necessary for every organization is different and can be determined through a collaborative effort between business owners and technologists. An executive sponsor should advocate an annual business impact assessment effort. It can be leveraged from already-captured information from an existing and updated enterprise risk management (ERM) program. The output from these efforts should provide clarity as to the needed technology assets based on business processes and customer expectations. This effort provides the operations resiliency team with sufficient data to define the resiliency factors for all assets based on the business processes they support, and return-to-operations requirements.

While the operations resiliency effort is meant to ensure that the organization can recover and survive the worst possible scenarios, the exercises conducted throughout the year verify the controls the organization relies on for meeting service-level agreements. The assurance achieved through such regular testing and continuous dialogue from the business groups ensures that as the organization changes, the business adapts accordingly. Financial

and operational negative impacts are defined throughout these collabora-
tions, and provide specific associated costs.

Organizations of all sizes worldwide should at least conduct the
following tasks:

1. Evaluate the criticality and sensitivity of technology operations and
   determine dependent and supportive resources (business impact
   analysis).

2. Institute procedures and safeguards to prevent and minimize damages
   or interruptions (develop and implement).

3. Document and publish the recovery plans (containing detailed guidance,
   published to all primary and secondary contacts).

4. At least annually, test the plan and verify that all business owners sign
   off on its sufficiency. (Plan maintenance should include updating as
   systems change.)[1]

Contributions from all members of the organization and documenting
the results of test runs are key to ensuring the operations resiliency controls
are effective for the organization's needs and efficiency, given the need to
apply resources where the appropriate.

Business Impacts

Impacts may include financial impacts, operational impacts, or technology-
related impacts as a result of a disruption to the processing ability of the
organization. Quantitative and qualitative valuations should be placed on
the technology assets through an enterprise risk management (ERM) or
business impact assessment (BIA) effort. These define the true impact the
organization can reasonably expect to sustain should a catastrophe occur.
When measuring these values, it is important to consider how the impacts
affect the organization when they occur in isolation (i.e., a single failure of
a single system). Impacts may occur in a cluster or affect all dependent systems, and this net impact of negative events should also be considered.

An organization can define financial impacts based on existing contracts it has for timely delivery of services. These contracts may provide
discounts to customers in the event of such a delay, and these discounts can
be calculated based on available service contracts. Contract-applied fees or
penalties or the inability to process transactions (sales orders or invoices to
customers) add an additional cost of capital to the organization. The financial impacts are market based and enforced through the market. In only
a few industries do government oversight bodies apply a financial fine to
organizations due to service disruptions.

Interruptions impact customers when call centers utilizing outsourced
services are unreachable due to technology glitches. They can result in a

loss of customer service capabilities, revenue, and goodwill. The inability to deliver timely information throughout the company can create a lack of trust or propensity to operate independently. The result of complex and inaccessible information is wasted resources, poor customer experience, and potentially harmful business decisions that affect the operations of the business. This loss of confidence in the operational capabilities of the organization can also impact the stakeholders of the company, external customers, regulatory agencies, and internal employees, and create a negative perception in the stock markets.

Business Case

BUSINESS SITUATION

An international airline carrier flies passengers from nearly every corner of the globe. To control costs due to skyrocketing oil and supply costs, the airline transferred the customer service centers to an outsourcing firm. The company heavily invested in creating customized connections to their reservation systems and other databases to ensure operators would be able to address caller requests. After nearly six months of operating successfully, a shipping accident occurs and severs the fiber optics used to transfer the voice-over-Internet-protocol (VOIP) traffic. Instantaneously all ticketing, rebooking, customer service, flight tracking, and customer-facing systems are unavailable.

ANALYSIS

The organization did not prepare a manual or secondary process to address the breakdown in technology. As the customer, the carrier must consider all risks and potential events that could interrupt its ability to service its clients. Failure to have any type of disaster recovery or secondary plan can be devastating to operations and staff during the event, costly afterward from litigation and regulatory review, and debilitating to the business as consumers associate capability of a call center with flying a jet.

SOLUTION

The identification of the call center as a core customer interface component would bring the contract, system, and supporting technology under the analysis of the business resiliency teams. A secondary channel—a satellite or a secondary call center provider—would be contracted and put into place. The failover of these systems would be tested, and the volume levels would be defined to support the worst-case scenario. The company can also request that a domestic call center be established as part of the agreement in case such a situation arises.[2]

A disaster that hits the organization resulting from dependencies across systems may negatively impact the technology itself. Given the expansion of virtualization around the world's data centers, organizations now rely on fewer systems that house multiple purposes. An event that displaces the service of a single system can cause a chain reaction throughout several other systems that rely on the impacted system. Impacted systems may be those that provide monitoring or preventive controls to the computing environment. If unavailable, a lack of trust in the remaining systems within the environment may develop. For example, the loss of a firewall at the perimeter may expose the internal systems to the public Internet. Such exposure would be considered serious under any audit and assessment and would create a need to fully vet each system that was exposed.

Loss of customers, forfeiture of vendor discounts, loss of confidence in the market, fines from partners for violating service-level agreements, internal mistrust regarding the ability to produce information, and the broad technical impacts on the technology assets are the major threats to an organization from a lack of operational resiliency.

Application

It is financially wasteful to institute the technology, procedures, and resources necessary to fully support the entire organization's business processes. The operations of the organization provide specific services to internal and external customers that are certainly necessary and important. The dependency between each process and the parties involved defines the value of the assets and support processes within the company. Every organization provides specific services that may be considered highly critical but also may not require a timely turnaround period to customers. By concentrating attention on specific business processes and relevant technology assets, the disaster recovery team has a more manageable set of responsibilities and a far more cost-effective and feasible situation.[3]

Prior to working with business owners, conducting a business impact assessment, or distributing questionnaires, the organization must assign the duty of the business continuity program to a permanent team. The team should be sponsored by an executive who understands and embraces the operations resiliency need and communicates its importance to all personnel. The sponsor also receives all reports regarding the identified critical assets, recovery times, and any negative findings in prior periods. The delivery team should be made up of members from different departments. A multidepartment team allows for easier interaction across the organization as well as exposure to more data sets and knowledge of more business functions.

Once the team is in place, it needs to determine the current capacity and resources relating to disaster recovery purposes and any available documentation. This part of the discovery phase does not define the scope or the direction of the team, but merely provides background on perceived needs of the organization and available resources. If an enterprise risk assessment exists, the team should strongly consider the findings identified in this report. Together the team incorporates the available works of others and develops a general prioritized list of business functions and assets.

Values can be assigned to assets in several ways, including order of productivity, a group work session with many business owners together, the distribution of questionnaires and surveys, or simply one-on-one interviews. Creating an atmosphere where business owners can collaborate on the interdependencies that exist within each other's business operations provides a greater likelihood of identifying the most critical assets and the true business contribution of each. Questionnaires and surveys are challenging because respondents tend to answer without introspection. Also, it is likely that a survey or questionnaire recipient does not fully understand the impact of a specific business process.

Finally, once a full understanding of the relationship of business functions to systems is reached and business functions are mapped to assets, the team can create a recovery strategy. It is likely that portions of the recovery strategy will be drafted by subject matter experts outside of the team, and these work products should be incorporated into the final documentation. The team will need to formally define their responsibilities given the types of systems, functions, and locations involved in the identified critical systems. Team members are assigned responsibility for a facility or business function, and work with other departments to institute a proper recovery process.

The team members must develop and document the procedures necessary for recovering the identified critical systems. Prior to the creation of the procedures, data migrations, technology deployments, adjustments to the regular processing by the business, and custom software modifications may be necessary to ensure that the organization adopts an optimal recovery plan. Procedures must be specific enough to allow for transferability to different personnel when the staff shifts or the organization expands.

A part of the formal implementation of the business resilience process throughout the organization must include training end users throughout the company. Training should communicate the need to adhere to policies relating to data management and understanding risks to the organization in the event of a catastrophe. An example would include an employee who disregards the regular testing of backup safeguards, and after a disaster, the company realizes that the backup media utilized for the past eight months is corrupt and all of the data are unrecoverable.[4]

Although the process of evaluating the needs of business owners and the implementation or configuration of redundancy safeguards is ongoing, the organization still must test the effectiveness of the established safeguards to ensure that the procedures are complete and that the organization truly is capable of sustaining a disaster. Studies show that organizations that are impacted by a disaster and do not have a plan to recover their systems are most likely out of business within 12 months.[5]

In Practice

Common control objectives include:

- A formal process is in place within the organization, sponsored by executive management, to develop, implement, and maintain a backup and restoration process.

- Procedures are documented concerning the sequence, resources, and contacts for restoring the operations of an organization.

- On-site and off-site backups are maintained, providing near–real-time backups that coincide with the organization's data management use.

- Recovery plans of the DRP/BCP are published and available to internal personnel.

- Sponsors and duties exist within the process outlining the responsibilities of each member. These assignments are kept up-to-date, and individuals are trained and competent in their area of coverage.

- Updates to the restoration process include a reevaluation of the processing needs of the identified business functions.

- Paper walkthrough testing is done at least semiannually, and full dry-run walkthrough evaluations are done on an annual basis.

- Management reviews DRP/BCP, the supported business functions, and the return-to-operations impacts. Management approves the proposed plan.

ENVIRONMENTAL SAFEGUARDS

Implementing a business resiliency process throughout an organization results in the full awareness of the importance of data and system assets across the enterprise. The institution of procedures and recovery plans allows the organization to respond to threats. Environmental safeguards are key to ensuring the organization's ability to manage threats resulting from human, natural, and environmental risks. These threats can include the accidental loss of power due to nearby construction errors or a tornado knocking out power lines. Regardless of the origin of the threat, the organization must consider and implement appropriate safeguards to prevent the total destruction or disablement of its computing capabilities as well as minimize threats to human life.

The risks an organization is susceptible to typically are captured by the risk management department of an organization. This team leverages multiple sources of trending data to calculate the likelihood of negative events and guides the organization in order to minimize identified risks. Generally a risk management department will champion all risk-transfer options through the acquisition of insurance contracts. In addition, the risk management department will play a role in the acquisition of new facilities, entrance to new sales markets, outsourcing of operational duties, and participating in disaster recovery scenarios. As a result, it is prudent to embrace the accomplishments of the risk management department when considering all risks to the business operations, as a tremendous amount of data and analysis are available in-house.

The organization must consider both its technical processing needs and its human component. In order for the organization to fully meet customer needs, both components are necessary at any given time. The technical processing needs of an organization rely on hardware that must operate within environmental ranges. These ranges are unique to the device and can be determined through vendor documentation. If the facilities do not maintain an environment within these ranges, systems will likely fail and processing errors will occur. Environmental conditions include consistent power for the systems without spikes or dips. In addition, a reasonable temperature, humidity, and air quality are also necessary to ensure the devices do not overheat or have sediment buildup. Such controls can be expected to operate on a daily basis and are monitored continuously.

Other environmental controls that support the technology processing abilities of the organization include onetime usage safeguards, such as fire-suppression systems. These fire-suppression systems are designed to extinguish fires that may occur within the computing environment. Some suppression systems are water-based and others are gas-based. The type employed should reflect the organization's abilities to have redundant systems. For example, if water-based systems are employed, extra hardware should be available to replace that which was drenched. (The hardware should be located somewhere other than where a separate sprinkler system is operating.) If the organization utilizes gas to extinguish flames, a facility must be robust enough to lock in the gases and must include internal cutoff switches in case people are inside when the system activates.

An organization's plan to switch operations to a backup facility at a remote site and restore the processing of customer requests addresses only the technical challenge in the event of an environmental incident. The personnel who manage the systems and complete the customer transactions must be considered in every environmental control. Such controls should include the use of sprinkler systems throughout the organization. (Sprinklers are much like security safeguards in an organization. They demonstrate their value when there is a fire, but otherwise they are a recurring cost. One would say the same for security devices: They are worth their expense as long as nothing penetrates the security defenses. If something does penetrate, another safeguard is needed—handheld fire extinguishers—to layer or enhance the effectiveness of the control. Sprinklers have become common, since insurance companies provide monetary discounts on premiums if they were present in a building, thereby providing a cost savings.) The environmental controls take into consideration the safety of the staff throughout the organization. The technology employed must reflect the number of staff on site.

Business Impacts

A catastrophe, such as a major fire that destroys the entire facility or a hurricane that floods the city, can have devastating effects on an organization; in fact, without proper planning and controls, it may not recover. Service interruption impacts can be as severe as a catastrophe or include a small grouping of applications. The difference is that the destruction of the technical systems, data, and applications of the organization compounded with personnel disruptions negate simple backup procedures. The absolute destruction of a data center forces an organization to rebuild all systems at a new facility and relocate the necessary staff to process the customer requests.

The business impacts can include loss of customers, breaches of contracts due to an inability to deliver services or goods within the prescribed time frame, loss of proprietary systems, expense of rebuilding all the systems, and expense of evaluating the data to determine the integrity and completeness of the restored systems. In addition, the use of third parties and services must be considered, such as the need for specialists to bring systems online rapidly and the use of secondary facilities as primary facilities during restoration. All of these impacts and more depending on the organization's business may be controlled to a tolerable level by leveraging environmental controls.

Application

Environmental and life safety controls for data centers and facilities in industrialized parts of the world are generally built in during the construction phase of any new facility. Only in rare cases do facilities lack the primary support systems required by organizations to maintain operations. Controls commonly need to be updated in older facilities, where they are not adequate for the needs of the organization or are not consistent with the laws of the area. Therefore, the application of physical and environmental protection measures may occur in several phases.

The first phase is a regularly occurring comparison of existing controls to the needs of the organization. This may occur yearly or every few years depending on the speed of business change. Such a review typically involves the risk management department, the results from the business impact assessment, and any relevant information from the enterprise risk assessment. Together these will provide sufficient awareness regarding the business function needs for systems and ensure that sufficient environmental controls are in place. This process focuses resources on the identified assets that provide the resiliency the organization requires and comply with the expectations of government laws.

Once assurances that all the environmental threats are understood have been received and the technical and human needs of the organization are captured, the organization should review the existing environmental controls to ensure the coverage is adequate. Power sources and backup and secondary sources must be sufficient, given the current needs of the organization and a reasonable growth period. As more devices are used within the organization, power requirements and temperature/humidity regulation needs also increase. Thus, the organization should consider the existing capacity of cooling and heating systems to ensure sufficient excess capacity exists to address growth as well as unusual climate conditions.

Existing environmental controls should be reviewed, maintained, and tested regularly. The sprinkler system does not have to be activated; rather, certified technicians must perform inspections to provide assurances that, when needed, the system will activate. These inspections should occur for the fire-suppression system, the HVAC systems, the power generation systems, and any monitoring systems. The results of these inspections should be reviewed and stored. These reviews should be provided to management that details the current capacity and responsiveness of the environmental control systems.

In Practice

Environmental business stability safeguards include:

- Air, temperature, and humidity system:
  - HVAC system maintains consistent temperature.
  - Humidity is maintained.
  - Monitoring system automatically notifies when conditions are beyond tolerance.
- Fire-suppression system:
  - Dry-pipe or chemical system.
- Stable, consistent, and clean power source:
  - Reliable power delivery grid.
  - Redundant power feeds that approach the facility in opposite cardinal directions and originate from separate grids.
  - Secondary backup systems: generators with sufficient time to safely shut down necessary systems.
  - Temporary power backup systems: UPS/APS or battery systems that provide power for a short period.
  - Conditioning of power to eliminate spikes and noise.

- Environmental hazards (Man-made/natural):
  ○ Location of facilities should consider seasonal threats to ensure full risk mitigation of natural event threat.
  ○ Avoid multiple locations in a tornado zone.
  ○ Avoid multiple locations susceptible to hurricanes.
  ○ Avoid multiple locations that may share a similar threat.
- Political and religious threats:
  ○ Facilities should not be located in areas susceptible to frequent civil uprising.
  ○ Facilities should not be located in areas that are considered high-value targets to terrorists or political activists.

COMPLIANCE

Business Resiliency

Operational resiliency is enforced mainly through market forces. Consumers will not conduct business with a company that is unavailable (consider how long your customer will wait for the checkout screen to load before they head to a competitor), and contractual partners will require compensation through fines or discounts for poor performance. In addition to causing general fines and loss of single customers, continual operating interruptions will result in canceled contracts and a viral effect throughout the Internet that is hard to undo.

Industry organizations and security professionals around the world define and mandate that organizations establish a means to maintain operations; in general, there are not many government regulations in this area. As a result, organizations must employ safeguards to ensure operations in order to maintain competitiveness, customers, partners, and the confidence of the auditors and oversight bodies when evaluating the technical control environments.

Industries that support human and health services, public utilities, and the finance sector do provide guidance and stipulate requirements around the resiliency of operations. Most guidance focuses on protecting the data when the systems are unavailable, but timely restorations of services are strongly encouraged.

Environmental

As mentioned, governments generally do not mandate environmental controls to ensure continuous operations or maintain the services delivery of the organization. The impetus for maintaining an ability to survive a catastrophic event lies with the business itself and its partners and/or customers. Nevertheless, market pressure is sufficient to ensure that organizations around the world institute environmental controls and rely on them on a daily basis.

While regulations do not mandate business services to be available to clients and therefore do not require redundant systems in this light, they do dictate that personnel safeguards should be in place. The environmental controls in this case are regulated to ensure that the company's employees are not exposed to additional threats resulting from the use of such controls (e.g., fire-suppression systems using certain gases that are deadly to humans). In addition, mandates require a risk management process that considers both naturally occurring risks (hurricane, tornado, earthquake) and those initiated by humans (terrorist attacks, chemical spills). Principle 4 is supported by a richer set of publications given the independent development and maturity of environmental controls and sustainability. Each core control is broken down as done in prior chapters. (See Exhibit 12.1.)

Exhibit 12.1   Principle 4 Matrix

Principle 4: Sustaining Operations[a]

Highlighted Global Core IT Controls:

- Operations Resiliency
- Environmental

Operations Resiliency: Relevant and Complementary Publications

AICPA, Trust Services
BS 15000-1, 2002 IT Service Management—Part 1: Specification
BS 15000-2, 2003 IT Service Management, Code of Practice for Service Management
BCI, Good Practice Guidelines
Business Continuity Management Good Practice Guidelines, 2005
CMS, Information Security ARS, Version 2.0
CMS, Policy for the Information Security Program
COBIT 4.1, Control Objectives, Management Guidelines, Maturity Models, IT Governance Institute
Corporate Governance in The Netherlands 2002: The State of Affairs
Executive Order on Critical Infrastructure Protection in the Information Age, October 16, 2001
FDA, CFR, Title XXI, 1999
FERC, RM01-12-00, Appendix G, 2003
FFIEC, Business Continuity Planning
FFIEC, Development Acquisition
FIPS 191, Guideline for the Analysis of LAN Security
FISMA
GAO/AIMD-12.19.6, Federal Information System Controls Audit Manual
GLBA, Privacy of Financial Information

HIPAA

Interagency Paper on Sound Practices to Strengthen the Resilience of the U.S. Financial System, 2003

ISACA, IS Standards, Guidelines, and Procedures for Auditing and Control

ISO 17799:2000, Information Technology—Security Techniques—Code of Practice for Information Security Management

ISO 27001:2005, Information Technology—Security Techniques—Information Security Management Systems—Requirements

ISSA, GAISP

MAGERIT Version 2.0, 2005

NASD, Rules 3510, 3520

NERC, CIP-008-1 Incident Reporting and Response Planning

NERC, CIP-009-1 Recovery Plans for Critical Cyber Assets

NFPA 1600, Disaster/Emergency Management and Business Continuity, 2007 Edition

NIST, SP800-34, Contingency Planning Guide for Information Technology Systems

NYSE, Rule 446

OCC, Circular 235

OCC, Thrift Bulletin 30

PAS, 56 Guide to Business Continuity Management

SP800-53, Recommended Security Controls for Federal Information Systems

SP800-100, Information Security Handbook: A Guide for Managers

Texas Department of Information Resources, Practices for Protecting Information Resources Assets

Title III of the E-Government Act of 2002, PL 107-347, December 17, 2002

Environmental: Relevant and Complementary Publications

CMS, Information Security ARS, Version 2.0

CMS, Policy for the Information Security Program

COBIT 4.1, Control Objectives, Management Guidelines, Maturity Models, IT Governance Institute

FISMA

GAO/AIMD-12.19.6, Federal Information System Controls Audit Manual

GLBA, Privacy of Financial Information

HIPAA

ISACA, IS Standards, Guidelines, and Procedures for Auditing and Control

ISO 17799:2000, Information Technology—Security Techniques—Code of Practice for Information Security Management

ISO 27001:2005, Information Technology—Security Techniques—Information Security Management Systems—Requirements

MAGERIT Version 2.0, 2005

NERC, CIP-006-1, Physical Security of Critical Cyber Assets

SP800-53, Recommended Security Controls for Federal Information Systems

Texas Department of Information Resources, Practices for Protecting Information Resources Assets

---

[a]See the acronym list for explanations of all acronyms.

ENDNOTES

1. NIST Special Publication 800-34, *Contingency Planning Guide for Information Technology (June 2002)*. URL: http://csrc.nist.gov/publications/nistpubs/800-34/sp800-34.pdf.

2. Andrew Waite and Andrew J. Waite, *A Practical Guide to Call Center Technology* (New York: CMP Books, 2001), 220.

3. K. H. Spencer Pickett, *The Internal Auditing Handbook* (New York: John Wiley & Sons, 1997), 473.

4. Atiba D. Adams and Michael R. Finley, "Bone Up on Backup," *LegalTimes*, vol. 26, March 10, 2003: "Sanctions for failing to preserve and produce data from backup tapes have ranged from monetary penalties to adverse jury instructions and judgment on the merits." ALM Properties Inc.

5. C. Guelke, "A Strategic Approach to Disaster Preparedness," *Proceedings, Engineering Management Conference, 2005 IEEE International* 2, September 11–13, 2005, 745–750.

13

Principle 5: Security and Assurance

Key Topics Addressed in This Chapter

Risk intelligence

Technology-secure platforms and networks

Validation and performance

OVERVIEW

The final principle identified from analyzing the world's regulations is security and assurance. Control and safeguards are not the sole responsibility or duty of the technology security department. In fact, the current model has dispersed such controls across many different management divisions. The security of the environment does ensure that the technical controls and systems processing data occur as expected, and that they provide a supportive and transactional role.

By understanding the threats faced by an organization, you have a way to balance the appropriate level of security with the cost to address them. The discovery and measurement is done through a risk analysis exercise that includes appropriate business managers in working sessions and survey methods described in Chapter 8.

The computing platform may consist of any piece of hardware or virtualized hardware environment that provides the base on which the developed or purchased software runs. The platform does not include the infrastructure that establishes the channel of communications; instead on the integrity of the processing platform. The governance program must include all administrative procedures established to ensure that all computing platforms operate efficiently and as expected in all situations. These safeguards must be resistant to malicious behavior and accidental processing errors. Through the introduction of a trusted platform an organization may place confidence in the technical controls and the data produced by these systems.

The integrity of the communication channels is critical to ensure that the data processed locally or remotely are completed as expected. The communication backbone of an organization is pivotal to supporting the processing and delivery of such information. The channels of communication have increased in importance as organizations distribute offices, business functions, and computing centers around the world. Confidence that the information remains intact and unaltered is paramount in order to trust the data inputs and outputs of the computing environment, and requires significant risk awareness, given the lack of trusted environments throughout the public Internet.

Organizations must continually monitor the progress and activities of the transactional application processes, the actors within the environment, and the controls themselves. This monitoring ensures that performance is improved operationally and that all functions occur as expected.

An incident response group also must exist in every organization. This team should encompass a cross-divisional and regional group that is both trained and prepared to address any type of negative event. A hierarchy regarding the appropriate response relating to the data and negative event must be established. Plans must be in place prior to any type of event and should be reviewed and accepted by the management annually.

The security and assurance of the organization is paramount for the proper processing and delivery of services. The use of information technology (IT) security raises the controls and effectiveness to a reasonable level of assurance. The global core IT controls that are highlighted within this principle include:

- Risk awareness
- Trusted computing platform
- Trusted communication and networks
- Monitoring and performance reviews
- Incident response capability

RISK AWARENESS

Being cognizant of the risks an organization faces physically, logically, and naturally is key to properly structuring a control environment that is both responsive and effective. While every organization is exposed to risks from multiple sources, most organizations practice an informal method of responding to and addressing risks. An operational hands-on approach was very effective when organizations had centralized systems due to proximity. Department and subject matter experts could be fully aware of the possible threats to the organization and have confidence in the risk management procedures in place. This reliance on proximity has become a liability as organizations expand globally, embrace virtualization across the enterprise, and leverage grid computing environments from such vendors as IBM and Sun.

As a result of this expansion, organizations have begun to seek mature methods of managing the risks they face in a more complete fashion. At some level, every organization has practiced risk management across the enterprise, as every process and procedure serves to mitigate a known risk. Management of risk benefits the organization through the development of a holistic, conscious, and systematic approach to managing risk. Enterprise risk management (ERM), the most familiar term for such a program, is an integrated and holistic approach to managing risks from the strategic perspective. Such a risk awareness program must achieve several milestones to address the risks faced by the global enterprise in an appropriate manner.

Companies around the world are recognizing the importance of discovering and managing these risks throughout the organization. Industry regulation groups and government legislation are beginning to recommend such self-evaluations. In addition, the value of understanding and managing risks is also becoming a weighted measurement used by Standard & Poor's (S&P) and others in their credit ratings.[1] In fact, companies with ERM programs in place receive a higher rating than those without them. When a single credit rating notch can mean billions of dollars in interest payments, the return on an ERM program is easy to see.

Business Impacts

Organizations that employ a risk awareness process create a culture in which the whole control environment embraces the strategy and the aggressiveness of the organization. The ability of the organization to compete effectively in the market reflects its ability to manage the risks it faces daily. An organization can sustain a negative event due to a lack of safeguards, or debilitate itself with burdensome controls that affect its ability to compete. A balance must be promoted and achieved that supports the organization as a whole consistently and confidently.

Organizations that do not fully understand the risks experience greater numbers of emergencies that result in projects being sidelined, staff working extra hours, and general failure to execute. According to some studies, technology projects fail 70% of the time, and these include everything from small divisional projects to enterprise-wide customer relationship management (CRM) initiatives.[2] An imbalance in the placement of controls of an organization results in strong controls being placed in certain areas and few in others. The result is extra expense and a complete failure to protect the assets that matter to the organization.

Financial impacts to the organization may come from higher operating costs due to excess controls and staffing. In addition, the organization is likely incur expenses such as being fined or penalized for not appearing risk-aware to credit agencies, regulatory bodies, and deep supply chain partners. Fines may result from breaches or negative events that occur to systems that were not properly protected: this negates the expense of the controls and introduces additional fees that may be applied in the future.

Application

The foundation of a strong ERM program is the inclusion of upper management, the risk management department, and the business owners. The process, as suggested in Chapter 8 and by industry luminaries such as Paul Sobel,[3] must be clearly defined and should establish the risk appetite of the organization, risk mitigation strategies, residual risk transfers, reporting, and continual management moving forward. In order to determine the risk appetite, the organization must be aware of the risks that may impact it internally and externally. This risk universe, or risk population, is the complete set of risks that face the organization based on trends, prior company data, and industry information. Parties from many levels of the company should be involved in the development of this risk population to ensure a complete accounting of all possible risks. The company should consider the impact each risk may cause independently and the net risk should more than one event occur simultaneously. The enterprise may rate each risk based on its relevance to the business and the ability of the enterprise to isolate the threats posed by each risk.

Based on the identified risk universe, the organization then determines its risk appetite through input from senior management, the board, and the business owners. Tolerance levels must be defined for a period of time that takes into account the loss of funds, functions, or the ability to deliver services to the market. The time period may be a year or reflect the existing schedule of strategy sessions. The tolerance levels may be different for each party, or parties may defer to those more closely involved with specific business functions. The team collects this information and averages the data together applying a weighted confidence method in order to determine the tolerance levels. The team must prioritize the concerns of all parties in a clear and logical way that does not diminish the concerns of any party. The tolerance levels must be defined based on fixed measures that reflect the nature of the business, and may include such items as budgets, regional revenue, or other financial measures.

Risk tolerances provide a measure that allows the project team to compare the current state of the organization to the target risk tolerance levels. Doing this helps the team to identify any excesses or deficiencies. This routine process of resetting risk tolerances must become embedded with the organization's strategy and corporate culture to ensure regular adjustments, as the business and market shift.

Upon identifying the risk universe and prioritizing the risks according to the company's strategic direction, the next step is to assess the risks themselves. Doing this involves determining the frequency of loss events, which may be scored simply as low, medium, or high. The severity of the impacts should be determined, which again may be scored as low, medium, or high, and finally the net effect of impact from risks should be assessed. Initially the values of these items may be assessed through roundtable discussions, one-on-one interviews, surveys, and historic data. Some data will be provided by authoritative sources and others may be provided by subjective observations. The team should consider a confidence value when assigning impact and frequency values. The team should determine this confidence value prior to collecting information. Confidence values provide the team with a mechanism to rate the quality of information received. These values allow a greater spread of information sources that may contribute to the final valuations. The product of the confidence values and the risk scores provides a weighted average calculation that ensures a balanced evaluation to ensure that a single source does not drive the whole evaluation.

The final weight-adjusted values should be brought together in a usable matrix that combines the data and considers both the thresholds and the result of calculating the frequency, impact, and confidence values. This information will demonstrate the ideal operational areas for the organization and provide a more strategic direction with regard to its risk controls. Finally, the team should perform an application gap analysis that compares the defined target risk values against the current control posture. The team does this using the completed risk matrix and evaluating the control safeguards in place. This evaluation should produce a current state report that indicates whether controls are below, above, or in line with the risk tolerance levels. In addition, it will identify whether further risk mitigation techniques are needed and, depending on the variance, whether risk transfer or avoidance is appropriate.

Upon completion of this process, the organization will continue operations for a period of time—months, quarters, years—before it conducts another thorough risk evaluation. During this period between evaluation efforts, the organization maintains the controls in order to manage the risks it faces. Monitoring and audit should occur regularly throughout the organization on an ongoing basis. This monitoring should capture the success of the implemented controls, their effectiveness, and the integrity of the applications. By auditing the control periodically against the risks, the organization should also detect whether the controls truly are mitigating the risks they target. All reports should be condensed and submitted to the executive sponsor on a regular basis. Any exceptions within the control environment or deficiencies should be highlighted and corrective action recommended.

In Practice

Implementing a risk awareness process throughout the organization requires coordination and support at the top, plus resources to ensure continuous monitoring. These 10 steps provide guidance to organizations seeking such a process:

Step 1. Enlist executive sponsorship (board member, executive).

Step 2. Demonstrate value for the process.

    a. Stress the importance of enabling senior management to monitor risk.

    b. Create a formal process to deliver information to the sponsor and receive feedback.

Step 3. Establish a regular dialog with business owners to develop risk tolerances and identify unknown risks.

    a. Explain ERM as a process to business owners.

    b. Develop a process to provide data to the business owners related to their business lines, the identified risks, and measurements against defined risk tolerances.

    c. Develop business value reports demonstrating the return the business owners experience throughout the process.

Step 4. Determine the risks facing the organization and collect data for analysis.

    a. Interview stakeholders and evaluate historical data.

    b. Utilize internal documents, data feeds from third parties, risks and vulnerabilities from the technology group, and any contractual risk thresholds established in contracts or regional laws.

    c. Produce a matrix with the values and risks identified and present it to all participants for acceptance, comments, or requests for more information.

    d. The review process should be cooperative in nature.

    e. Determine tolerance levels, risks, frequencies, impacts, and confidence levels.

Step 5. Evaluate the sources and risks to the organization and create a process to capture data for measurement.

    a. Capture data that indicate the posture of the control environment.

    b. Compare data against the accepted risk tolerance levels.

    c. Establish a plan to mitigate risks through risk management methods.

d. Address risks and refine controls to meet the required level of toler-ance throughout the organization.

e. Establish an ongoing monitor and audit process to ensure the organization operates within defined thresholds, and exceptions are communicated to the appropriate party.

Step 6. Establish an escalation process throughout the control environment to ensure transparency in the process.

Step 7. Define frequency and assign responsibilities for validation of controls throughout the environment.

Step 8. Develop reports that can be made available to the sponsor, the man-agement team, internal audit, risk management, and the independent auditors on request.

Step 9. Assign job performance metrics to the ERM tolerance levels.

Step 10. Schedule updates to ERM in conjunction with strategic objective set-ting by the executive team.

TRUSTED COMPUTING PLATFORM/SYSTEM CONTROLS

Trust established within the control environment is assured by constraints applied from the system on the user environment and on the system itself. Such constraints provide the administrator, user, management, and auditor with confidence to rely on the transactions of the environment. Systems within the organization provide several functional services, including stor-ing information, processing information, or transmitting it to be processed further. These simple foundational services highlight how systems interact across vast distances, and reinforce the business necessity for a structure in which to assess the wider universe of business technology. A primary con-cern of system users and business stakeholders who depend on the accuracy of the computing results is that the integrity and reliability of these systems are dependable.

The storage of data within systems, whether these are enterprise data-base solutions or simple flat files, is integral to the long-term viability of the systems and applications involved in the business operations. Providing assurances that the data captured within, for instance, the general ledger are the same data as provided during the previous time frame allows for confidence in accounting for the cash flows of the organization. The lack of integrity regarding information storage brings into question, in this exam-ple, the organization's ability to forecast financials and can allow damaging frauds to be perpetuated.

Stored data may be attacked by crackers (malicious individuals who are seeking to inflict damages or steal data for profit) who can leverage malicious software to include viruses, worms, and web-based attacks. These attacks leverage user or system account permissions; the integrity-monitoring system would catalog an authorized person's making changes. Implementing network- and system-level safeguards, such as antivirus programs, provides a level of protection. Given the speed with which online attacks occur, it is best to institute behavioral and cultural policies to limit the possibility and degree of such impacts.

No system operates in a vacuum. Although the era of centralized computing is beginning to creep back into organizations, as is evident in the widespread adoption of virtual data centers and the thin client approach promoted by Google and other web-based companies, the need to transmit information across systems remains a priority of every organization. This is especially true given the wide adoption of virtual networks set up between business process outsourcing (BPO) and other providers that manage data around the world. Organizations need to ensure that the transmission of the information occurs in a manner that protects its integrity and in most cases its confidentiality. In addition, the administration of these virtual platforms must be considered.

Business Impacts

Not being able to trust the data within our electronic databanks is a scary proposition. A simple power outage demonstrates the great importance organizations place on these systems. Such an event shows the extent to which the organization's productivity relies on technology. When the data processing services of an organization are no longer trusted, it loses productivity and customers, and service agreements are broken.

The costs can be calculated in many ways. One way is simply to measure the cost of restating earnings for a period of time, as was done by thousands of companies after the institution of the Sarbanes-Oxley Act (SOX) in the United States. What is the cost of losing a contract with Dell, for example, due to misunderstanding the number of processors required for a specific delivery date? Such manufacturers or retailers in the competitive marketplace do not tolerate mistakes of that nature, no matter the reason for the confusion. Another approach would be the cost in person-hours to rebuild systems from a backup.

The impacts to the business can be clearly determined in monetary values and the long-term viability of the organization. The impacts defined and their financial values exclude the organization's duty to regulatory and oversight bodies. Nor does the loss of trust in system integrity describe the impacts to goodwill or quality of life that can occur to the organization's stakeholders, employees, and customers. The social effects can be extreme if the information systems (instead of processing impersonal items) were determining the correct dosages of medicine for critically ill patients, for example. The need for integrity and trust within the operations of a system is absolute. The impacts on greater areas of the business and technology environment illustrates the importance of even a single system operator.

Application

Ensuring the integrity of the operations within an environment has many facets, and the specific approaches are unique to every organization. The ability to evaluate an organization's control environment should be established and maintained internally. As the organization itself is able to control, measure, and respond to incident cases throughout the year, a more balanced and measured approach is possible. In addition, the organization able to fully address the risks and reduce the impacts of some of them has a better strategic position in an ever-expanding and electronically hostile world.

Specifically, an organization may consider instituting a system that provides information of the technology management team regarding threats to and known vulnerabilities of systems found within the organization. This vulnerability management system should be incorporated with the help desk ticketing systems and allow for cross-references to identify trends within the organization. Such a system should encompass at least a patch, vulnerability, and baseline configuration management focus.

Timely receipt of information and validation are prudent controls to actively manage a technology environment. Data services should be acquired that communicate vulnerabilities and industry threats to the business. This simplifies the capture of such information and ensures that a lapse does not occur. These services are freely available online, included in a maintenance fee from vendors, and a pure third pay service. Notification identifies known threats, but not configuration or unique vulnerabilities. To address these risks a third-party regular assessment is worthwhile. These should evaluate all critical systems at least annually, and more regularly as they change in the environment.

The establishment of integrity checking on systems ensures notification of changes but does not in most cases prevent such changes. Organizations should enforce directory- or file system–level restrictions on systems to restrict access to managed administrative accounts. Doing this ensures that systems are protected from accidental modification. An extension of restricting access to systems would be to leverage the intelligence identified under Principle 1 and limit the amount of information that requires such restrictions in the first place. Doing this would entail reducing the amount of data that service providers are delivering to the corporate systems and that are being transmitted to other providers from the corporate systems. A simple vetting of this information and then application of restrictive controls ensures that safeguards are in place where necessary.

Stored data are susceptible to modifications that are both authorized and unauthorized. Some form of integrity monitoring system, a logging solution, or a malicious code detection and prevention system can identify such modifications on the network or hosts. The wire monitoring should consider the source, context of data, and requested actions. Through the establishment of policies the system can report to or act on the behalf of the company when violations or anomalies occur.

Intentional attackers can utilize the Internet to launch malicious code at an organization and its systems. These attacks can occur over open or insecure company wireless access points, or via Internet attacks. The software utilized in these attacks subverts the safeguards on the systems of the company, and provides a beachhead for the attacker to further exploit the environment. These attacks leverage internal user permissions, human behavior, and poor security configurations. The attacks, in some cases, can exploit the company desktop web browser and use it to steal company information.[4] Establishing a proper policy, as described in Chapter 9, and through security awareness the organization may limit the success of these types of attacks. Additional safeguards can be deployed to restrict access through user privileges and network segmentation that can also minimize these impacts.

Organizations seeking to reach a reasonable level of assurance on Internet communications and transmitted files may rely on encryption solutions. The use of encrypted tunnels that rely on certificates and PKI can provide assurances that the data passing through the channel are both unmodified in transit and kept confidential. Beyond the establishment of such communication channels, organizations utilize hashing techniques. Hashing creates a fixed string of characters that represent a one-way computation of the source file. These values are unique to the files themselves, and provide a mechanism for the receiving party to trust the integrity of the file—so long as the hashes match. These two methods provide assurances that the data passed between the parties are correct and accurate.

In Practice

System software controls include:

- Deploy systems without the default configurations, usernames, and access settings.
- All unauthorized attempts at accessing the system must be detected, captured, reviewed, and addressed.
- Establish a monitoring process that identifies flaws in the software platforms, and may include inputs from:

- End-user support/feedback tickets

- Vendor/third-party security feeds (example: BugTraq)

- Security assessment results: in-house or third party

- Incident response reports

- Continuous monitoring systems

- Log aggregators identifying errors in processing

- Establish a central management process for collecting and distributing updates automatically.

- Maintain an accurate accounting of the information systems, patch levels, and the progress of any remediation efforts.

- Deploy automated solutions that monitor and report unauthorized modifications of protected or restricted-access files on a system utilizing integrity-checking technologies.

TRUSTED COMMUNICATIONS AND NETWORK

The world has become dependent on the ability to communicate in near-real time. The ubiquity of high-speed network connections and always-connected systems has enabled businesses to reach beyond their core facilities for processing, expertise, and partnerships. Industry research groups project that 75% of the United States will be online using high speed by 2011.[5] Even the smallest of operations have networked their computer systems, fax machines, copiers, and phone systems together to lower costs and extend features. The explosion of wireless networks that span entire geographical regions and continents expands the remoteness of associates and extends the sensitive information of the organization to well beyond its walls. The richness of the data is growing for organizations through collaboration across associates and partners. The utilization of virtual computing centers and grid computing also is growing; these functions disperse the processing operations of a single organization across hundreds and even thousands of systems shared by many different organizations.

The ability to reach beyond the defined walls of an organization enables it to access resources to which they would normally not have access—for example, small organizations are able to rent time on supercomputers or collaborate online with the top minds of an industry at only a fraction of the usual cost. Today it is not enough merely to be networked within the global marketplace; only an evolution of the networked environment that leverages global knowledge systems will deliver a marked advantage to companies. This evolution involves expanding business operations and enhancing existing business processes to take advantage of extended computing power, large pools of human capital, and efficiencies gained through more integrated computing systems. As with any major business decision, the organization must weigh the costs and benefits of reaching beyond the confines of the physical walls to rely on environments that it does not own.

An organization's architecture includes the traditional wired network environment that is the backbone of the operation. This wired architecture is manageable using existing methods due to the fact that network traffic can travel only where the physical cables are placed and not farther. (Although scientific research has demonstrated that the noise from cables can be interpreted, such a threat is reserved more for government agencies, secret agents, and heavily funded criminal organizations and is far beyond that to which most organizations are subject.) Organizations employ physical separations in a wired environment, or logical access control restrictions. Wireless architectures must be deployed with consideration for the information transmitting from the host system (i.e., when laptops are in the field and using hotspots) and the office configurations that allow guests and associates to access the network.

Interconnecting networks that result from BPO agreements, extended virtual networks, or the commission of grid computing introduce a level of complexity that the organization must consider. These relationships generally depend on other systems, networks, controls, people, and control environments specifically to protect the integrity, confidentiality, and availability of the services required. The lack of ownership by the originating corporation creates a method to define more carefully the data that are being shared and a way to ensure that the originating corporation's control needs are addressed completely. Given that the originating corporation does not own the systems and must expect additional customers of the BPO to utilize those systems (customers who may include competitors), an adaptive approach to refining and evaluating controls is necessary.

Control assurances may be established through both technical and procedural requirements regardless of who owns the asset. Organizations must consider the contractual agreements established between BPO and other third-party service providers. It is in the best interest of both parties that beyond a standard agreement on performance metrics, an agreement on safeguards and control structures also is in place beyond a standard SAS 70 report. Specifically the organization may consider creating a vendor audit program that mirrors the principles and control tests of its own attestation reports.

Technical safeguards may include the deployment of security monitoring tools, robust authentication, and network attack prevention systems. Procedural enhancements may establish escalation procedures and breach notification activities. The substance of such agreements and audit programs should relate to the needs of the originating corporation and focus on the subject without requiring burdensome controls on the organizations providing the services.

Business Impacts

The ability to communicate depends on the availability of the parties, the reliability of the received messages, and assurance of confidentiality when required, such as when communicating competitive or sensitive information. The organization's network and communication systems transfer valuable and highly sensitive information of the company. As organizations expand and further integrate with vendors, their information becomes more accessible. Controls must exist to ensure the integrity of the information and that all departments, partners, BPO organizations, and other third-party service providers maintain safeguards to validate the integrity. The establishment of controls that limit access and obfuscate information limits the threat exposure of sensitive information results in fines, civil lawsuits, and competitive disadvantages.

By utilizing external service providers, the organization may inadvertently have exposed data to competitors in the marketplace and have had research and other information stolen. The impact of an exposure is equal to the criticality of the data involved; therefore management and monitoring of the information in transit, the safeguards in place, and careful review of third-party relationships are important for IP and sensitive information.

Application

Organizations can establish greater trust in the networked environments through better awareness of the traffic, content, and users of the systems. Restricting the data throughout the network limits the possibility and impact of breaches, Trojans, virus attacks, and worms within the organization. In addition, the proper segmentation of networks and limiting of traffic between groups and segments limits the capability of these threats to impact the entire enterprise. Networks should be segmented at a functional level that considers operations and user roles. This process should include business owner input on the proper association of roles to operations. This linkage then can be logically applied to the infrastructure, and a network segmentation effort can be completed. Then a secondary effort to restrict access by service level should be conducted, using a similar input process from business owners and managers. By limiting inbound and outbound traffic to all devices, the organization will gain a superior advantage against malicious attackers from any front, internal or external.

The wireless network must be treated as an untrusted network. This architecture is designed to place all wireless users on a segmented network that is separate from the general corporate assets. Organizations require users of the wireless medium to authenticate and connect to the corporate assets as if they were connecting as remote users; an encrypted tunnel and generally two-factor authentication are required. Wireless networks may include 802.11, Bluetooth, cellular, microwave, or even satellite.

It is important to verify that segmentation and the enforcement of device-, service-, and user-level controls throughout the network is done at all points where sensitive data are processed. This segmentation may be further enhanced through the implementation of network-level preventive and detective controls.

Organizations should employ preventive systems wherever possible and employ detective solutions only as a secondary measure to provide automated alerts through triggers to a security group. Preventive solutions include network intrusion prevention systems and the deployment of malicious software controls. Intrusion prevention technology is designed to remove harmful traffic from a network without human intervention, thereby eliminating any threats in real time. Malicious software controls include antivirus, spam, and malware applications that strip harmful messages and traffic prior to reaching the targeted host. Malicious software controls should be installed on all workstations and systems that allow connections to these systems. A company policy and specific network access rules will be necessary to ensure that end users utilize the protected systems and do not bypass the controls through third-party mailing systems, such as Gmail.

Despite the proper placement of network security applications and a fully communicated policy on acceptable use on the network, additional network-level controls are advised. Behavioral signatures are unique to an organization, but sophisticated anomaly detection may be employed to identify unusual network traffic. These anomalies are identified through the deployment of intelligent network trending systems or through a system that aggregates the data of long periods of traffic. Anomalies may consist of surges of traffic in the middle of the night for an organization that operates no after-hour batches. This example may not be an anomaly for an organization that runs full-system backups; the resulting traffic may be from the backups. Other anomalies may consist of large database queries, continuous traffic from specific hosts, large amounts of DNS queries to destinations that are out of the usual traffic, or unusual activity of remote users at odd hours. Interestingly, such anomaly detections can also identify malicious malware activity or peer-to-peer networks based on networking patterns, and may be used to locate and eliminate such instances.

In order to detect anomalies, the organization must employ some form of behavioral or content monitoring system that is able to identify and present the information for analysis. As stated, one organization's anomalies may be another's usual traffic. Therefore, it is important to investigate all abnormalities fully prior to taking any restrictive action. The types of anomalies may indicate specific threats or attacks to the organization. Some examples of anomalies and their causes follow.

- *Large database queries.* An internal employee's user account was compromised, and thieves were pulling all customer records and reselling them.

- *Continuous traffic from specific hosts.* After opening e-mail with malware, the user's system opened a port 6667 or 31337 encrypted tunnel to a hacker's system.

- *Large amounts of DNS queries to destinations that are outside of the usual traffic.* An internal user configured an SSH tunnel through DNS packets to bypass the network security safeguards.

- *Unusual activity of remote users at odd hours.* User accounts were compromised, and a hacker entered the system after hours to avoid a user-account-busy error.

Safeguards in environments where the organization does not own the systems, such as grid computing, should initially include a vendor agreement that defines the performance levels expected by both organizations. It should also include a right to audit by the company and establish a defined set of principles the organization must comply with at all times, including data privacy management, data security procedures, breach notification procedures, and disaster recovery facilities. These principles generally state that the organization will practice and adhere to the same controls and safeguards as the company does itself (e.g., *Treat my data as I treat my data*). The type of safeguards implemented depends on the data classification. Such data management allows the organization to specify the level of security required by third-party providers and even determine whether the data are processed by third parties or split between several providers to ensure all the data are never exposed at once.

Safeguards surrounding the virtual assets of an organization must be deployed beyond that which exists on the general hardware and software of an organization. These safeguards must address the host-and-guest operating system relationship and third-party middleware. In addition, a host of additional granularity and management is possible on virtual systems given their operation within a controlled environment.

The organization should establish an automated system that determines the performance of third parties against service-level agreements and presents an annual report on the status of the safeguards placed, as required by the vendor audit guidelines. The results of these regular measurements should be made available to management and be included in the enterprise risk management (ERM), business impact assessment (BIA), and data classification strategy sessions.

In Practice

Virtual/grid computing[6]/vendor audit control requirements include:

- Integrated policies and procedures address the account management found on the administrative, host (master), and virtual systems.

- Controls are in place to evaluate system and user permissions (regression testing) after modifications are made to the environment.

- All accounts with access to company data are centrally managed, reviewed, regularly reapproved, and audited.

- Least-privilege and separation-of-duties practices are applied to all accounts.

- Security settings are active (including identification with LDAP/directory linkups) and default profiles are removed.

- Architecture encrypts files and transmissions of data between points.

In Practice

Network security controls include:

- Maintain a clear description of the security attributes of all network services and protocols used by the organization.

- Perimeter firewall (ACL) devices should be configured to deny connections from all known and untrusted networks, countries, and organizations.

- VPN uses encrypted tunnels to ensure the privacy and integrity of the data passing over the public network.

- A published, vetted, and accepted standard encryption is used to protect the confidentiality of sensitive or critical information.

- A well-defined policy on the use of network services exists.

- Authorization and approvals are regularly provided by management for network services and access to end users.

- External access provider contracts include consideration of security responsibilities and procedures.

- Verify network security is adequately addressed by authorizing and monitoring:

  ○ System interconnections

- ○ Protocols and services on devices connected to the network
- ○ System and event logs for suspicious, unauthorized, and illegal behavior
- ○ Analyzing data and customer support requests for patterns and trends
- Evaluate controls over the management of remote equipment.
- Confirm that network and communication controls appropriately mediate access between security domains:
  - ○ Consider security device topology and architecture.
  - ○ Types of firewall (ACL) devices utilized (packet filter, stateful, application, behavioral, signature).
  - ○ Physical placement of components.
  - ○ Placement and monitoring of network monitoring and protection devices, including intrusion detection system (IDS) and intrusion prevention system (IPS) functionality.
  - ○ Determine whether appropriate controls exist over the confidentiality and integrity of data transmitted over the network (e.g., encryption, parity checks, message authentication).
- Ensure remote access devices and network access points for remote equipment are appropriately controlled.
  - ○ Remote access requires management authorization.
  - ○ Additional management authorization is required for all users who access, manage, or transport sensitive data remotely.
  - ○ Authentication is of appropriate strength (e.g., two-factor for sensitive data sets).
  - ○ Remote access devices are appropriately secured and controlled by the entity.
- An enterprise antivirus, spam, and malware solution should be deployed and be made available for all systems that support end-user computing. (Servers should have some form of malware protection, but the default desktop configuration may not be appropriate or available for some server platforms.)
  - ○ Systems automatically update the malware libraries and are distributed at regular intervals throughout the entire organization.

FIREWALL/ACCESS CONTROL BEST PRACTICES

☐ A firewall should exist. All Internet traffic inside to outside, and vice versa, must pass through it.

☐ A firewall exists and all network traffic to third parties and remote satellite facilities must pass through the device.

☐ Publicly accessible services and systems must not make sensitive information or information systems vulnerable to compromise.

☐ All network sessions transmitting sensitive information should use encryption when traveling beyond the established firewalls.

☐ The firewall will be configured to deny all services not expressly permitted and will be regularly audited and monitored to detect intrusions or misuse.

☐ Message notifications from the firewall and other access control devices shall be directed to a central logging system. Triggers notify the staff in real time when defined thresholds are exceeded.

☐ Firewalls should operate on dedicated hardware, and all superfluous services, software, editors, installation packages, and documentation files should be deleted or disabled.

☐ After a failure, all firewalls will fail to a secure configuration.

☐ Source routing will be disabled on all firewalls and external routers.

☐ The firewall will not accept traffic on its external interfaces that appears to be coming from internal network addresses.

☐ The firewall will provide detailed audit logs of all sessions. These logs will be reviewed for any anomalies.

☐ Firewalls will be tested offline and the proper configuration verified.

☐ Firewalls will be configured using Network Address Translation (NAT) and shall proxy all outbound services.

☐ Firewall documentation will be maintained on offline storage (digital permissible) at all times. Documentation should include: the network diagram, IP addresses of all network devices, IP addresses of routers, DNS servers, CCU, change control tickets, associated policy and procedure documents, and network policy security configurations.

☐ Configuration parameters such as packet filter rules will be up to date and reflect all configuration changes with attached management approvals.

☐ The firewall implementations must be part of the regular backup schedule to ensure immediate recovery to the most recent management-approved policy.

MONITORING AND PERFORMANCE REVIEWS

Organizations must evaluate the quality of a company's control environment over time and take action as necessary to ensure it continues to address risks and operational needs. The monitoring controls of an organization provide a closed-loop system that delivers feedback and regular updates regarding the policies, procedures, and technical controls deployed by management. The lack of such feedback prevents management from identifying inefficiencies and the means to address risks before they become significant.

The monitors placed throughout the control environment provide the necessary information to measure the existing controls and provide reports to management. The measurements are based on the risk tolerance thresholds determined by executive management. While the continuous measurement of all controls may not be achievable given the involvement of multiple parties, the organization should institute a program that provides feedback from all controls relative to their importance on a reasonable recurring schedule.

The performance of the information technology environments maintained internally and processed through third parties should be monitored. Such monitoring may be achieved through feedback based on customer service tickets, downtime, and comparisons against stipulated delivery windows. The internal audit department itself should also be evaluated by an outside party; this is recommended and a good practice encouraged by the Institute of Internal Auditors.[7] Beyond performance and the practices of the internal audit department, the organization must evaluate its ability to meet contractual and regulatory requirements. These evaluations should be done with the company's legal department to ensure that all mandates are identified and interpreted properly. The organization also should monitor the deployment of IT controls and their effectiveness. Although internal staff can perform part of this assessment, to be completely free of influence and bias, an independent third party should do this monitoring.

Logs and audit trails prove the accuracy and completeness of the data provided for the monitors. These logging events must provide sufficient transparency into the actions taking place within the organization's applications and business functions. Beyond transparency, these audit trails assure that actions taken are recorded and that accurate and appropriate corrective actions are taken in the future based on these records. Organizations must ensure that audit trails include their operating system, applications, and database stores to ensure that all access points to the data are monitored and sufficiently safeguarded. An additional value of a robust monitoring system is the ability to analyze historical data in the future to identify trends or to support a forensic investigation.

Business Impacts

While a monitoring function is meant to discover both deficiencies and excesses, lack of such a process results in the eventual decay of a control environment. Establishing a regular review process where the implementation, integration, and acceptance of controls are evaluated ensures that adjustments occur in a timely manner. Organizations that do not monitor have a higher likelihood of controls being overridden by both management and end users. This may be the result of a control that is not properly configured, given the needs of the business, or some more malicious intent of the parties involved.

Organizations that do not achieve contractual or regulatory compliance risk both penalties and loss of contracts. Some regulatory mandates are examined only in the event of a security breach, at which point it is obvious that the organization is lacking mandated controls and will accrue fines and penalties. Attributed damages as discussed before will also include contract cancellations, operating licenses may be revoked, or access to certain trade information may be limited.

Application

The organization may institute tactical monitoring and feedback procedures through simple staff rotations and management review of produced reports. It may also consider instituting independent reviews of technical findings of staff. The use of a feedback line (whistleblower hotline) is prudent to ensuring open communication without undue pressure. Such feedback lines should be advertised as valuable ways to disclose unethical behavior as well as information regarding the controls in place throughout the organization and their effectiveness.

A wealth of information is available to the organization through the company technical support lines where employees report system-level problems and availability issues. In addition to the data captured in these support ticketing systems, when security and network anomalies are compared, they provide greater information regarding the performance and effectiveness of the control environment itself. These data sometimes are lost through the use of BPO contracts, so it is necessary to ensure that a feedback loop is included in any contracts.

Logging systems must be established on all technical and environmental assets and controls. The output of these systems should be sufficient to provide forensic and troubleshooting teams enough evidence to develop the correct conclusions. The level of monitoring will vary on devices, but information such as the time, user account, command, and any content returned are normal attributes to include. The logs should be centralized in a system that is itself protected from the organization administrators. This system should protect the data it receives from modification by any party and provide evidence to support the integrity of the logs themselves. Most solutions today produce an encrypted hash of the time periods and can verify whether data logs were modified. The retention of logs is critical, as inappropriate rotation and destruction of backup logs may eliminate any ability to recover or investigate any situations. The retention period on all data elements should be determined based on data classification and legal requirements; however, organizations should consider a backup retention period that at least allows a full recovery of all important systems for 12 months.

Facility visits are a key way to ensure that organizations both fully communicate the seriousness of controls throughout the enterprise and validate their institution. Periodic site visits should determine whether procedures are followed as intended. Outsourced facility centers and partners that handle sensitive systems also should be visited. Each visit should focus on the primary controls in place at the organization.

All reports should be submitted to management and eventually to the executive sponsor charged with the control environment. Irregularities discovered during monitoring and site visits should be highlighted with the cause of the event specified. Corrective action should be implemented as quickly as possible. The lack of solid controls for whatever reason places the entire control environment at risk.

Every three years the organization should conduct a quality audit of the internal audit function. This cooperative engagement is meant to improve the organization's ability to manage risks and the control environment. Final reports should be made available to both the chief audit executive and the senior management team.

A third-party organization may be needed to assess the effectiveness of the organization's technical controls against any defined risks. These technical engagements should be done from both outside the network and inside, to determine the level of vulnerability that exists from authorized individuals and external attackers. Such engagements may include network vulnerability assessments, web application assessments, database assessments, penetration tests, wardialing (phoneline assessments), wardriving (wireless assessments), social engineering, and physical penetration assessments. Such technical engagements are beneficial in their ability to determine the organization's capacity for current threats and whether secondary and compensating controls are sufficient, given the threats and the criticality of the data and environment.

Addressing risks is successful only when the parties tasked with instituting controls are aware of all the requirements and threats to the organization. The internal audit team should routinely examine governmental and industry requirements placed on the organization to determine if all required compliance needs are addressed. The legal department and the risk department should work together to identify all mandates and report any new findings to management.

All deficiencies and exceptions discovered during the controls evaluation must be responded to. If there are instances of policy and control violations, the organization must enforce the defined penalties. Such follow-through is critical for ensuring that future negative events do not occur. It also demonstrates to future auditors and regulatory bodies that the organization swiftly and consistently addressed any control weaknesses once discovered.

Once considered and measured, all monitoring and feedback loops should be specified in a report to the directors of the organization from the sponsor of the team. This report should be used to determine the adequacy of all controls and any necessary adjustments.

In Practice

Leading practices to maintain monitoring and assurance controls:

- Automated technologies are employed that continuously assess the security configurations and posture of critical areas throughout the environment, and report these in real time to the proper individuals.

- Indicators of performance for systems, applications, and services provided by third parties should be identified by management and agreed on by all parties.

- Once the target threshold is determined, it should be examined at least semiannually.

- Compliance within thresholds should be examined quarterly or more often based on the criticality and sensitivity of systems and data involved.

- Performance reports must be published and made available to management in a timely fashion. The reports may include these metrics:

  ○ System and application usage.

  ○ Network and services availability: response time, connect times.

  ○ Fault and error notices.

  ○ Staff should be rotated in duties on a regular basis.

  ○ Third-party technical reviews should occur regularly.

  ○ The effectiveness of whistleblower programs should be determined based on call volume, closure rate, and satisfaction surveys.

  ○ Third-party service-level agreement performance measurement, review, and action: failure to meet contractual agreements must be addressed in a timely fashion.

  ○ Quality audit evaluation should occur every three years for the internal audit department.

INCIDENT RESPONSE CAPABILITY

An incident response (IR) program enhances the existing technology controls and procedures established throughout the control environment. Executive management determines the primary emphasis of an IR program: Should it focus on the restoration of services to a normal secure state utilizing a problem determination and resolution method, or conduct the recovery effort in a manner that may facilitate a legal forensic effort? A forensic investigation allows the organization to collect evidence and quarantine systems in a manner that is recommended by the governing legal systems. All evidence collected may be submitted into a legal proceeding.

The IR team should investigate all security incidents or suspected incidents. The goal of establishing an IR program and team is to ensure that the organization's assets are adequately monitored and protected. The level of response and the type of methods employed may depend on the data classification of the information. The incident response program is supported by the IDS, IPS, emergency response policies and procedures, and corporate policies.

Generally an incident response program contains methods of alerting the IR team, procedures for identifying the incident and the affected systems, a containment approach, corrective actions, and a follow-up analysis. The organization must consider local laws regarding any disclosures required for different types of sensitive information (depending on the nation and industry, these types may be government secrets or personally identifiable information), and should incorporate these communication requirements into the existing IR plan.

The value of an incident response program and its team lies in its ability to recover operations, maintain compliance with regulations, ensure the confidentiality of sensitive systems, and limit any potential damages to the organization. This ability has grown beyond the traditional technical drivers to understand and rectify system failures. Today an IR program is a business imperative enforced through domestic and international legislation. Privacy legislation and breach notification laws occur throughout the world, but terms—*breach, sensitive information, notification*—are not consistently defined. The United States alone has at least 34 separate mandates that address these areas uniquely. No matter the specific requirements of these laws, each requires the corporate entities to respond competently to each suspected incident. Laws relating to privacy and breach notification will proliferate, and it is prudent to leverage an existing IR program to address these compliance needs.

Business Impacts

An active and capable incident response program provides many benefits. A traditional benefit has been the ability of such a program to identify root causes of technical failures. These failures may be the result of poor change management testing or simply environmental impacts. The traditional support in case of technical failures and the response tasks in most organizations are the responsibility of an in-house or outsourced technical support team; only exceptions to processing controls and possible security incidents are the responsibility of the IR team.

The ability to identify security situations limits the number of negative impacts on the organization. The length of time an intruder is in control of a system is directly proportional to the amount of damage that he or she may cause. Several levels of damage exist. The physical hardware and software that the intruder had access to must all be taken offline, and possibly preserved for use as evidence in a criminal prosecution. New hardware must be configured and deployed. In addition, degradation of services occurs due to downtime and operating on backup systems that may be several hours, days, or weeks old.

In addition to these costs, users may lose confidence in the integrity of an organization's control environment. Auditors rely on the fact that computing systems within the organization process data the same way reliably throughout the year; this fact allows for reduced sampling sizes and single-sample testing.

Application

The people in an organization provide the ingenuity and the strength to compete in a global marketplace. These same individuals have innate knowledge of the organization's systems, processes, and operational activities. As a result of this knowledge, these employees are able to isolate significant systems and are capable of recognizing anomalies in general activities.

Staff knowledge of significant systems allows the organization to employ specific monitoring solutions and enhanced controls where they are required. In an era in which employees may simply add dashboard widgets that indicate the health of e-commerce sites and provide database utilization data, everyone in an organization plays a part in protecting system integrity through active observations and being alert to anomalies. Management, through the receipt of executive-level reports and dashboards, further encourages an environment that is aware of the operational activity levels within the organization.

In order to support its natural ability to self-monitor, the organization must establish communication methods that inspire, encourage, and enable all employees to recognize unusual behavior. In addition to relying on associates recognizing anomalies, published thresholds and activity reports should be distributed to provide greater intelligence of situations. A method of response is necessary for each query by an associate to provide closure and to indicate each request is taken seriously. It is striking how many organizations have excellent feedback centers with staffed support personnel, online web forms, and anonymous whistleblower lines but fail to provide any form of response to the originator. If an organization fails to provide the proper positive encouragement, it is unlikely that users will continue to supply information.

The organization's response protocol must be communicated and fully understood throughout by everyone. This may include a sliding scale defining the type of response that is dependent on the type of information being stored on specific assets. For example, a system that contains highly sensitive information may require the assets to be switched off or disconnected from a network the instant an attack is detected. This is the approach the U.S. government took when a security attack was executed against the Office of the Secretary of Defense (OSD); in response, nearly 1,500 computers were disconnected.[8] Less sensitive data may be part of a process that continues to stay online to assist intelligence agencies to investigate the crime in progress without alerting the attackers. The organization should make it clear as to the manner in which any level of response is undertaken.

The entire company represents an organization's single best form of identifying and responding to threats. A dedicated IR group that is trained and capable of following through on these notifications must mirror the organization's unique characteristics. A team should be made up of individuals across the entire organization from all points of service and background. This breadth of culture, experience, and geographical reach provides the team with the ability to interact and respond to identified threats with flexibility, regardless of the department, system, or global location. The team does not necessarily have to be dedicated full time, but participation should be included in job descriptions, bonus structures, and career planning.

Automation is important to managing large expanses of systems and is especially vital to organizations that heavily leverage technology throughout the business. The greater the dependency on technology to handle ever-expanding portions of the business, the greater the need for additional technology to manage the business systems. The tools employed throughout the organization may span across all levels of complexity, from in-house–developed dashboard and filtering systems to enterprise collectors of system data that parse out events exceeding predefined thresholds. An organization should consider employing automated technology that, at least, automatically collects data, filters through information based on organization-specific custom settings (an industry default or vendor default configuration will not properly address the risks of your organization and will likely result in excessive alerts), notifies specified parties, and captures the result of any actions undertaken by the notified parties.

In Practice

Common controls include:

- Technical support, incident tickets, and user-feedback systems are in place and operational.

- Users are aware of and utilize support, incident tickets, and user-feedback systems to report availability, integrity, potential security breaches, and other issues without fear of negative penalty.

- The support teams have established procedures to escalate items that relate to potential breaches and availability issues.

- Automatic triggers exist and are operational within the feedback systems to alert the incident response group regarding potential breaches.

- Network activity is monitored, and anomalies are investigated and documented.

- Intrusion prevention and detection systems are employed on sensitive network segments.

- IPS/IDS are monitored, and alerts are responded to in a timely fashion.

- Aggregated system event and security logs are reviewed, and action is taken; automatic filters and triggers are ideal.

- Intrusion response procedures are reviewed by legal, risk management, and top management, and are approved by management prior to adoption.

- Performance, capacity, availability, and incidents are tracked and reported in regular IT group reports to management.

- Automated tools intercept intruder attempts to violate corporate policies.

- Develop, gain acceptance, and distribute security guidelines and machine lockdown procedures.

- In-house training is conducted with all businesses through workshops.

- Staff continually researches new security technologies, risks, and trends.

- The organization centrally aggregates the data and conducts analysis to identify enterprise-wide trends.

- Automatic thresholds are deployed to limit the negative exposure caused by malicious software in the environment (automatic segmentation of networks in a network access control scenario).

- The monitoring solutions fully evaluate bidirectional traffic to properly protect the organization.

COMPLIANCE

Information security controls are recognized around the world as an imperative for every organization that conducts business online or relies on digital networks. The absence of such controls exposes the business to unavailable assets and a high probability of sabotage. Beyond the imperative to have security controls to "keep the lights on," organizations must demonstrate confidence in the functions of the business that rely on these technology controls. As a result, many of the safeguards organizations adopt to be compliant are the same ones they need to be secure.

Unfortunately, there is no direct correlation between compliance and security; in fact, organizations that focus on being compliant, at the minimum level required by law, are not secure. Therefore, organizations must balance applying regulations with the risks of the business. This balance must achieve a reasonable level of compliance that addresses the business risks, and sufficiently safeguards the organization from security threats.

Risk Awareness

Establishing a risk-aware company, from the executive level on down, demonstrably reduces costs and enables the more precise placement of controls. Beyond operational benefits, many regulations throughout the world strongly advise organizations to have an enterprise risk program. In some regions the use and incorporation of such a program for all aspects of the business's control environment is mandated.

Trusted Computing Platform

Most countries require that organizations demonstrate adequate controls on systems and applications, as a means of supporting the automated control solutions implemented in them. Organizations that adhere to best practices and continuously monitor and respond to the systems may furthermore demonstrate effectiveness in the control environment and ensure a level of trust that third parties and the organization itself can rely.

Trusted Communications and Network

Integrity of communications and assurance of confidentiality for sensitive information resonates around the world's legal circles. While the laws differ on the definition of sensitive information, all state that it is the corporation's duty and responsibility to protect such information in a fair and appropriate fashion. The legal statutes are less concerned with the organization's corporate secrets. To governments, typically, "sensitive information" concerns citizens and national security issues.

Organizations must demonstrate compliance annually through on-site evaluations by government auditors and through third-party organizations.

In the event of a security breach, additional audits will be required, and possibly additional security safeguards. Regardless, the organization must maintain security on these communications to protect the information, to demonstrate sufficient controls during regular audits, and in the event of a security breach.

MONITORING AND PERFORMANCE REVIEWS

Industry and professional groups require reviews of both performance and activities by internal audit and other control environment components. While failure to comply with these may not result in a penalty or lost business, professionals within the organization will look poorly on those failures and may consider leaving to secure a more professional position.

General laws around the world do not emphasize the need to monitor the performance of organizations, but most do cite that the effectiveness of controls must be monitored and assessed at regular intervals. This focus on management attestation often includes ensuring that the technical safeguards are operating in a proper control environment. Therefore, organizations must consider the regulatory mandates regarding control effectiveness and ensure that a mechanism exists to report on such efforts.

INCIDENT RESPONSE CAPABILITY

The ability to detect, respond, and follow through on security infractions resulting from internal or external violation of corporate policies is of primary importance in many regulations. In addition to the ability of organizations to detect such events, the existing laws specify precisely what procedures must be followed as a result. Compliance requirements within both the United States and the European Union detail the type and method of notification to the owners of such data. Corporations have recently begun to contractually require all partners and vendors to include them in every notification, due to both the influence of government legislation and a need to satisfy internal stakeholders.

The scope and interpretation of how an organization manages security events are flexible through many regulations with a few specific exceptions. Organizations must establish a mechanism to identify breaches to company policy, and this mechanism should be applied to all sensitive data. In addition, a mechanism should exist to determine the extent of any such breach and that owners of any breached information are notified. Organizations should fully assess their ability to address such events and continue to support the activities necessary to be capable of responding; regular training for staff, cross-organizational teams, and executive buy-in with full communication to all parties is ideal. Exhibit 13.1 provides the most complete reference to international publications. The sheer amount of information produced on this single principle highlights the necessity for a methodical and diligent approach from design, develop, and through adoption. Practitioners should carefully review each reference, and develop an adoption process that fits the organization. The publications highlighted within the five principle chapters, and condensed into a single listing within the appendix, provide *a global reference guide* that will accelerate any organization that operates with the assistance of information technology.

Exhibit 13.1   Principle 5 Matrix

Principle 5: Security and Assurance[a]

Highlighted Global Core IT Controls

- Risk Awareness

- Trusted Computing Platform/Systems

- Trusted Communications and Network

- Monitoring and Performance Reviews

- Incident Response Capability

Risk Awareness: Relevant and Complementary Publications

12 CFR, Part 30, Appendix A, II (Operational and Managerial Standards), B
AICPA/CICA, Privacy Framework
AICPA SAS 94 (AU Section 319), Effect of Information Technology on the
Auditor's Consideration of Internal Control in a Financial Statement Audit
AS/NZS 4360—1999, Risk Management 1.3.32
Basel Capital Accord (Basel II)
Bill 198, Ontario, Canada, Keeping the Promise for a Strong Economy Act
(Budget Measures)
BS7799-3, Risk Management, ISO 27005
CERT, OCTAVE
CMS, Information Security ARS, Version 2.0
CMS, Information Security Business Risk Assessment Methodology, Version 2.1
CMS, Information Security Risk Assessment Methodology, Version 2.1
CMS, Policy for the Information Security Program
CMS, Reporting Standard for Information Security Testing, Version 4
COBIT 4.1, Control Objectives, Management Guidelines, Maturity Models, IT
Governance Institute
Corporate Governance in The Netherlands 2002: The State of Affairs
COSO, ERM Framework
COSO, Integrated Framework

Exhibit 13.1   (*Continued*)

EU 92/242/EC

EU95/46, Article 17 of the European Data Privacy Directive

EU 2002/58/EC, Directive on Privacy and Electronic Communications, Articles 4, 6

FIPS 191, Guideline for the Analysis of LAN Security

FIPS 199, Security Categorization of Federal Information

FISMA

GAO/AIMD-12.19.6, Federal Information System Controls Audit Manual

GLBA, Privacy of Financial Information

HIPAA

HKICPA, Internal Control and Risk Management—A Basic Framework

IIA, GTAG, Guide 3: Continuous Auditing: Implications for Assurance, Monitoring, and Risk Assessment

IIA, GTAG, Guide 5: Managing and Auditing Privacy Risks

IIA, GTAG, Guide 6: Managing and Auditing IT Vulnerabilities

IIA, GTAG, Guide 7: Information Technology Outsourcing

IIA, GTAG, Guide 8: Auditing Application Controls

ISACA, IS Standards, Guidelines, and Procedures for Auditing and Control

ISO 17799:2000, Information Technology—Security Techniques—Code of Practice for Information Security Management

ISO 27001:2005, Information Technology—Security Techniques—Information Security Management Systems—Requirements

ISO/IEC 13335-1:2004, Information Technology—Security Techniques—Management Information and Communications Technology Security

ISO/IEC 21827:2002, Information Technology—Systems Security Engineering—Capability Maturity Model (SSE-CMM), 2002

ISO/IEC TR 15443:2005, Information Technology—Security Techniques—A Framework for IT Security Assurance—Part 1: Overview and Framework, 2005

ISSA, GAISP

ITIL, Security Management

J-Sox, Financial Instruments and Exchange Law

MAGERIT Version 2.0, 2005

NERC, CIP-002-1, Critical Cyber Asset Identification

OCC 12, CFR 30, Safety and Soundness Standards

OECD, Guidelines for the Security of Information Systems and Networks: Towards a Culture of Security

PCI DSS v1.1, Payment Card Industry Data Security Standard Security Audit Procedures

SAS No. 109, Understanding the Entity and Its Environment and Assessing the Risks of Material Misstatement

SP800-30, Risk Management Guide for Information Technology Systems

SP800-33, Underlying Technical Models for Information Technology Security

SP800-53, Recommended Security Controls for Federal Information Systems

SP800-100, Information Security Handbook: A Guide for Managers

Texas Department of Information Resources, Practices for Protecting Information Resources Assets

UK and Wales, Internal Control: Guidance for Directors on the Combined Code (Turnbull Report)
U.S. Department of Commerce, EU Safe Harbor Privacy Principles

**Trusted Computing Platform/Systems: Relevant
and Complementary Publications**

AICPA, Trust Services
CMS, Information Security ARS, Version 2.0
CMS, Policy for the Information Security Program
COBIT 4.1, Control Objectives, Management Guidelines, Maturity Models, IT Governance Institute
FISMA
GAO/AIMD-12.19.6, Federal Information System Controls Audit Manual
HIPAA
IIA, GTAG, Guide 4: Management of IT Auditing
IIA, GTAG, Guide 6: Managing and Auditing IT Vulnerabilities
ISACA, IS Standards, Guidelines, and Procedures for Auditing and Control
ISO 17799:2000, Information Technology—Security Techniques—Code of Practice for Information Security Management
ISO 27001:2005, Information Technology—Security Techniques—Information Security Management Systems—Requirements
ISO/IEC 18028-1:2006, Information Technology—Security Techniques—IT Network Security—Part 1: Network Security Management, 2006
MAGERIT Version 2.0, 2005
NERC, CIP-005-1, Electronic Security Perimeter(s)
NERC, CIP-007-1, Systems Security Management
OCC 12 CFR 30, Safety and Soundness Standards
OECD, Guidelines for the Security of Information Systems and Networks: Towards a Culture of Security
PCI DSS v1.1, Payment Card Industry Data Security Standard Security Audit Procedures
SP800-14, Generally Accepted Principles and Practices for Securing Information Technology Systems
SP800-41, Guidelines on Firewalls and Firewall Policy
SP800-53, Recommended Security Controls for Federal Information Systems
SP800-100, Information Security Handbook: A Guide for Managers
Texas Department of Information Resources, Practices for Protecting Information Resources Assets
U.S. Department of Commerce, EU Safe Harbor Privacy Principles

**Trusted Communications and Network: Relevant
and Complementary Publications**

AICPA, Trust Services
AICPA/CICA Privacy Framework
ANSI X9.79, U.S. Regulations for Digital Signatures
CMS, Information Security ARS, Version 2.0
CMS, Policy for the Information Security Program

Exhibit 13.1   *(Continued)*

COBIT 4.1, Control Objectives, Management Guidelines, Maturity Models, IT Governance Institute

COSO, Integrated Framework

DISA, Field Security Operations V6R4.4, Network Checklist

ETSI, TS 101.456, European Regulations for Digital Signatures

EU, Directive on Privacy and Electronic Communications 2002/58/EC, Article 4, 6

FIPS 191, Guideline for the Analysis of LAN Security

FISMA

GAO/AIMD-12.19.6, Federal Information System Controls Audit Manual

GLBA, Privacy of Financial Information

HIPAA

HKICPA, Internal Control and Risk Management—A Basic Framework

IIA, GTAG, Guide 4: Management of IT Auditing

IIA, GTAG, Guide 7: Information Technology Outsourcing

ISACA, IS Standards, Guidelines, and Procedures for Auditing and Control

ISO 17799:2000, Information Technology—Security Techniques—Code of Practice for Information Security Management

ISO 27001:2005, Information Technology—Security Techniques—Information Security Management Systems—Requirements

ISO/IEC 18028-1:2006, Information Technology—Security Techniques—IT Network Security—Part 1: Network Security Management, 2006

ISO/IEC 18028-4:2005, Information Technology—Security Techniques—IT Network Security—Part 4: Securing Remote Access, 2005

ISO/IEC 18043:2006, Information Technology—Security Techniques—Selection, Deployment and Operations of Intrusion Detection Systems. 2006

ISO/IEC TR 18044:2004, Information Technology—Security Techniques—Information Security Incident Management, 2004

ITIL, Security Management

MAGERIT Version 2.0, 2005

NERC, CIP-005-1, Electronic Security Perimeter(s)

NERC, CIP-007-1, Systems Security Management

OCC 12, CFR 30, Safety and Soundness Standards

OECD, Guidelines for the Security of Information Systems and Networks: Towards a Culture of Security

PCI DSS v1.1, Payment Card Industry Data Security Standard Security Audit Procedures

SP800-14, Generally Accepted Principles and Practices for Securing Information Technology Systems

SP800-33, Underlying Technical Models for Information Technology Security

SP800-53, Recommended Security Controls for Federal Information Systems

SP800-58, Security Considerations for Voice Over IP Systems

SP800-97, Guide to IEEE 802.11i: Establishing Robust Security Networks

SP800-100, Information Security Handbook: A Guide for Managers

SR 943.032.1, Swiss Regulations for Digital Signatures

Texas Department of Information Resources, Practices for Protecting Information Resources Assets

U.S. Department of Commerce EU Safe Harbor Privacy Principles

**Monitoring and Performance Reviews: Relevant
and Complementary Publications**

12 CFR, Part 30—Appendix A, II (Operational and Managerial Standards), B
AICPA, SAS 94, (AU Section 319), Effect of Information Technology on the
Auditor's Consideration of Internal Control in a Financial Statement Audit
AICPA, Trust Services
Basel II
Bill 198, Ontario, Canada, Keeping the Promise for a Strong Economy Act
(Budget Measures)
BS 15000-2: 2003, IT Service Management, Code of Practice for Service
Management
Canada, Combined Code on Corporate Governance
CERT, OCTAVE
Clinger Cohen Act
CMS, Information Security ARS, Version 2.0
CMS, Policy for the Information Security Program
CMS, Reporting Standard for Information Security Testing, Version 4
COBIT 4.1, Control Objectives, Management Guidelines, Maturity Models, IT
Governance Institute
Corporate Governance in The Netherlands 2002: The State of Affairs
COSO, Integrated Framework
DoD 5015.2-STD, Design Criteria Standard for Electronic Records Management
Applications, Version 3
EU Directive on Privacy and Electronic Communications 2002/58/EC, Article 4, 6
EU95/46, Article 17 of the European Data Privacy Directive
FFIEC, Audit
FFIEC, Information Security
FIPS 191, Guideline for the Analysis of LAN Security
FIPS, PUB 200, Minimum Security Requirements for Federal Information and
Information Systems
FISMA
GAO/AIMD-12.19.6, Federal Information System Controls Audit Manual
GISRA
GLBA, Privacy of Financial Information
HIPAA
IIA, GTAG, Guide 4: Management of IT Auditing
IIA, GTAG, Guide 5: Managing and Auditing Privacy Risks
IIA, GTAG, Guide 6: Managing and Auditing IT Vulnerabilities
ISACA, IS Standards, Guidelines, and Procedures for Auditing and Control
ISO 15489-1, Archiving/Records Management
ISO 15489-1:2001, Information and Documentation—Records Management—Part 1
ISO 15489.2-2002, Records Management—Part 2: Guidelines
ISO 17799:2000, Information Technology—Security Techniques—Code of Practice
for Information Security Management
ISO 27001:2005, Information Technology—Security Techniques—Information
Security Management Systems—Requirements
ISO/IEC 18043:2006, Information Technology—Security Techniques—Selection,
Deployment and Operations of Intrusion Detection Systems

Exhibit 13.1   *(Continued)*

ISO/IEC TR 14516:2002, Information Technology—Security Techniques—
Guidelines for the Use and Management of Trusted Third Party Services
ISO/IEC TR 18044:2004, Information Technology—Security Techniques—
Information Security Incident Management
ISSA, GAISP
ITIL, Security Management
J-Sox, Financial Instruments and Exchange Law
MAGERIT Version 2.0, 2005
NASD 3110
NERC, CIP-005-1, Electronic Security Perimeter(s)
NERC, CIP-006-1, Physical Security of Critical Cyber Assets
NERC, CIP-009-1, Recovery Plans for Critical Cyber Assets
NIST, SP800-26, Security Self-Assessment Guide for Information
Technology Systems
NIST, SP800-37, Federal Certification and Accreditation
OCC 12, CFR 30, Safety and Soundness Standards
OMB Circular A-130, Appendix III
PCI DSS v1.1, Payment Card Industry Data Security Standard Security Audit
Procedures
Presidential Decision Directives 63
Sarbanes-Oxley Act of 2002, Public Company Accounting Reform and Investor
Protection Act of 2002
SEC Rules 17a-3, 17a-4
Sedona Principles, Best Practices Recommendations & Principles for Addressing
Electronic Document Production, 2005, 2007
SP800-53, Recommended Security Controls for Federal Information Systems
SP800-66, Resource Guide for Implementing the Health Insurance Portability
and Accountability Act (HIPAA) Security Rule
SP800-100, Information Security Handbook: A Guide for Managers
Texas Department of Information Resources, Practices for Protecting Information
Resources Assets
U.S. Department of Commerce, EU Safe Harbor Privacy Principles
UK and Wales, Internal Control: Guidance for Directors on the Combined Code
(Turnbull Report)

Incident Response Capability: Relevant and Complementary Publications

BS 15000-1, 2002 IT Service Management—Part 1: Specification
BS 15000-2, 2003 IT Service Management, Code of Practice for
Service Management
CMS, Information Security ARS, Version 2.0
CMS, Information Security Incident Handling Procedures
CMS, Policy for the Information Security Program
COBIT 4.1, Control Objectives, Management Guidelines, Maturity Models, IT
Governance Institute
EU Directive on Privacy and Electronic Communications 2002/58/EC, Article 4, 6

FIPS 191, Guideline for the Analysis of LAN Security
FISMA
GAO/AIMD-12.19.6, Federal Information System Controls Audit Manual
GLBA, Privacy of Financial Information
HIPAA
ISACA, IS Standards, Guidelines, and Procedures for Auditing and Control
ISO 17799:2000, Information Technology—Security Techniques—Code of Practice
for Information Security Management
ISO 27001:2005, Information Technology—Security Techniques—Information
Security Management Systems—Requirements
ISO/IEC 18043:2006, Information Technology—Security Techniques—Selection,
Deployment and Operations of Intrusion Detection Systems, 2006
ISO/IEC TR 18044:2004, Information Technology—Security Techniques—
Information Security Incident Management, 2004
MAGERIT, Version 2.0, 2005
NERC, CIP-008-1, Incident Reporting and Response Planning
OECD, Guidelines for the Security of Information Systems and Networks: Towards
a Culture of Security
PCI DSS v1.1, Payment Card Industry Data Security Standard Security Audit
Procedures
SP800-53, Recommended Security Controls for Federal Information Systems
SP800-61, Computer Security Incident Handling Guide
SP800-100, Information Security Handbook: A Guide for Managers
Texas Department of Information Resources, Practices for Protecting Information
Resources Assets
U.S. Department of Commerce, EU Safe Harbor Privacy Principles

[a]See the acronym list for explanations of all acronyms.

ENDNOTES

1. Prodyot Samanta, Standard & Poor's, "Evaluating Risk Appetite: A Fundamental Process of Enterprise Risk Management." URL: www2.standardandpoors.com/portal/site/sp/en/us/page.article/2,1,1,0,1148332051802.html?vregion=us&vlang=en Published on 10/31/06.

2. Bob Lewis, "The 70-percent Failure,"*InfoWorld* (2003). URL: http://archive.infoworld.com/articles/op/xml/01/10/29/011029/opsurvival.xml.

3. Paul J. Sobel, *Auditor's Risk Management Guide: Integrating Auditing and ERM* (Chicago: CCH, 2005).

4. "Browser-based Attacks on the Up," (2004), *The Register.* URL: www.theregister.co.uk/2004/04/13/browser_security_woes.

5. Vikram Sehgal, "Emerging Economies Catalyze Future Growth" (June 21, 2007), JupiterResearch. URL: http://www.jupiterresearch.com/bin/item.pl/research:concept/75/id=99411.

6. World Community Grid. URL: http://www.worldcommunitygrid.org.

7. External quality assessment engagements are recommended every three years. There are self-assessment materials available at the IIA. URL: www.theiia.org/guidance/quality/the-external-quality-assessment-process.

8. Robert McMillan, "Pentagon Shuts Down Systems After Cyber-Attack,"*PCWorld* (June 21, 2007): "The Department of Defense took an estimated 1,500 computers offline after a security breach in the Office of the Secretary of Defense." URL: www.pcworld.com/article/id,133301-pg,1/article.html.

PART FOUR

LOOKING FORWARD

The vast possibilities of our great future will become realities only if we make ourselves responsible for that future.

—*Gifford Pinchot*

14

This is Not the End

BRINGING IT ALL TOGETHER

Change is ever present in today's world. This text has presented several independent forces that contribute to the importance and relevance of technology controls and safeguards. These forces stem from both contractual and regulated pressures and include natural business perseverance motivations. Businesses are just beginning to grasp the implications of a globalized marketplace that includes access to larger numbers of customers, partners, and competitors. The ability to redefine business structures by leveraging these international resources allows companies to outsource and create joint partnerships that were not possible a decade ago.

Globalization has also expanded the responsibilities of companies in regard to local cultures and laws. The operation of businesses abroad is not new, but the depth of this expansion into international markets is unique. Today companies, regardless of size, can deliver services and products to consumers around the world. Many, however, are not initially prepared for the vast differences in culture and legal practices. Governments have committed resources to redefining their laws in order to allow businesses to fit into this new structure.

The level of interaction between foreign companies and citizens of nation-states around the world has given rise to a new customer, the global citizen. To serve this new customer, companies are instituting technology and strategic governance efforts alongside increasingly popular good-neighbor practices. This dual effort is an effective way to avoid the introduction of onerous legislation, to increase profit, and to limit legal liabilities.

A clear pattern that has emerged regarding technology is that it begins as a supporting element to business and evolves into a new industry. The disruptive effects of technology have been seen in hundreds of revolutions: from navigation essentials like the compass, to transportation inventions such as the railroad and steam engine, to today's silicon chips and components. Over the past 100 years, technology has provided a way for companies to grow to unprecedented size, employ hundreds of thousands of individuals, operate in hundreds of countries, and deliver consistently. These innovative and technology-supported processes have become critical to the long-term growth of any business enterprise.

The enhancements in communication networks, including the Internet, have bridged the gap of culture and language. The ability to collaborate with experts on a topic regardless of time zone, language, culture, and family status can only advance the mission of these individuals. The ability to maintain this capability requires continued vigilance in open communication, boundary-free networks, and independence from political allegiances, both within the United States and abroad.

Today, IT systems have vast responsibilities. Technology is part of or oversees the creation, delivery, maintenance, and disposal of nearly every consumer and business product. Users of such systems require verifiable evidence of quality and capabilities. Likewise, administrators of such systems, including the business owners, the data custodians, and the technologists, are accountable for the information assets. Definitions of effective operations will continue to be sought. For a simple example of how a small lapse in assurance can impact a business, consider a generic example of a widget manufacturer. If a supplier of a minor component to the latest widget misses the required specs, and the quality control is not working properly, the entire product line might have to be recalled. Controls are not merely for the assurance of third parties operating in connection with your organization. They are vital to the longevity of the company itself.

Testing internal technology controls has grown in importance, in parallel to the growth of technology within businesses. While the need for testing is critical within businesses of all types, forces external to the organization also require it. The emphasis on technology environments will continue as more business functions are integrated into computing environments and these system environments become more transparent in society as consumer experiences are more supported by technology.

Past growth, fueled both by mandates and business necessity, has led organizations to silo duties between each department. Today, however, this siloed focus has begun to shift to a centralized effort, similar to the way insurance, risk management, and legal duties shifted from individual divisional responsibilities to a centralized specialized unit within a corporation.

Governments are enacting more legislation regarding the safeguarding of information and requiring strategic and enterprise control programs, a process that will continue as whole societies rely on these technology infrastructures.

In response to the growing number of regulations, businesses need to understand their technology environments better. This need has given rise to a growing number of technology organizations and voluntary associations that have published recommended standards and guidance. These publications provide a sufficient repository of knowledge for most industries, and some organizations embrace them wholly as a complete approach. As discussed earlier, though, this approach is wasteful and likely to fail. No single organization is exactly exposed to all the risks or has all the same operations that these publications address. If such cookie-cutter operations existed, companies would offer little value over their competitors.

Understanding the shortcomings of published guidance along with a global effort to define, measure, record, and evaluate technology controls and processes assures the resiliency and agility of a business. A focused evaluation of business needs and risks helps explain the unique challenges of a specific business. A top-down enterprise-risk approach is preferred and may be conducted in any number of ways. The key to success is to include the business owners and the technology teams to ensure full transparency in the methods and clarity in the true requirements of the business. Considerations must include all of the influencers of the business and the likely risks each strategic decision may incur.

Corporations that unify the governance requirements can establish a manageable and appropriate level of control that provides sufficient clarity on organization priorities and allocates resources accordingly. This is measured and assured through current-state gap analysis efforts designed to include all sources of intelligence. The formal identification of the five principles and their associated controls provides the structure on which any organization can build and manage a unified governance program.

FIVE PRINCIPLES

Development of the Five Principles

The principles and their respective controls are timeless and appropriate for all technology-enabled organizations. This broad applicability is based on the cross-industry and cross-nation alignment that was undertaken to ensure these principles and related controls addressed the concerns of companies around the world. The principles themselves maintain the most critical operational requirements of each company and are presented in a fashion that may be expanded on, given each organization's unique position.

The method described within the convergence section on international standards, discussed at a high level in Part I and in detail in Chapter 8, is the same process applied to developing the principles and controls. This process, however, considered the most diverse and internationally active companies: essentially a nightmare scenario for a company, reserved only for the true global conglomerates. The principles and the alignment were developed over several years of field engagements. In addition, numerous attestation reports for different industries and regions of the world were reviewed and identified to support these principles. This is not to say that the process or the principles are free from the biases attributable to other frameworks; however, they have been vetted. Ironically, the process identified several operational gaps that are of paramount importance to businesses: the necessity of business resiliency, or availability, and aspects of security within the organization. Enhancements were made to the security and continuity sections to address the operational needs of companies to remain online to deliver services and to repel malicious attacks.

The process of unifying multiple requirements from various sources and then applying these requirements to the business is an ideal way to approach the business operational and global assurance demands. This belief is rooted in the notion that businesses and technology excel at instilling predictable and repetitive processes, and this enables the business to manage these requirements through a single test and then reporting to many environments.

Summary of Principles

The five unique principles provide the anchor points for any organization managing technology control environments. The first principle, *technology strategy orchestration*, focuses on the top-level governance needs of an organization, including such areas as policies and ethical conduct. An important control detailed under Principle 1 concerns the technology intelligence that lays the groundwork for understanding value in today's digital world. Along the same lines, *life-cycle management*, Principle 2, provides further structure but relates directly to the handling of technology, including development, modification, and of course support.

User management is addressed under Principle 3, *access and authorization*, and includes the logical and physical areas of the organization. The breakdown of the controls under this principle highlights various aspects of the logical computing environment and the concerns that exist today regarding physical access in a distributed computing environment. The assurance necessary for individuals operating with sensitive data is also highlighted.

Principle 4, *sustaining operations*, focuses on an area that is addressed in a very limited fashion by government regulations but is heavily emphasized in supply chain agreements. This principle highlights operational resiliency, and environmental safeguards for the organization are highlighted and various approaches discussed.

Principle 5, *security and assurance*, addresses an area that is growing in importance as more aspects of the business are being placed online. Online expansion and technology adoption is escalating both at the business-consumer level and also in regard to the nation state–foreign citizen situation, such as when Chinese hackers were identified as breaching Germany's computer systems.[1] Understanding risk and then establishing trusted environments are supported and illustrated by the methods outlined in Chapter 8. The final sections of this last principle focus on monitoring and the ability to respond to incidents as they arise.

In total, the five principles are designed to handle any business. They are flexible enough to address technological leaps and unforeseen threats to the organization.

Challenges and Caveats

The world is a complex place with constantly shifting priorities of companies, countries, investors, and untold additional outliers. These challenges exist regardless of the focus of the business, but vary today more than at any other period as a direct result of the unprecedented interwoven world economy. Despite this interdependency and the lack of awareness within most boardrooms and government legislatures, companies are progressing toward more resilient environments capable of weathering future storms. The political stances of countries change with each new election or lack thereof, and directly impact companies' ability to sustain operations in different parts of the world. This political environment threat is obvious when nations nationalize the assets of private companies and demonstrate extreme shifts in the political climate that must be considered.

The severity of legislation and its enforcement is related to the political parties in power and to the economic status of the nations themselves. Companies should establish operational plans to respond when political and public opinion make it difficult to conduct business.

The importance and management of influencers on the company require support from top management and active participation from all business owners. This is essential to ensuring that the survey efforts isolate all of the influencers and that efficiencies gained do not have unintended negative effects. Gaining access to these individuals can be challenging given their busy schedules, and staff members working on these assessments must be flexible. Despite this challenge, there is no substitute for management participation and executive support.

It takes time for a program that spans the enterprise and considers all aspects of operations, from political climate to technology service agreements, to become fully integrated into the organization. Sometimes these programs end up being treated like cancers in the organization, avoided and shunned. To make the program a part of the organization, it must be adapted to fit the corporate culture; in some cases, the culture has to be adjusted.

Modifying the behavior of a struggling company is hard; modifying that of a successful company can be very difficult. Success may require a phased integration to show quick wins to the parties involved and gain adoption.

Continuous development and enhancements of public and private standards ensure a constant supply of leading practice approaches that may be incorporated into defined global core controls, as detailed within this book, and sufficient implementation guidance from similar institutions to address the tactical challenges of technology and operational difficulties. This continuous march of data has the potential to bury the organization in constant revisions, crippling the program. Programs should be updated on a defined schedule so that updates also adhere to the development and review process supported by the principles themselves, thereby perpetuating the cycle of technology within the organization.

REFLECTION ON INFORMATION TECHNOLOGY INTERNAL CONTROLS

Evolution of Internal Technology Controls

Over the past 100 years, ebbs and flows resulting from market booms, or the introduction of technology, or leaps in innovation have been followed by professional enhancements in techniques, then by fraud or some negative event, with political remedies soon following. Over time, strict professional and political efforts generally are rolled back somewhat to reflect the organizational drive for efficiency and effectiveness.

The establishment of government bodies, work groups, and oversight boards and the publication of professional trade group standards demonstrate the natural ability for the parties involved to provide the tools necessary to assure the operations of organizations. Unfortunately, as frauds over the past 100 years have shown, greater vigilance is required of many forms and functions. It is clear that the existing approaches are not sufficient, and continuous legislative efforts to predict future events by reacting to the past are illogical.

Despite a mature profession and many public references surrounding control development, management, and testing there is no single solution. Evaluating controls within an organization is a learning process, and it too must adapt to shifts in technology and business. Therefore, it is important that people within organizations are themselves subject to the fate of the business, and thus true stakeholders. The knowledge workers within the organization need to have the responsibility and resources to prepare for those unique risks that have yet to be discovered or legislated.

Future of Internal Technology Controls

The future itself is unknown. Today's economies have enjoyed unprecedented and nearly uninterrupted growth and development for many decades.

Throughout this period, industries, technologies, countries, and companies have come and gone. The technology controls of the future must be agile for a company to be assured of consistent operations. The biggest trend that will continue is legislation regarding the digital-information environment. Legislative efforts will impact all companies at one point or another, as partnerships and supply chain relationships experience trickle-down and trickle-up regulations. As described, the political party in power will impact the volume and depth of regulations. So will any future violations of good corporate citizenry. Companies must act professionally and equally in all markets, so that controls and safeguards are applied across all parties susceptible to risks. Equality demonstrated by enterprises establishes an expected level of service and limits the need for oversight and regulations.

In conjunction with increased legislation, a process of convergence will be taking place around the world on adopting and managing these requirements. The simplifying and merging of mandates is the result of a maturing of controls and consensus between government bodies (international acceptance is surfacing as a requirement, and laws are being crafted to reflect these cross-boarder effects) across the world business market and the acceptance of leading practices by third parties. Convergence will play a part in the legislation itself and the enforcement agencies that can explicitly highlight complementary standards, laws, and guidance. Convergence will also come into play within the audit profession, where a natural aggregation of controls will introduce a test-once, report-to-many capability. It may also lead to generally accepted technology controls practices, as is defined formally for accounting under the generally accepted accounting principles (GAAP) method.

A shift in the perception of technology, the controls, and the applied standards will also occur. Technology today is a subtext in the business function, more a tool and means. The business owners do not consider the technology to be the company. This misinterpretation will be tested and eventually will evolve as technology and the necessary controls become more visible components of daily business. This change will be more widely understood as negative events—power outages, for instance—occur and the true importance of technology is realized. The importance of complying with the standards will differ by business owners and by geographical location. In some parts of the world, a standard may be considered a performance metric; in other parts, it may be considered a matter of law and something taken very seriously. The difference between a control being considered a bonus versus an operational imperative is striking, and the efforts taken by those considering it an operational imperative are rewarded with more efficient operations and simpler demonstration of compliance to legislation.

Incentives that exist today are focused on efficiency and effectiveness, but perks and rewards are beginning to be established around the world.[2] Private institutions are offering reduced operating fees or rewards for those within the supply chain that follow a technology safeguard. In the public equity markets, better debt ratings are attributed to companies that can demonstrate strong enterprise resource management and technology controls. Perks to achieve a level of assurance generally are given in the information technology control environment.

The future will see greater expansion of principles and legislation requiring better transparency and reliability throughout all aspects of technology environments. This role is likely to increase as globalization requires better processes and more consistency in companies operating in the international arena and as the costs of such implementations become more affordable.

Trends

Merger and acquisition (M&A) activity in the mid-2000s has been explosive as a result of massive liquidity in the market and a world economy that provides ever-expanding markets for internationally capable and diverse companies. This activity was overshadowed only by the privatization of firms through private equity buyouts. Despite their different business structures, both M&A and private equity acquisitions require that technology is fully vetted during the due diligence. Whether a firm or a management group is purchasing a company, assurance regarding the integrity of its financials and the expandability of its operations is necessary.

A parade of divestitures is likely to follow the huge M&A market. Regardless of the changes in business structure, technology controls will be important for ensuring the assigned market value is fair. Acquisitions rely on technology to ensure the organization gains efficiencies in operations and to merge the two organizations' systems and knowledge sets. If redundancies are not eliminated through integration of technology control environments, inefficiencies are more likely and can damage the return on acquisition rate.

Siloed architecture will disappear in favor of enterprise approaches. Enterprises will gain better insight into all technology efforts within the business, and individual tactical projects will be better controlled through central management and orchestration. Overall, this will allow better management of the technology and ensure that the business operates under a single strategy.

The focus on transparency and oversight, originally created by the high-profile, destructive frauds that occurred in the 2000s, will continue. It will move from credit and financial institutions to their immediate partners, eventually expanding to business customers over time. This increased participation by financial providers will serve to protect bank investments, which will be achieved through better risk calculations on the part of banks. Relying on public disclosures and third-party evaluations, the public equity markets and private industry will apply these calculations of technology control risk.

The beginnings of this trend can be seen in firms developing and enforcing business-to-business security control mandates. These requests were once satisfied through the public accounting audit reports, such as Statement of Accounting Standards 70. These reports, however, were deemed insufficient to cover the technology concerns that firms had regarding their business and consistency of operations.[3] Today many businesses complete at least five vendor audits a year. These are contractually enforced by the business relationships. The value of the audit efforts is clear: Breaches of contracts identified and reported in the audit reports can result in predetermined fines and likely a loss in business.[4]

There is no doubt that more regulations will be put into place as new frauds or disruptions in business occur. This is not to say that the business should simply ignore or stall until the legislation loses favor; rather, the business should recognize these trends and measurably respond to these mandates in a manner that optimizes all party requirements. Say a regulation is ignored one year. A company may decide to drop related controls from its control environment, only to have to reinstate the same controls in a few years when they are again required, as the regulation may arise in a separate piece of legislation in the same nation or another. The cost of removal and replacement may be deemed unacceptable and unnecessary given any identified business improvements.

ENDNOTES

1. John Blau, "German Government PCs Hacked,"*PCWorld* (August 27, 2007). URL: www.pcworld.com/article/id,136421-c,hackers/article.html.

2. "Visa USA Pledges $20 Million in Incentives to Protect Cardholder Data," Visa.com. URL: http://usa.visa.com/about_visa/press_resources/news/press_releases/nr367.html.

3. Vendor audits do not necessarily focus solely on the technology or the ability to produce a quality product but include the manner in which operations are delivered. This area was historically reserved for quality management. An example of these extensions is illustrated nicely in this text regarding GMP auditing: James L. Vesper, *Quality and GMP Auditing: Clear and Simple* (Boca Raton, FL: CRC Press, 1997).

4. The PCI Security Standards Council maintains the payment processing standard (PCI DSS) established by the five major credit card associations, and the security mandates apply to all systems that store, process, and transmit cardholder data.

15

Building a System of IT Compliance and Controls

Key Topics Addressed in This Chapter

Keys to success

Impact of change on assumptions and influencers

Operating one century at a time

GETTING STARTED

The most common question asked by anyone seeking to apply a process or embrace a program always seems to be where to start. While this is a great question, the problem is that it implies a beginning and an end. It may also imply the assumption of a clean slate, which hardly exists in a venture start-up company and certainly is nonexistent in an established enterprise. If we accept that an organization is a constantly evolving entity that is subject to the whims of an incalculable number of variables, then we can embrace the idea that to start *anywhere* is a move in the right direction.

Given that organizations are constantly evolving, it follows that those organizations that are the most agile and receptive to change will have incredible competitive advantage in the marketplace. Building an effective system of information technology (IT) compliance and control requires a high level of participation throughout the organization. To get full buy-in across all levels, people must be able to see the benefits of participating. Whether these benefits are the achievement of performance targets, managing long-term capital expenditures, or ensuring low-to-reasonable turnover in high-knowledge-worker centers of the organization, the entire organization excels when technology is leveraged to the needs of the business. Therefore, if a first step must be taken, and it certainly may be a small step, it should be centered on *business technology intelligence.*

Business technology intelligence requires communication between IT and the various functions of the organization (i.e., legal, marketing, customer service, manufacturing, etc.). The goal of this communication should be to establish how each function can best serve the customer and/or the business and how technology can help. The value of technology must be recognized at the board-of-directors level by presenting the information from technology via a team lead of information technology executives in an actionable and approachable manner. This identification of value and communication may be initiated by the chief information officer (CIO) participating regularly at board meetings. The board, management, and business owners must establish benchmarks for metrics, such as uptime of technology systems, integrity of electronic cash transactions, regulatory mandates, supported business function value generation, or self-imposed metrics meant to ensure competitive advantage in the marketplace. The values provided by technology and the controls can be explicitly defined as direct financial values and indirect contributory values. Direct valuation of technology and controls is based on clear revenue generation and cost savings by the introduction of technology. Indirect valuation requires the acceptance of technology as a *general-purpose technology* (electricity and the internal combustion engine are accepted examples). Valuations should be based on the business's extended use of what technology allows, not just technology by itself.

Audit reports, both internal and external, are tremendously valuable. Leverage these valuable reports and create a fuller understanding of the organization's interrelationships and existing business process functions as they relate to the technology centers. Many people do not consider audit reports to be reusable, and they are missing out on a great opportunity. Most organizations consider annual independent audits to be a validation of technology deployments, both for compliance with requirements and for secure operations. Unless there is active participation in the audits and awareness of the scope of the engagements, reliance on audits can be misleading. Organizations should actively participate in defining this scope. Then the findings should be built into a compliance program and communicated to all affected business owners.

Audit reports are produced after what should be exhaustive evaluations, evidence collection, analysis, formatting, and report production. These reports allow the organization to bypass the legwork required to understand the business and determine its attributes and controls. Those charged with improving the organization's control environments both for operating efficiency and for maintaining a compliant and secure environment should request full access to these reports. The team should, in fact, review the workpapers developed by the independent auditor. The team can leverage the data into the business intelligence effort and use it to map the business process functions.

The end result of this exploration of available reports enhances the current effort and saves the heavily taxed technology department and those charged with maintaining daily operations time by not forcing them to repeat and reexamine previously addressed concerns, processes, and business imperatives.

PITFALLS

A failure in the deployment of an enterprise program assumes complete loss of all benefits. More simply, if we failed to accomplish a task (the goal), we must write off the entire effort. If everyone thought this way, today's world would be quite different. It is a mistake to believe that efforts undertaken provide zero value if the goal is not achieved. Consider the development, production, and marketing efforts undertaken for any available solution, technology, or product. Not one of these originated from a single effort that experienced zero failures, and most likely the largest percentage of innovations were not ones that were the intended goal but in fact were the interesting result of a separate effort.

If there is inherent value in the process of innovation and invention, it is important to realize that the institution of a truly global control computing environment that is operationally appropriate and adheres to international mandates can provide similar advantages to the enterprise. Of course, the long-term goal is to institute a program that can survive with the business for decades, providing additional benefits. There are lessons to be learned from the efforts of those who have gone before. Your effort will be more successful if you recognize the failures of others and the unique business risks and plan for them; and your own learning experiences will be a boon for those who come after you.

Business/Technology Disconnect

The classic pitfall experienced by organizations is a disconnect between the business strategy/vision and technology controls and platforms. This disconnect can be the result of a lack of communication between teams, an inconsistent governance program, or simply a misalignment of duties spread between business and technologists. This challenge will cause an organization to have either too much or too little technological capability and will result in the business operations failing to meet market demands. In some situations this disconnect with strategy can result in costly capital expenditures or simply a lack of corporate agility.

These costly expenditures can result where a technology department scales back its ability to support multiple locations and reduces both headcount and equipment only to realize that the organization is expanding operations around the globe over the next 12 months. These expenditures may also be the result of excesses, as when a technology team develops an environment that can operate redundantly around the globe to sustain a multiweek outage, eventhough such capability is not really needed. I have seen both examples firsthand. Each can happen in any organization that does not include IT in its business strategy.

Capturing the current human capital is the first step to ensure that business objectives and input are sought out first and that all parties have a voice, greatly reducing the likelihood of losing valuable information. Interestingly enough, the disconnect that can exist between technology and the business strategy also may result from the expansion of technology centers for technology's sake. This is a common sore point in organizations that overengineer their technology infrastructures for the sole purpose of acquiring the latest and greatest. In retrospect, many technologies that were employed rapidly could have been pushed out several years. The benefit of these additional years is that they allow for business cases to be defined, technology to become cheaper, and technological kinks to be worked out. Also the organization would have access to a greater number of experienced individuals who are familiar with the technology. I am not recommending that you ignore the next Internet or e-commerce market or turn a blind eye toward innovations; instead, all parties should fully evaluate how the business can benefit from technology today and in the future and then align these benefits with the organization's strategy.

Avoiding Real and Imagined Red Tape

Technologists and managers have an underlying fear that a mountain of paper and red tape will destroy the organization's ability to deliver and will foster a very uncreative and unpleasant work environment. In some cases this fear is based on experience and is justified. Yet, in order for the program to be accepted, this perception has to be addressed as a risk to the program. Eliminate this perception of the program through communications and the inclusion of all stakeholders to ensure true value is provided.

One primary driver of the negative experiences with programs is that often they are shoved onto organizations without consideration of the operating culture. If a control program developed by an organization without customizing the controls, thresholds, metrics, and management is added to the business processes it will be treated like a cancer. The entire ecosystem, human capital and external service providers, of the company will challenge it with all their strength until everyone associated with it is exhausted and defeated. It is the duty of those charged with improving the organization's operational efficiency to realize that the adoption of this type of program must be promoted internally by all corners of the organization. Ensuring that the program addresses the business operational needs and, most important, supports and complements the existing culture of the organization allows this adoption to take place. Organizations must not blindly adopt a generic framework; they should create a control framework that reflects the energy, operational needs, and technology environment of the organization as a whole in a single effective program.

Watch for Complacency

Complacency can occur in spite of the organization's efforts to avoid all the previously discussed pitfalls. In the beginning, the passion exhibited in rolling out a new program and the energy captured as the entire organization's infrastructure, business operations, audit programs, and culture evolve are incredible. There comes a time, however, when teams rotate from positions, budgets become misaligned, and priorities become disconnected from those understood by the operational groups of the organization. The success of the organization in the past can breed a feeling that nothing bad will happen. The fallacy of this mindset can be seen regarding the purchase of insurance for an organization. That money can seem like a waste in a year when there are no adverse incidents: no car wrecks, no lawsuits, no floods, no natural storms. Yet it would be incredibly shortsighted to stop purchasing insurance based on that logic. Technology controls and compliance should also be seen in this light.

Complacency can also arise within the control environment itself. The control environment must undergo a life-cycle management process, where controls and business functions are examined continuously. The process should include challenging all aspects of the control environment, examining new risks, and refreshing the environment's visibility into the business itself. Doing this ensures that as new strategies are introduced—business shifts from domestic to international, business outsources 30% of technology operations—the organization has sufficient capabilities to enhance them.

The circular relationship that exists among the technology control environment program, the business, and its processes is a key determinant of success. The whole program must be adhere to its own standards. Only then can the organization be sure that its custom control program is appropriate for its own needs and sustainable. This self-evaluation process also maintains the health of the program by allowing for constant feedback and shifts appropriate to the business direction.

OPPORTUNITIES

People Power

The organization's success is based on its ability to execute, fortune's favor, the abilities of the people involved, and other factors that are best examined by the likes of Mr. Drucker and Mr. Maslow. The most telling sign that people play a large role in an organization's longevity and success is clear when we review companies that have been in operation for more than 100 years. These organizations are built on principles that have worked from the beginning of the enterprise, and have been carried forward by the culture and character of each succeeding generation. It is therefore reasonable to credit these same individuals with creating an environment where a business can succeed in a world of change and competition.

Having a team of individuals who are passionate about the organization and aligned with its mission is the key to an ongoing successful operation. The term *success* encompasses both profitability and achievement of business objectives. Business objectives range from engineering healthy drugs, to curing disease, to developing computer chips. The key people are the ones we rely on to institute good controls throughout the organization; entrust with our corporate secrets, intellectual property, and future plans; and who ultimately make the organization succeed. The institution of organic controls by these trusted individuals is formalized through the publication of documentation in response to legislative mandates.

Yet we must return to the classic *trust-but-verify* concept. Managers around the world agree that without metrics, an organization cannot be successful. The need to verify does not imply that work is being delivered unethically; verification is an operational and strategic measurement that enables full execution of business objectives. Routine measurements enhance the operation of the organization; they are not mere window treatment. Metrics for an organization, division, and department should be restricted to a single screen or 8.5 × 11-inch sheet of paper to ensure that reams of information are not produced.

Once we accept that smart people are a part of our team, it is also a fair statement that smart individuals can be found in other parts of the business or on the outside. This recognition, particularly in regard to internal sources of talent, enables us to expand the pool of resources to deal with challenges. Engaging these individuals requires seeking to understand their business functions and bridging the gaps between each department to find valuable areas of collaboration.

Audit Opportunity

A common misperception that causes great harm to an organization is that an audit is a single event in which auditors are presented with a bounty of information and then business continues as usual afterward. The treatment of an audit as a single event, a nuisance, or as an exercise in stonewall defense techniques damages the business and the opportunity that audits present. Organizations today have more at stake during audits than ever before. Vendor and customer deals depend on successful evaluations and therefore enhance the confidence in established business relationships. Today's audits are more like management risk evaluations and less focused on isolated segments of the company.

An organization should not need to ramp up or put on a show for the auditors. So much waste and lost revenue can occur during these periods that they can materially damage the organization's ability to meet shareholder expectations. Organizations should embrace audits as ongoing exercises instead of single events. The more audits are integrated into the operations of the business, the more likely efficiencies of testing can be achieved. In addition, audit report findings allow operational improvement targets to be reset.

Redefining IT

Businesses should redefine the mindset of those who manage the IT environments as well as those who rely on them throughout the company. Open communication and collaboration should be the focus for IT and the various departments. Objectives and incentives should be modified to support this new mindset and reward its achievement.

The technology infrastructure also needs to be refocused to bring all teams together around common goals. Only in IT are there job descriptions that are complete contradictions of each other. For example, the network infrastructure team is tasked with keeping the computing environment operating in the quickest and most highly available manner possible. In contrast, the security team is tasked with restricting and inspecting every single packet crossing the network with the sole intent of stopping as many as possible. Each team seeks to meet its objectives, but success can occur only at the expense of the other team. Either the network team will have fast packets, or the security team will block as many as desired and slow down the network. In a possible win-win situation, capital expenditures year after year support a large enough infrastructure with the fastest IT equipment and fastest security equipment, allowing both parties to meet their goals, but at considerable expense for the company. Often what results from this tug-of-war between technology objectives is an overly complex system that is cumbersome to business users.

Opportunities exist to equalize the objectives of all parties by focusing on delivering services to customers, internally and externally. This understanding is achieved by aligning the objectives of the business with those of the contractual obligations. Together the controls can provide the bridge that closes the gap among the needs, the technology desired, and the stakeholders' assurance.

OBJECTS IN MIRROR ARE CLOSER THAN THEY APPEAR

Oncoming events and shifts in the business marketplace are unavoidable and natural. To maintain the vitality of the business, it is necessary to be aware of the influencers to the business and the impacts they have. How much of a difference does it make when one of the influencers or assumptions of the business shifts, and to what extent does this change impact the business?

Only recently have the effects of globalization begun to be understood. Consider the effects on a small town when a rare natural resource is discovered.

Suddenly, large amounts of capital and different cultures and ethical systems converge onto one small area. The effects can be extremely positive, but they also will cause a major shift in the population's culture and perception of the world. This effect is occurring around the world in newly emerging markets as language and cultural barriers are being broken down. The general shift away from European business and cultural conditions will also create new opportunities for businesses to excel and contribute to emerging nations.

The need for international agreement and protections will likely become a hot topic and a key focus of business leaders and political leaders. In order to protect both businesses and people, safeguards regarding proper business practices, privacy, consumer rights, governance, and human rights are all required. Many of these concerns are regulated through international treaties, but enhancements and extensions will be necessary as these newly accessible nations become part of the global economy. These clarifications and expansions of protections are important to solidify outsourced supply chain operations and international client expectations.

The political makeup of a country influences the ability of corporations to profit within a given region. The specific political party in power also strongly influences the enactment and enforcement of regulations. Therefore, it is important for businesses to be aware of both the political climate and the agendas of the countries in which operations are located. This is necessary both in emerging markets, which tend to experience more dramatic shifts in political party beliefs, and everywhere else. In cases where power shifts are violent, it is likely that existing company assets and investments may be lost.

The exposure to these events can be easily quantified when you are an oil company and a nation-state dictator nationalizes the oil production. These are fixed assets with expected cash flows that can be calculated. The loss is equal to the amount expended for labor, plus hard materials, plus lost cash flows. Cost assessments are more challenging for telecommunications companies. Say the backbone fiber-optics trunks are within such a country, and the dictator threatens to nationalize the entire system. The entire Internet ecosystem is at risk: all of the e-commerce, the telecommunications, and the business processes. The provider of this backbone component may be able to calculate its losses, but the countries that depend on that link may not be so lucky or aware.

A major risk in this fictional though highly probable situation is that organizations often rely on technology under the assumption that it will exist in the future. The loss of a major connection would impact millions of companies and potentially billions of people. The changes to the infrastructure resulting from political actions, war, posturing among Internet providers, or simply an accident are massive and require forethought to ensure that the organization can recover. Awareness can be developed by understanding not only where the firm's offices and data centers are located physically, but also where their customers and suppliers are, and what, if any, chokepoints exist. The Internet was built on sending packets through a network to find the optimal path and specifically designed to withstand the major disconnects just described. However, it works only if key international points of connection allow for the natural redundancy of many connection points.

Organizations depend on technology in a more open manner; leased lines are generally replaced with VPNs; manual procedures to process organization services are no longer possible due to the elimination of staff members who originally were trained but were let go as technology replaced their job functions. In addition, the organization may now process a volume that exceeds its capacity to deliver with a manual system.

The continued adoption of the Internet by businesses, consumers, and media companies may also introduce instability into the network. This instability may arise not from a cataclysmic event or an accident, but instead merely from growth. The Internet may become overburdened by the continual load and outages may develop. This may create a situation where individuals who pay the most are given priority, similar to systems that allow those who pay more to board a plane first. Another result may be the introduction of *private internets,* separate from that of the general public and available only to specific clients. Such a development would negatively impact information accessibility and the population a company can offer services to, but it is a possible shift.

The net result for the world is that change will continue and that prior assumptions will be wiped away by a new innovation or truth. Organizations constantly must be aware of the influencers on the business as well as those that are not directly affecting it currently. Simply said, organizations must have their eyes open and keep looking side to side, lest they and their staff get hit by a truck—that is, business and technology leaders must seek out government and stakeholder requirements proactively and aggressively enhance the program as required.

OPTIMIZATION

Management and companies around the world constantly seek to optimize operations and business processes. Optimization describes the correct balance of risk and reward in all aspects of the business. In the context of technology and controls, it can be interpreted in two entirely different ways. The organization itself determines the optimal efficiency of its operations through both research and trial by fire. While the book has interjected research approaches that will place the organization at a threshold that is only a degree or two beyond optimal, the organization can achieve remaining advantages by exploring the alternatives. Two separate but related requirements of the business can determine optimization: operational efficiency and legal mandates.

Optimization of the technology operations is a business requirement. That is, the operational goals of efficiency and effectiveness in controls are required for the organization to continue to operate in the future. Rarely can an organization exist that fails to meet customer demands. So, business optimization is a necessity for continued operations. That fact must be considered when resources and effort are being allocated. The regulatory environments in which the company does business may provide other optimization drivers, quantified through the valuation processes and prioritization efforts detailed in Chapter 8.

Failure to meet regulatory requirements results in very specific penalties, unlike operational requirements, where there are no transparent costs that are predictable or fully understood. This clarity regarding regulatory requirements causes businesses to be evaluated in a cost-benefit analysis. Because the penalties are known and calculable, organizations can compare costs of compliance with the requirements with costs of failure to comply. In some cases, executives who are bound by a fiscal duty to maximize stakeholder equity can be expected and even legally required to accept the possibility of fines and reprimand as a cost of doing business.

Applying a risk-based evaluation of regulatory concerns identifies the business need to meet specific regulations, and provides alternatives when such compliance efforts are not appropriate. Lack of compliance, however, does have implications beyond fines posted on government buildings, and includes soft and unknown costs. Legal defense and dialogue from harmed parties will increase the financial impact of the regulation itself. Other costs can include negative public image and the perception of moral failure within the organization. Costs associated with regulatory compliance can far exceed any detailed estimates by the government agencies themselves, and therefore projections based on penalties applied to other firms must be included in the cost analysis. In the end, regulatory compliance may be more an operational requirement given the organizational indirect costs and less likely to be considered unnecessary.

The organization that seeks to optimize both the regulations and the operational requirements can gain advantages at many levels. These advantages can be identified in the organization's functioning control environment, which is designed to respond to all of the business operations and compliance requirements. Eliminating duplicate controls, technology, and processes provides efficiencies that benefit the organization. By centralizing and standardizing controls, the organization can conduct fewer testing efforts on its assets. Unified governance and unified reporting to all parties, internal and external, are other benefits.

Centralizing and optimizing the monitoring, measurement, collection, analysis, and reporting of auditable areas and making the information available is a huge advantage to a company that is seeking to understand costs and operations, and examine expansion feasibility plans. By optimizing the control environment itself and the reporting functions, the organization also can determine weaknesses and instill proactive safeguards. The ability to respond proactively rather than to react results in tremendous savings to both resources and budgets.

General efforts may be taken per direction from the board and executive management to move the organization toward a more optimized process of technology controls. Adhering to a risk-based model of control application and monitoring allows an organization to focus on the areas that matter and vigorously test them. However, it is also important to apply controls on these identified areas sufficiently to fully address the requirements. Doing this ensures that third parties will deem the environment adequate, so the organization will not incur unnecessary audit fees. Regularly monitoring these safeguards, the audit requirements, and the influencers allows the organization to promptly reset its controls and processes. Finally, in order to truly close the gap of optimization within the organization's technology control environment, clear accountability is required. Job descriptions, management responsibilities, and consequences are in place to vigorously remind and penalize anyone who fails in his or her duties with respect to the organization.

LONGEVITY AND VITALITY: THE NEXT 100 YEARS

Organizations must consider multiyear plans instead of quarterly reporting periods; from there they must envision several decades beyond the multiyear plan; finally they must plan a century ahead. Although practical management oracles would question anyone's ability to plan beyond a few years, I believe that planning and vision beyond the near term are critical to the operational success of the organization. Although we cannot predict what technologies will be popular in 100 years, we must consider the future in order to establish and create a culture that moves beyond just *making the numbers*—infact, one that is *making the business*—a philosophy espoused by numerous studies, executives, and independent research groups.[1] In an effort to achieve such a long-term approach, an organization must establish the basic scaffolding to allow it to grow and excel.

An organization must establish ownership that must transcend all levels from the board to the administrators of systems and factory associates. All the wonders of governance and control are for naught if the leaders do not drive the organization's culture of assurance and longevity. It is the board's duty to define this responsibility to the executive principals. The board does this in a fashion that considers the candidates' past successes when reviewing for succession, establishes financial incentives for the long-term success of the business, defines metrics that the organization reviews and revises, and ensures that accountability is exercised when necessary. Establishing a tone at the top where the organization operates with conviction and morals ensures that all reaches of the business are equally supportive.

The establishment of the tone at the top and accountability at the highest levels is leveraged throughout the organization by communicating clearly the principles of both management and the board and their vision of the future of the company. Providing accurate and current information to all stakeholders allows everyone to fully understand the organization's mission and creates champions. Communicating consistently ensures that all parties are aware of the value and importance of all areas of the business. The technology leaders must communicate the determined value and contribution of technology, the control environment, and how these impact the operational needs of the business. This communication is necessary as a lack of knowledge can lead to waste and unnecessary risk exposures for the business.

This is especially timely in areas of the business that have evolved beyond their original value proposition. Today they include the technology infrastructure and those around the internal audit teams. Technology once was like the pavement in the parking lots or the PBX systems in the back room running the phone systems. They were considered an operational backbone that was always on and simply a medium to conduct business on; more descriptively, technology was similar to paper. The business could operate with the paper by calling people and through separate channels of operation. Today is different. The technology is different, and businesses have backup operations of technology with more technology. Technology affects all aspects of life. I recently attempted to make a purchase when the retailer's point of sale system (running the most popular operating system) went down, and the staff was forced to dig up paper sales sheets. Although the shop had a paper backup system, the staff had no idea how to use it, so the sales process took at least three times as long, and the store easily lost half the customers who intended to make a purchase.

To succeed in the future, organizations must consider the principles outlined in this book and the method of converging business and contractual obligations. Organizations must manage the rollercoaster of change just like any other part of the business. The best way is to adopt the necessary requirements in a steady but measured manner. I am not endorsing becoming noncompliant or avoiding the advantages gained through technology innovations; rather I believe that a steady and sure approach is better than sudden drastic changes. In a business where the long term and the *really* long term are part of the business plan, such leaps are rarely necessary.

Philosophers and academics often ponder the culture of an organization, but rarely do they credit it with ensuring the viability of the business. The culture of an entity is built on how the business drives for success, and what the purpose of the organization is stated to be regarding the customers and the community. The driving of purpose and the establishment of a mission or purpose in a field of service are core to growing a culture within an organization. Much has been written about developing and identifying the best culture. I simply advise that a further effort be made to determine the culture of the organization. A culture audit can show whether the business is made for the long term or whether people are merely working in the environment, drawing on all its energy and value, and planning to move on.

It is interesting to think of a company in increments of decades and centuries instead of quarterly earnings reports. The idea that our actions today will play out over centuries to come brings a perspective that is rare in companies. This lens of time allows for organizations to consider the best actions for the business, the community, and the market itself. The actions of short-term profiteering are replaced by sensible business management where profits and returns are balanced across the whole ecosystem. One European company has been producing a wonderful port for nearly two centuries. More than 50 years ago, the company put away a special stock to be opened on its two hundredth birthday. Consider the culture and confidence of this management team: Everyone contributes to an organization that will live on and where their works will be enjoyed by those who will come after. I hope to instill such a long-term perspective in today's organizations, so that they too may contribute positively many centuries into the future.

FINAL THOUGHTS

The yin and yang of predictable events and the course of human history can be summed up in two common phrases: *History repeats itself* and *Prior events do not indicate future events*. To believe in only one would be foolish; to believe them both can lead to schizophrenic tendencies. We cannot base an organization solely on what has happened in the past, but we must also realize that the habits of old will return. In nearly every decade over the past 100 years there has been a financial fraud, a scare in the credit markets, market booms, and market busts. Companies have died, been reborn, and died again. These tendencies only highlight the fact that there are certain risks and events that, while remote, can and will occur again. A business seeking to achieve operational efficiencies must consider safeguards that limit the impacts of these events.

An organization must establish monitoring systems both to detect the adequacy of the controls implemented and to minimize risks. An efficient control environment is one that lives in the present by ensuring all regulatory requirements are being met. Just as importantly, the environment learns from the past while looking to the future, using a controls-based approach. The processes outlined in the previous chapters provide an implementation model that will help organizations achieve this balance and set a chart for ongoing success in the years and decades to come.

ENDNOTE

1. "Built to Last: Focusing Corporations on Long-Term Performance," report of the Committee for Economic Development (June 27, 2007): The basis is that "an increasingly short-term focus by many business leaders is damaging the ability of public companies to sustain long-term performance." The report specifically recommends that "companies voluntarily refrain from issuing short-term guidance." URL: www.ced.org/docs/report/report_corpgov2007.pdf.

Supportive Publications

See the acronym list for explanations of all acronyms.

12 CFR, Part 30—Appendix A, II (Operational and Managerial Standards), B

AICPA SAS 94 (AU Section 319), Effect of Information Technology on the Auditor's

AICPA, Trust Services

AICPA/CICA, Privacy Framework

ANSI X9.79, U.S. Regulations for Digital Signatures

AS/NZS 4360—1999, Risk Management 1.3.32

Basel Capital Accord (Basel II)

BCI, Good Practice Guidelines

Bill 198, Ontario, Canada, Keeping the Promise for a Strong Economy Act (Budget Measures)

BS 15000-1: 2002, IT Service Management—Part 1: Specification

BS 15000-2: 2003, IT Service Management, Code of Practice for Service Management

BS 7799-3, Risk Management, ISO 27005

Business Continuity Management Good Practice Guidelines, 2005

Canada, Combined Code on Corporate Governance

CERT, OCTAVE

Clinger Cohen Act

CMS Information Security C&A Methodology, Version 1.0

CMS, CSR

CMS, Information Security ARS, Version 2.0

CMS, Information Security Business Risk Assessment Methodology, Version 2.1

CMS, Information Security C&A Methodology, Version 1.0

CMS, Information Security Incident Handling Procedures

CMS, Information Security Risk Assessment Methodology, Version 2.1

CMS, Integrated IT Investment & System Life Cycle Framework
CMS, Policy for the Information Security Program
CMS, Reporting Standard for Information Security Testing, Version 4
CMS, SSP Methodology, 2003
COBIT 4.1, Control Objectives, Management Guidelines, Maturity Models, IT Governance Institute
Commission of the European Communities ITSEM, Version 1.0, MAGERIT Version 2.0, 2005
Corporate Governance in The Netherlands 2002: The State of Affairs
COSO, Enterprise Risk Management—Integrated Framework, 2004
COSO, Internal Control—Integrated Framework, 1992
DCID 6/3
DISA Field Security Operations V6R4.4, Network Checklist
DoD 5015.2-STD, Design Criteria Standard for Electronic Records Management Applications, Version 3
DoD, Policy 8500
ETSI, TS 101.456, European Regulations for Digital Signatures
EU 2002/58/EC, Directive on Privacy and Electronic Communications, Articles 4, 6
EU 92/242/EC
EU 95/46, Data Privacy Directive, Article 17
EU Directive on Privacy and Electronic Communications 2002/58/EC (Article 4, 6)
Executive Order on Critical Infrastructure Protection in the Information Age, October 16, 2001
FDA, CFR, Title XXI, 1999
FERC, RM01-12-00, Appendix G, 2003
FFIEC Management
FFIEC, Audit
FFIEC, Business Continuity Planning
FFIEC, Development Acquisition
FFIEC, Information Security
FFIEC, Management
FFIEC, Operations
FIPS 191, Guidelines for the Analysis of LAN Security
FIPS 199, Security Categorization of Federal Information
FIPS, PUB 200, Minimum Security Requirements for Federal Information and Information Systems
FISMA, Federal Information Security Management Act
GAO/AIMD-12.19.6, Federal Information System Controls Audit Manual
GISRA
GLBA, Privacy of Financial Information
HIPAA
HKICPA, Internal Control and Risk Management—A Basic Framework
IIA, GTAG, Guide 1: Information Technology Controls

IIA, GTAG, Guide 2: Change and Patch Management Controls: Critical for Organizational Success
IIA, GTAG, Guide 3: Continuous Auditing: Implications for Assurance, Monitoring, and Risk Assessment
IIA, GTAG, Guide 4: Management of IT Auditing
IIA, GTAG, Guide 5: Managing and Auditing Privacy Risks
IIA, GTAG, Guide 6: Managing and Auditing IT Vulnerabilities
IIA, GTAG, Guide 7: Information Technology Outsourcing
IIA, GTAG, Guide 8: Auditing Application Controls
Interagency Paper on Sound Practices to Strengthen the Resilience of the U.S. Financial System, 2003
Internal Control 2006: The Next Wave of Certification—Guidance for Management
ISACA, IS Standards, Guidelines, and Procedures for Auditing and Control
ISO 15489.2-2002, Records Management—Part 2: Guidelines
ISO 15489-1:2001, Information and Documentation—Records Management—Part 1
ISO 17799:2000, Information Technology—Security Techniques—Code of Practice for Information Security Management
ISO 27001:2005, Information Technology—Security Techniques—Information Security Management Systems—Requirements
ISO/IEC 13335-1:2004, Information Technology—Security Techniques—Management Information and Communications Technology Security
ISO/IEC 15288:2002, Systems Engineering—System Life Cycle Processes
ISO/IEC 18028-1:2006, Information Technology—Security Techniques—IT Network Security—Part 1: Network Security Management, 2006
ISO/IEC 18028-4:2005, Information Technology—Security Techniques—IT Network Security—Part 4: Securing Remote Access, 2005
ISO/IEC 18043:2006, Information Technology—Security Techniques—Selection, Deployment and Operations of Intrusion Detection Systems, 2006
ISO/IEC 18405, Common Criteria for Information Technology Security Evaluation Version 3.1
ISO/IEC 21827:2002, Information Technology—Systems Security Engineering—Capability Maturity Model (SSE-CMM), 2002
ISO/IEC 9126-1:2001, Software Engineering—Product Quality—Part 1: Quality Model
ISO/IEC TR 14516:2002, Information Technology—Security Techniques—Guidelines for the Use and Management of Trusted Third Party Services
ISO/IEC TR 15443:2005, Information Technology—Security Techniques—A Framework for IT Security Assurance—Part 1: Overview and Framework, 2005
ISO/IEC TR 18044:2004, Information Technology—Security Techniques—Information Security Incident Management, 2004
ISSA, GAISP

ITIL, Security Management
ITSEM Version 1.0, Commission of the European Communities, Information Technology Security Evaluation Manual
J-Sox, Financial Instruments and Exchange Law
MAGERIT Version 2.0, 2005
NASD 3110
NASD, Rules 3510, 3520
NERC, CIP-002-1, Critical Cyber Asset Identification
NERC, CIP-003-1, Security Management Controls
NERC, CIP-004-1, Personnel & Training
NERC, CIP-005-1, Electronic Security Perimeter(s)
NERC, CIP-006-1, Physical Security of Critical Cyber Assets
NERC, CIP-007-1, Systems Security Management
NERC, CIP-008-1, Incident Reporting and Response Planning
NERC, CIP-009-1, Recovery Plans for Critical Cyber Assets
NFPA 1600, "Standard on Disaster/Emergency Management and Business Continuity Programs, 2007 Edition"
NIST, SP800-26, Security Self-Assessment Guide for Information Technology Systems
NIST, SP800-34, Contingency Planning Guide for Information Technology Systems
NIST, SP800-37, Federal Certification and Accreditation
NYSE, Rule 446
OCC, 12 CFR 30, Safety and Soundness Standards
OCC, Circular 235
OCC, Thrift Bulletin 30
OECD, Guidelines for the Security of Information Systems and Networks: Towards a Culture of Security
OMB Circular A-130, Appendix III
PAS, 56 Guide to Business Continuity Management
PCI DSS, v1.1, Payment Card Industry Data Security Standard Security Audit Procedures
Presidential Decision Directives 63
Sarbanes-Oxley Act of 2002, Public Company Accounting Reform and Investor Protection Act of 2002
SAS No. 109, Understanding the Entity and Its Environment and Assessing the Risks of Material Misstatement
SEC Rules 17a-3, 17a-4
Sedona Principles, Best Practices Recommendations & Principles for Addressing Electronic Document Production, 2005, 2007
SP800-100, Information Security Handbook: A Guide for Managers Systems
SP800-14, Generally Accepted Principles and Practices for Securing Information Technology Systems
SP800-26, Security Self-Assessment Guide

SP800-30, Risk Management Guide for Information Technology Systems

SP800-33, Underlying Technical Models for Information Technology Security

SP800-41, Guidelines on Firewalls and Firewall Policy

SP800-53, Recommended Security Controls for Federal Information Systems

SP800-58, Security Considerations for Voice Over IP Systems

SP800-61, Computer Security Incident Handling Guide

SP800-66, Resource Guide for Implementing the Health Insurance Portability and Accountability Act (HIPAA) Security Rule

SP800-97, Guide to IEEE 802.11i: Establishing Robust Security Networks

SR 943.032.1, Swiss Regulations for Digital Signatures

Texas Department of Information Resources, Practices for Protecting Information Resources Assets

Title III of the E-Government Act of 2002, PL 107-347, December 17, 2002

U.S. Department of Commerce, EU Safe Harbor Privacy Principles

UK & Wales, Internal Control: Guidance for Directors on the Combined Code (Turnbull Report)

List of Acronyms

Acronym	Explanation
ARS	Acceptable Risk Safeguards
BCI	Business Continuity Institute
C&A	Certification and Accreditation
CICA	Canadian Institute of Chartered Accountants
COBIT	Control OBjectives for Information and related Technology
COSO	Committee of Sponsoring Organizations of the Treadway Commission
DCID	Director of Central Intelligence Directives
DISA	Defense Information Systems Agency
FERC	Federal Energy Regulatory Commission
FFIEC	Federal Financial Institutions Examination Council
FIPS	Federal Information Processing Standards Publication
FISMA	Federal Information Security Management Act
GAISP	Generally Accepted Information Security Principles
GLBA	Gramm Leach Bliley Act
GTAG	Global Technology Audit Guide
HIPAA	Health Insurance Portability and Accountability Act
HKICPA	Hong Kong Institute of Certified Public Accountants
IIA	Institute of Internal Auditors
ISO	International Standards Organization
ITIL	Information Technology Infrastructure Library
ITSEM	Information Technology Security Evaluation Methodology
MAGERIT	Metodología de Análisis y Gestión de Riesgos de los Sistemas de Información
NASD	National Association of Security Dealers
NFPA	National Fire Protection Association

(*continued*)

Acronym	Explanation
NIST	National Institute of Standards and Technology
NYSE	New York Stock Exchange
OCC	Office of the Comptroller
OCTAVE	Operationally Critical Threat, Asset & Vulnerability Evaluation
OECD	Organisation for Economic Co-Operation and Development
PCI DSS v1.1	Payment Card Industry Data Security Standard Version 1.1
PCISC	Payment Card Industry Security Council
SSP	System Security Plans

Index